PSALMS

For 2,500 years the Psalms have been a source of inspiration and solace, but also bewilderment and doubt, as readers struggle with their often strange language and occasional savage demands for revenge. They reflect the traumas and triumphs, fears and festivals of the Jewish people from David to Qumran. From obscure origins in the long-vanished Temple of Jerusalem their influence, both religious and poetic, has spread through western culture. What do they mean in the modern world? How can we read them anew? Can we appreciate their poetry today?

Psalms offers new approaches to these old questions. Beginning with a consideration of the criteria for choosing an English version, it examines the needs of readers and the various techniques used to inform a wide range of interpretations. Part I explores the theory of reading, including a review of structuralist and postmodern approaches. A sevenfold interpretative scheme is described (including attention to historical, social and liturgical matters) and applied in Part II to the detailed analysis of individual psalms. In Part III the theory is tested on a complete group – the Psalms of Ascents (120–34).

Alastair G. Hunter is Senior Lecturer in Hebrew and Old Testament Studies at the University of Glasgow. He is the author of *Christianity and Other Faiths in Britain* (1985).

PSALMS

Alastair G. Hunter

London and New York

First published 1999
by Routledge
11 New Fetter Lane, London EC4P 4EE

Simultaneously published in the USA and Canada
by Routledge
29 West 35th Street, New York, NY 10001

Routledge is an imprint of the Taylor & Francis Group

Typeset in Garamond by Keystroke, Jacaranda Lodge, Wolverhampton
Printed and bound in Great Britain by TJ International Ltd, Padstow, Cornwall

British Library Cataloguing in Publication Data
A catalogue record for this book is available from the British Library

Library of Congress Cataloging in Publication Data
Hunter, Alastair G.
Psalms / Alastair G. Hunter.
(Old Testament readings)
Includes bibliographical references and index.
1. Bible. O.T. Psalms – Criticism, interpretation, etc.
I. Title. II. Series.
BS1430.2.H85 1999
223'.206 – dc21   98–54242

ISBN 0–415–12769–6 (hbk)
ISBN 0–415–12770–X (pbk)

Dedicated to the staff and students of the PERSETIA
theology summer school at the Fakultas Theologia UKIT,
Tomohon, North Sulawesi, Indonesia,
13–24 July 1998,
and in particular to Robert Waworuntu, with grateful thanks.

CONTENTS

CONTENTS

ILLUSTRATIONS

Figures

Tables

PREFACE

Anyone who embarks on a study of the Psalter must be conscious both of the enormity of the task and the long tradition in which they stand. Texts like the Psalms, central to the liturgies of both Judaism and Christianity, surrounded by a host of commentaries and by theological and personal interpretations, and cherished by countless individuals as a source of personal inspiration, can never be subsumed under a single interpretative methodology.

What this book attempts is a broadly literary approach to the Psalms in English which takes seriously the words of the poems and the way they are structured. The choice of translation is fundamentally important, and for this reason the first two chapters deal with this issue in some detail. While the outcome will not please everyone, I hope at the very least that the logic behind it will be persuasive. The standard biblical versions receive consideration in Chapter 2; readers might also be interested to consult Davie (1996), Frost (1977), Gelineau (1965), Jackson (1997), Levi (1976) or Slavitt (1996) on the matter.

In essence the aim of this book is to encourage readers to develop their own approaches to the Psalms, and so my emphasis is on providing a broad method. I offer both theoretical discussion and practical application, the selected Psalms being treated in reasonable depth. This is therefore not a commentary (only twenty-one Psalms are explicitly covered – 2, 8, 24, 29, 74, 82, 120–34) but a meta-commentary; that is, a discourse which should (if I have been successful) enable the reader to shape his or her own commentary. While a wealth of earlier work forms the largely unseen foundation for every modern interpretation, it is important not to let the process of reading become mired in an endless and pedantic résumé of past opinion. I suggest therefore that those who wish to engage with this journey of exploration equip themselves with a basic survival kit consisting of: the text itself (in the preferred version (see below), with others for comparison); a concordance; access to the basic commentaries (see section 1 of the bibliography); and collections of relevant ancient near-eastern texts (for example, *ANET* or *NERTOT*). A potentially interesting new resource, which I have unfortunately been unable to consult, is Hallo and Younger's *The Context of Scripture. I: Canonical Compositions from the Biblical World* (Leiden–New York–Cologne: Brill, 1997).

Throughout this book I have used the NRSV translation of the Bible, unless otherwise indicated, and chapter and verse references are always to the English version.

Finally, I would like to record my thanks to a number of people: successive classes at the University of Glasgow whose members have acted as unwitting guinea-pigs as this approach to the Psalms developed; those students at the PERSETIA summer school in Indonesia in July 1998 to whom I delivered parts of this book in a course of lectures, and who made a number of helpful suggestions; my colleagues and former teachers Robert Davidson and Robert Carroll, who did so much to encourage my interest in the Hebrew Bible – and the patient editors at Routledge to whom I made the same lame excuses for late submission that I have so often heard from students in respect of essays! But most of all, to Maggie, both différance and supplément.

ABBREVIATIONS

ANE	ancient Near East
ANET	Pritchard (1969) *Ancient Near Eastern Texts Relating to the Old Testament*
BCE	Before the Common Era (= BC)
CE	Common Era (= AD)
ET	English Translation
ICC	International Critical Commentary
JB	Jerusalem Bible
JSOT	*Journal for the Study of the Old Testament*
KJV	King James (or Authorised) Version
MT	Masoretic Text
NEB	New English Bible
NERTOT	Beyerlin (1978) *Near Eastern Religious Texts Relating to the Old Testament*
NIV	New International Version
NJB	New Jerusalem Bible
NRSV	New Revised Standard Version
REB	Revised English Bible
RSV	Revised Standard Version
SOED	*Shorter Oxford English Dictionary*

Part I

THEORY AND PRACTICE

1

TRANSLATING AND READING

Preliminary comments

> You are urged therefore to read with good will and
> attention, and to be indulgent in cases where, despite our
> diligent labour in translating, we may seem to have
> rendered some phrases imperfectly. For what was originally
> expressed in Hebrew does not have exactly the same sense
> when translated into another language. Not only this work,
> but even the law itself, the prophecies, and the rest of the
> books differ not a little as originally expressed.
>
> (Sirach: The Prologue [RSV[1]])

These words, translated from Greek written nearly twenty-two
centuries ago, and themselves a comment on a translation from
Hebrew into Greek, indicate the fundamental dilemma confronting
any proposal to embark upon a literary reading of the Psalms. Quite
simply the 'Psalms' which are under consideration are neither
hatt^ehilim – the Hebrew title of the collection found in standard
editions of the Jewish Bible[2] – nor those *psalmoi* with which the
writers of the New Testament were probably familiar. However
regrettable it may be, we have to acknowledge that our study is at
most second-best: a reading, or series of readings, of material which
has already become distanced from its sources.

The question we must begin with is simply this: 'Is translation
either possible or appropriate?' Much ink and effort has been spilled
or spent on this probably unresolvable quandary. The question may
be put with different degrees of severity, from absolute embargo to
the modest requirement that the reader note the difficulties. The
translator of Sirach no doubt belongs to the moderate part of that
particular spectrum. The problem also varies according to the status
of the material we wish to translate. A simple request for directions,
or a friendly greeting, can no doubt be expressed in many different

languages with limited loss of comprehension. Instructions as to how to make things work ought to be susceptible to accurate translation, assuming both linguistic and technical competence on either side. The difficulties increase, however, with growth of sophistication in linguistic use. Jokes are a real hazard because they depend upon both verbal double entendre and cultural context. But it is when we encounter anything which merits, at whatever level, the label 'literature' that those who object to translation have a strong case.

What is the point, they might say, of deceiving ourselves into thinking that anything important of the Greek epic known as the *Iliad* survives a rendering into English? No doubt there is an English work – or rather a number of such works – of this title; but it is a fundamentally different composition. Far better that we should cut our losses and recognise that we simply cannot have access to literature in languages with which we are unfamiliar. In the religious realm, it is often claimed that the Holy Qur'an is of this kind: there may exist interpretations in other languages, but the Qur'an itself is and must remain Arabic; and Arabic of a particular time and place. Even a native speaker of some modern branch of the Arabic language may be considerably distanced from the Qur'an.

There is undoubtedly a genuine point to be made here, but in its most uncompromising form it surely excludes more than is necessary, and is overly pessimistic about the ability of people of different languages, cultures and ages to communicate at quite subtle levels. A similar debate takes place over such issues as black experience, feminism and the situation of the oppressed, where there are those who argue for the exclusive rights of blacks to speak on the subject of discrimination on the basis of colour and of women to comment on feminist affairs. The legitimate reservation to be entered in both cases is that the extreme position tends to dismiss the fact of shared humanity as being of no importance. Can it not reasonably be held that some communication can take place across all barriers? The alternative implied by the purist stance is that we resign ourselves to mutual silence – a counsel, surely, of despair. For if it were to be taken to its natural conclusion, we would be barred from the literature not only of those whose language is not ours but of those whose distance from us in time or place renders them mute. If the belief is well founded that the literature of those long dead can still be meaningfully read, it is reasonable to apply a similar logic to other forms of separation and to allow ourselves access not just to the mundane and the pragmatic, but to the subtle and the profound.

A more common, but in the end similarly erroneous, approach is to assume (almost always without discussion) that there are no difficulties which a healthy pragmatism will not resolve. Found in both scholarly and lay circles, this attitude characterises those who, while accepting that translation is imperfect and that nuances are lost, believe that the principal essence is preserved and that we can gain assured access to the author's intended meaning, given professional competence on the part of the translator. Unfortunately, while having the appearance of a judicious working basis, this too turns out on closer examination to be seriously flawed.

The reasons lie at the heart of what this book is concerned with: the *uncertainty of meaning* in all but the simplest of literary texts, and the *self-destruction* of the notion of '*authorial intention*'. The former results from the realisation that the kinds of texts we are dealing with, dense as they are with metaphor and other linguistic tropes, do not refer to simple facts or to notions of merely superficial character, and so the idea of the competent translator requires not just knowledge of the Hebrew word for 'heart', for example, but some sensitivity to the way in which that word functions in Hebrew metaphorical usage.[3] Such sensitivity cannot be communicated lexicographically; it is developed bit by bit, through what could be described as a process of continuous feedback involving both the individual translator, the corpus of the language under scrutiny, the larger tradition of translation, and the contemporary societies of those carrying out the work of translation. But even given the sensitive application of the skills thus indicated, the 'meaning' eventually constructed remains exactly that: a construct which is in no way to be identified with the Hebrew original. Whatever we, in the late twentieth century, think or imagine we are doing when we scan a page of the Psalms in English, we are absolutely not sharing an experience with pious (or, for that matter, impious) Jews of 2,000 and more years ago.

If meaning is uncertain, the author is a wraith vanishing in an autumn mist. It may be a matter of sorrow that we have to dismiss as the purest fantasy those affecting pen pictures of David composing Psalm 51 in a spirit of deepest repentance at having sinned in the matter of Bathsheba. We may regret the loss of the poet-king of Israel whose personal life is touchingly represented in Psalm 23. But dismiss them, lose them, we must. For there is, let it be clearly stated, not the slightest shred of evidence that would justify our believing we are in touch with the mind or minds of the author or authors of these hymns, laments, liturgies and processionals which have found their way into the Psalter. When the dust of the debate over postmodernism has settled, one ineluctable reality will remain: the meaning of a text cannot depend absolutely upon its author's intention. Not only is this a consequence of our not knowing what authors did in fact intend; it is indicated by the realisation that even if an author had left us a statement of what he or she intended in a particular passage, that statement would itself be problematic. It might be (probably would be) opaque; it might be accidentally misleading; it might be mischievously misleading. (Imagine, if you will, Anthony Burgess leaving us in his will directions for the interpretation of *A Clockwork Orange*!) And, in any case, why should it be authoritative? It is not for nothing that both stage and screen directors prefer to keep authors (especially living ones) at a distance. They tend to interfere with the reading. Our case is perhaps simpler, since in all but the rarest of cases in the Jewish Bible we have no idea who the author may have been, and in any case cannot interrogate those whose names we have. It follows that we must firmly reject the notion that the author's intention is the principal or only means of recovering the meaning of the text, for most of those readings which claim such authority are circular. The 'author' is inferred from his or her supposed writings, is attributed an authorial 'character' on the basis of these inferences (together, it must be said, with a good seasoning of imaginary biography), and the resulting pleasing fiction is then brought to bear in support of further interpretations.[4]

We thus find that the pragmatic approach fails for (ironically) the pragmatic reason that its ambitions are, for practical purposes, impossible to fulfil. It is important to register, however, that we have not foreclosed on the question of access. To say that it is not possible to achieve a generally acceptable translation by the use of accessible and transparent skills is not the last word. For what we confront is a body of literature which, while remaining closed to us in important ways, is nonetheless susceptible to the application of a variety of readerly techniques (including translation!), each less than adequate, some incompatible with others, but all in different ways allowing the reader a window into the text, casting a partial light on its pages. At one level this is not a controversial observation. Those who read the Psalms today, whether in translation or by using their acquired knowledge of Hebrew together with a standard edition, have a variety of reasons for doing so. A survey of some of these reasons will help to clarify the processes involved.

Patterns of worship

Some may belong to a religious tradition which integrates the Psalms into its own patterns of worship. The Scots' Reformed Kirk, with this in mind, produced the Metrical Psalms, a remarkable and original rendering, but no more authentic as a translation than is Fitzgerald's *The Rubáiyát of Omar Khayyám* of its Persian original. The comparison drawn here is intended to be apt, not pejorative: both works have a justly celebrated place as cultural products of the English language, and the success of both is due not least to their freedom (I am almost tempted to write 'cavalier attitude') with respect to the originals, whose relationship to the end-product is much more that of inspiration than of control. The Gelineau Psalms (1965), a fresh translation set to modern chants, and the use of the King James Version with traditional Anglican chants, equally reflect a creative borrowing which successfully transposes (but does not translate) the Psalms from one medium to another.

There is no intention to deny the legitimacy of such transpositions; indeed, in one sense at least they are truer to the originals than many literary or theological interpretations, for there is little doubt that where psalms were used in worship[5] they were accompanied by music and by musical instruments. Several titles indicate this, and though the titles are certainly later additions, they undoubtedly reflect ancient practice. Thus, for example, Psalm 6: 'To the choir-master: with stringed instruments; according to The Sheminith'. The mysterious final phrase (and others like it at the head of other Psalms) is usually taken to refer to the name of a particular chant or musical motif. Within some psalms we find references to perform-ance involving musical instruments and dance – and in the case of Psalm 150 the ancient equivalent of a symphony orchestra appears to be indicated![6] In 1 Chronicles 15:16–24 David's instructions to the Levites to provide musical accompaniment for a procession of the Ark are reported, while permanent arrangements for temple worship are given in 1 Chronicles 25. Recently at least two serious attempts have been made on the basis of musicological interpretations of the accent marks found in Hebrew texts from the sixth century CE and later to recover the chants which are presumed to have been sung in the post-exilic temple.[7]

Historical criticism

Perhaps the most familiar of modern approaches to Psalms study is that of historical criticism, by which is meant the process of asking

7

– and seeking answers to – a whole range of broadly speaking historical questions. When were the Psalms written, and by whom? To what social or cultural context do they belong? Can they be related to known historical events, or to events which can be plausibly reconstructed? What is the status of the various introductory headings found attached to many, though not all, Psalms? Does the division into five Books, and the overall order, have any historical significance?[8]

Attempts to answer these and similar questions have generated a huge literature. What they all share is the characteristic of being external to the text itself. The answers, should they be forthcoming, will not enable us to interpret any particular psalm; though they might provide contextual material which will shape a particular reading. Thus if (as is commonly held) Psalm 74 was composed in the light of the destruction of Jerusalem and its temple by the Babylonians in 587 BCE, certain features of the text can be appropriately interpreted. But such historically constrained readings do not necessarily exhaust meaning, and can stifle interpretation by consigning such psalms to the category of historical curiosities. Moreover, it is rare indeed for anything like a plausible historical setting to be available; if we were to confine our readings to those informed by history we would have remarkably little to say.

It is not the purpose of this study to engage in more than a passing way with the historical approach; though it will form one stage of interpretation in the formal process set out in Chapter 5. Since most commentaries survey the historical proposals more or less thoroughly, it will be sufficient to leave the reader to consult the various commentaries with a view to gleaning any useful background of a historical nature. An annotated selection of the main commentaries is provided in section 1 of the bibliography.

Literary criticism

In the field of biblical studies it is common to refer to a set of approaches, which in other disciplines would be regarded as broadly historical, by the title *literary criticism*. This convention is somewhat confusing, since outside the field literary criticism has a rather different meaning. What is indicated in fact is a concern with three rather specific techniques which emerged largely in the nineteenth and early twentieth centuries in response to the particular character of the Jewish Bible. They are: the study of form and genre; the study of sources; and the study of the editorial process (redaction criticism) or the history of tradition. Since these are regularly described and discussed in almost every basic account of modern biblical studies[9] I will not detail them here, but will simply indicate how they have impinged upon study of the Psalms, and how my description of them as essentially a branch of historical criticism may be justified.

Almost every commentary published since the late nineteenth century has devoted considerable space to historical and literary criticism in the terms defined above, dealing at some length with plausible, or not so plausible, historical contexts, but most importantly offering a categorisation of each psalm in form-critical terms. This became a virtual *sine qua non* of Psalms commentaries following Gunkel's groundbreaking work of 1930 which brought significant order to what had seemed – in critical terms – random material. Reinforced by Mowinckel's magisterial *The Psalms in Israel's Worship* (ET 1962), which effectively brought Gunkel's form-critical thesis into harmony with a festival-based reconstruction of how the Psalms were actually used, it is no exaggeration to say that it is only in the last few years that the composite paradigm thus created has begun to be radically questioned. The paradigm is undoubtedly an attractive one, bringing together as it does several seemingly natural assumptions: the Psalms were used in some kind of worship; they have their origins mostly in the period of the monarchy; the form or genre of a particular psalm gives us access to its particular role or function in the liturgy of ancient Israel. Using this approach Mowinckel postulated a festival of the enthronement of Yahweh; A. R. Johnson (1955) argued on the basis of sophisticated linguistic analysis of the details of individual psalms that Israel practised a ceremony similar to the ritual humiliation of the king in Babylon; and Artur Weiser (1962) assumed throughout his commentary that a covenant festival lay behind the collection of Psalms. None of these supposed ritual or cultic events can be identified either in the narratives and laws of the Pentateuch or in the Prophets. Yet they are confidently assumed in commentary after commentary and in numerous learned articles. The reason for this acceptance lies in the nature of form criticism, whose essential aim is to recover an appropriate *Sitz im Leben* (setting in life) for each unit, or 'form'. Since the primary task of allocating a genre to the psalm or part-psalm under discussion has a clear relevance, it tended to be accepted that the longer-term project was also justified. To take a simple example: there is little doubt that the genre of Psalm 2 is that of a coronation liturgy. What does not so readily follow is any conclusion about its actual use. The piece could indeed have been retrieved from some actual coronation ceremony, though its historical location remains unknown; but it could just as well have been composed as a sort of pastiche, mimicking a familiar genre for the writer's own purposes. The fact that Psalm 2 forms part of the introduction to the whole Psalter,[10] that it makes explicit reference to the anointed (Hebrew *mashiach*) messiah, and that it uses exalted language for the relationship between the king and Yahweh – 'You are my son: today I have begotten you (2:7) – might very plausibly be taken to demonstrate that Psalm 2 is one of those post-exilic writings (parts of Chronicles belong to the same type) which idealises the long-vanished Davidic monarchy in terms of an apocalyptic hope. The fundamental mistake made by too many form-critical approaches is to assume that the Psalms have been collected directly from ancient cultic use, so that the only *Sitz im Leben* ever considered is that of the religious festival or ceremony. Only if external evidence for the liturgical event exists can we with any confidence associate a given psalm with it; the problem with the 'lost festival' approach to the problem is that it assumes that the Psalms contain evidence for these rituals, and then proceeds to interpret the Psalms in terms of them. This evident circularity seriously weakens, even if it does not absolutely destroy, the usefulness of the hypothesis.

An interesting variant on this approach is to be found in a series of studies by Michael Goulder.[11] He has produced ingenious accounts of four of the major sub-collections in the Psalter (Korah: 42–9, 84–5, 87–8; David: 51–72; Asaph: 50, 73–83; Book V: 107–50) in which he reconstructs both historical and liturgical contexts in relation to the major historical narrative traditions of the Jewish Bible. Like Johnson's 1955 study, Goulder's work demonstrates impressive expertise and versatility in decoding details of the Hebrew text, and has certainly put very firmly on the scholarly agenda the requirement that we take seriously the groupings within the Psalter, rather than simply dismissing them as evidence of later and irrelevant editorial activity. But in so far as Goulder's work depends on a rather literal reading of the historical traditions, it falls foul of much current historical work which tends to undermine the reliability of those accounts which underpin his approach. In the case, for example, of the Korahite Psalms, few would now endorse the idea of a northern kingdom group bringing its festivals to Judah after the fall of Samaria; and at a time when the very existence of David and his supposed empire is being questioned by serious scholars[12] it is a bold act, if not one of defiance, to explain a Davidic collection of Psalms on the assumption of a festival re-enacting significant events of his reign. Goulder has made the interesting suggestion that the mysterious rubric *selah* which appears in a number of psalms is an indication that at these points a lection was to be read; he then goes on to speculate that these 'readings for the day' are none other than pertinent sections of the appropriate historical book. This is a fascinating, but completely unsupported proposal, and may owe more to his long-standing interest in scripture's lectionary role in the early church[13] than to its inherent probability.

Source criticism and tradition history have had less importance in Psalms study. The existence of 'Yahwist' and 'Elohist' sub-collections[14] in which at least one psalm is repeated with the divine name YHWH replaced by the generic *'elohim*, suggests that sources might have been combined from separate origins. More generally the repetition of psalms or part-psalms within the Psalter and in other parts of the Jewish Bible indicates a process in which smaller collections were merged, with concomitant editing. Recent studies have begun to open up this avenue of research, suggesting that there is purposeful editing behind the order and form of the collection as we know it.[15] Inevitably these studies become rather technical, and I will not deal with them in this book except where they impinge on my particular remit. When we come to look at Psalms 120–34 (the so-called Psalms of Ascents) in Part III I will have cause to refer to some of the editorial theories which have recently been proposed.

Theological questions

Undoubtedly the Psalms have had a profound theological influence on the Christian tradition, and it is important therefore to acknowledge that approach to Psalms study which addresses theological questions. The Psalms contain messianic references, both explicit and implicit – consider, for example, Psalms 2, 110 and 132; and, whatever their original meaning, they have readily been adapted to Christian doctrines of the Christ. Psalms are quoted at key points in the Gospel accounts of the life of Jesus,[16] where they seem to have prophetic force. This has led to a much more extensive use of the Psalter as a rich source of 'prophecies' about the messianic character of Jesus, and has given the Psalms a theological significance in Christianity which they simply do not possess in Judaism.

The Christological use of the Psalms is a matter of some debate even within Christian discourse. There are many who are made profoundly uneasy by the assumptions which underpin this form of interpretation. While there may well be psalms which refer to David (at least in the mind of the composer; it is less likely that any were composed by him), this does not establish any causal link with the person of Jesus. To effect that link it is necessary to bring in some such theory as the *Heilsgeschichte*[17] – that explanation of the history of the Jews which sees it as the continuous working out of a divine plan for the salvation of humankind – or 'typology' – whereby characters and events in the Old Testament are regarded as presaging or fore-shadowing their 'antitypes' in the New. Both of these are equally at odds with conventional and scholarly understandings of history, and have tended to be marginalised in historical-critical studies. Yet they have been, and continue to be, extraordinarily influential in Christian circles. Two millennia of messianic appropriation of the Psalms have given them a central place in the worship, teaching and contemplative orders of the Church throughout the world. It is not necessary to share this view (or even to sympathise with it) to recognise its legitimacy, within its own terms, as a reading.

Personal inspiration

For many lay people, certainly within the Christian tradition, it is their value as a source of personal inspiration which gives the Psalms their lasting importance. The familiar, yet still reassuring sentiments of Psalm 23, or the example of personal contrition and forgiveness provided by Psalm 51, give these ancient compositions an imme-diacy for the individual which is undeniable. And at another point of the spiritual spectrum, the sense of awe created by Psalm 139,[18] and the more familiar mood of praise engendered by Psalm 100 (most commonly in its metrical form, 'All people that on earth do dwell'), ensure their continuing vitality. Such verses have contributed incalculably to the personal and spiritual development of many for whom theology is a remote abstraction and critical biblical study an obscure pedantry. We may, as scholars, feel uneasy when we come upon such a 'misprision'[19] as 'I to the hills will lift mine eyes, from whence doth come mine aid' which succeeds in exactly reversing the probable sense of the Hebrew.[20] Worse, it has encouraged an endless stream of mawkish reflections on the experience of God or the numinous to be had on mountain tops (particularly in Scotland, whose preachers rarely miss an opportunity to combine religious sentimentality with a puff for the Highlands and Islands Tourist Board). Yet we cannot simply ignore them or treat them contemptu-ously as mere ill-informed piety. For, however much a certain type of scholarly mind may suffer as Psalm 23 is intoned (yet again) to the tune *Crimond* as part of a public ceremony of a quasi-religious order, there is an undeniable authenticity to pious readings so long as these are clearly understood to be personal in character.

It might be helpful to summarise the point we have reached in this quest for a literary approach to the Psalms. From an initial recognition that the Psalms form a body of literature in a long-dead language, I noted that there exists a lengthy and complex tradition linking that literature, in many different ways, with our own time. I have claimed that anything other than an approximate translation is effectively beyond our reach, and that the original author or authors are equally inaccessible, thus ruling out the possibility of successfully appealing to intention as a means of interpreting or explaining the texts. In fact, even a brief survey has shown that there are a great many types of reading, generated by the needs or interests of a variety of readers. Some of these are theologically constrained, others are deeply subjective; some focus on rather pedantic points of linguistic or historical interest, while others engage in the bold venture of seeking to reconstruct the setting and use of the Psalms in their own time. The primary desideratum with which this study will proceed is that of achieving some sort of public, shared discourse with which to address the contemporary task of 'reading the Psalms'.

There is one other, perhaps naive, question which should be put: what sort of material are we dealing with? Are the Psalms poetry, or heightened prose? If the former, is their reference religious or everyday (if indeed it is proper to make such a distinction in the world of the ancient Near East)? Is their character, even if poetic, that rather specialised poetry which is familiar to us from hymnaries and liturgies? It is clear that the Hebrew Psalms meet the various criteria usually taken to define poetry in that language, and the translations and versions almost without exception present the Psalms in the typographic form of verse. There is some evidence from manuscripts found in the Dead Sea area, dating mostly from the first century BCE and the first century CE, that the scribes who produced these documents were conscious of a quite subtle distinction. We find, for example, that fragments of the Psalms, and also a portion of Deuteronomy 32, which is often referred to as 'The Song of Moses', are written in such a way that lines end on the parchment where the natural poetic line-breaks occur. By contrast, the Scroll of Isaiah, containing prophetic oracles whose linguistic *form* in Hebrew is largely similar to that of poetry, is written in prose form. Could the ancient scribes have been aware of a genre difference (not that they would have used that term) between the Psalms and the Prophetic literature which matches our own sense that poetry is a rather special kind of composition?

The question of the nature of the Psalms as poetry is discussed in more depth in Chapter 4; but I end this preliminary account by proposing a framework for the reading of the Psalms within a broadly literary context, which will be examined in detail in Chapters 2 and 3. I propose to assume, with appropriate discussion, an agreed translation, a definition of a set of readers, textuality as our *modus operandi*, a means of providing some critique of readings, and an ongoing dialogue among and between

(a) sets of readers
(b) sorts of readings and
(c) translations and 'the text'.

2

WHICH TRANSLATION?

The decision to engage upon a literary study of the Psalms pre-supposes that an acceptable version has been agreed upon. For the great majority of readers this is a far from simple matter: what physical textual object should we assume to be either literally or metaphorically before us as we read?

If we – the presumed author and his or her readers – were able to read classical Hebrew with equal facility, the answer would be relatively simple: we could agree to use the Hebrew text.[1] This is, unfortunately, simply impractical; for whatever the desirability of acquiring a knowledge of classical Hebrew, the company of those who have an interest in the Psalms is vastly greater than that of readers of Hebrew. It is necessary, therefore, to decide upon an English version with which to engage; and it is here that a further set of problems emerges. It would no doubt be possible to provide new translations of those Psalms which are under discussion. While this would make it easier to display the poetic and other literary features in which we are specially interested, it would be in effect a series of highly personalised texts – private readings which might be of satisfaction to myself (or my ego), but which would have no public reputation to recommend them. Further, they would share certain unhelpful features with the Hebrew originals, in that most readers would be ill-equipped to discern whether the individual translations offered were more or less true to the Hebrew than any of the wide range of existing public translations. These at least are supported by a range of scholarly expertise, and those who *could* judge the merits of my new versions might just as well go straight to the Hebrew.

In the light of these observations it is surely more appropriate to adopt an existing widely available and widely used version as our basic text. Certain criteria can be identified to guide the choice: does the version explicitly seek to provide a 'faithful' translation, or does it have the frank aim of interpreting the original more freely? Are there academic or theological presuppositions built in to the work of the translators which may have skewed the result?[2] Is the translation honest – that is, do the translators reveal, through footnotes or addenda, those places where unresolvable ambiguity in the original precludes an authoritative interpretation, or where the original is simply incomprehensible? It is surprising how often these matters are ignored or glossed over, and smooth versions produced in English which belie what can be described only as the anarchy of the original. It is important also to be clear that there is nothing specially privileged about the version we settle upon. The choice will be made on the kind of intelligently pragmatic grounds indicated. What we are seeking is a 'best fit', appropriate to the concerns of a literary approach; there is no implication that those not chosen are to be dismissed out of hand. A choice must be made; others may choose differently, and there is little more to be said. It may be helpful to observe that the problem of identifying an 'authorised' text is not confined to the Bible. There are various editions of most of Shakespeare's plays; the text of *Ulysses* is notoriously the subject of rather acrimonious debate;[3] and it would be a rash scholar who would claim to be confident of the 'authentic' edition of Wordsworth's *Prelude*.

Having adopted an edition, however, it will none the less fall to the responsible interpreter to bring to bear upon it a certain limited special privilege based on the Hebrew text. For it is necessary to clarify (for instance) why the version is as it is at particular points, or why certain alternatives have been rejected. There are places also where the Hebrew employs a particularly striking structure, or achieves a notable effect which cannot be reproduced in English, and these ought to be pointed out – but only on a strictly limited basis. This exercise of discipline is required lest a private translation be slipped in, as it were, through the back door. In any case, many of the points that it might be necessary to make will be found through a judicious survey of the major technical commentaries. A careful use of these sources will help to provide much of the relevant information of use to the reader of the Psalms in English. Too much detail is likely only to obscure the issues, while the major questions are fairly systematically covered. In my discussion of individual psalms in Part II and the Psalms of Ascents in Part III I will adopt this approach.

Which versions, then, are the likely candidates? Several come to mind almost immediately: the King James, popularly known as the

Authorised Version (KJV); the New International Version (NIV); the Revised Standard Version (RSV); the New English Bible (NEB). Each of the last two has been the subject of thorough updating and revision in recent years, without affecting the characteristic tone. Thus we should also consider, respectively, the Revised English Bible (REB) and the New Revised Standard Version (NRSV). Finally, account should be taken of the two major translations from the Catholic tradition – the Jerusalem Bible (JB) and its recent successor the New Jerusalem Bible (NJB). Certain 'free' translations, like the Good News Bible and the Living Bible have been deliberately left out of consideration. Since the admitted purpose of each of these is to paraphrase, they have ruled themselves out in terms of the kind of principles elucidated in Chapter 1. We require for our use a version whose stated intention is to render the Hebrew into English which, within the inevitable limits, provides a fair and accurate expression of the original. This is not in the least to go back on earlier comments about the likelihood of success in such an enterprise; but not even to attempt the task takes us into the realms of what are best described as compositions 'inspired by' or 'suggested by' the Hebrew, and not in any sense that matters representative of the language of first composition.

Given that whichever we use must be strongly positioned (that is, having a wide readership and general acceptance) we can safely narrow the choice to the following short leet:[4] the KJV, the NIV, the RSV (and the NRSV), the NEB (and the REB), and the NJB (and the JB). The chronological order of the last two reverses that of the other pairs, not least because the JB is, as a scholarly production, on a different footing from the others. It might also be appropriate to bracket the NIV with the KJV, since part of its stated intention is to return to the language of the King James wherever possible. In order to refine the choice further, it will be helpful – and revealing – to consider what they have to say for themselves. Such declarations of intent are typically to be found in the translators'[5] Prefaces, to which I now turn. In particular, I will return to the three 'diagnostic questions' which were posed at the beginning of this chapter, in the hope that they will provide a framework within which to assess the extent to which these different versions satisfy our requirements.

Is a 'faithful' translation intended?

This might seem to be the least problematic question. Since we have deliberately excluded examples of free interpretation, and since all the versions we have looked at claim, in one way or another, to be as true to the original as current knowledge and skills permit, we might reasonably take this criterion as having been met. The King James Version may speak for all when its translators give their reasons for what they are about:

> But how shall men meditate in that which they cannot understand? How shall they understand that which is kept close in an unknown tongue? . . . Translation it is that openeth the window, to let in the light; that breaketh the shell, that we may eat the kernel; that putteth aside the curtain, that we may look into the most holy place; that removeth the cover of the well, that we may come by the water.
>
> (KJV: 3a)

The language is perhaps a little florid, but the sentiment is a fine one, shared by all who engage upon the task. That they are professional and responsible in their approach to the work of translation is equally clear:

> [W]e never thought from the beginning that we should need to make a new translation, nor yet to make of a bad one a good one . . . but to make a good one better, or out of many good ones one principal good one. . . . The work hath not been huddled up in seventy two days[6] but hath cost the workmen, as light as it seemeth, the pains of twice seven times seventy two days, and more. Matters of such weight and consequence are to be speeded with maturity: for in a business of a moment a man feareth not the blame of convenient slackness. . . . But having and using as great helps as were needful, and fearing no reproach for slowness, nor coveting praise for expedition, we have at length, through the good hand of the LORD upon us, brought the work to that pass that you see.
>
> (ibid.: 7a,b)

This methodological statement (which, in its full form, makes clear the translators' dependence upon a host of prior work – commentaries; earlier translations; Aramaic, Hebrew, Syriac, Greek and Latin originals and versions) establishes a scholarly dynasty of translation to which each of our versions belongs. Given also that many see themselves as standing in the KJV tradition,[7] and all defer to it, we can readily appreciate the seminal character of that monumental work for all future responsible biblical translation.

There are, however, some reservations to be entered. When, for example, the Preface to the KJV speaks of 'divine authorship' and 'inspired penmen',[8] is something introduced which might skew the translation – an assumption made, for example, which owes more to a (hidden) theological assumption than to a proper presentation of the text's own evidence? This is particularly true of the handling of what might appear to be unacceptable statements concerning the status of God. For example, the Hebrew of Psalm 82 begins 'God ('elohim) stands in the assembly of 'el' (the name of the chief deity of the Canaanite pantheon); the KJV has 'God standeth in the congregation of the mighty'. The NRSV, still avoiding the issue, at least flirts with the unthinkable: 'God has taken his place in the *divine* council' (similarly the JB and NJB: 'divine assembly').[9] A more striking example is that of Ruth 1:15–16. In verse 15 Naomi urges Ruth to return to 'her people and to her gods' (NRSV), while in the next verse Ruth avers that 'your people shall be my people and your God my God'. The KJV is substantially the same, as is the NIV; in the JB and NJB, however, the translation reads 'Look, your sister-in-law has gone back to her people and to her god.' In fact the same Hebrew word is translated 'gods' and 'God' (a consequence of the fact that the common generic form 'elohim, though grammatically plural, is used in both singular and plural contexts). Where there is a difference in the English it lies in two theological assumptions: that Naomi, as an Israelite, must have been monotheistic; and that Ruth, as a Moabite, must have had a plurality of gods. Neither of these is indisputably true of the period which is assumed for the story, the time of the Judges.

These may seem to be pedantic points, but they cut to an important issue of principle which is implicit in my second question – the part played by theological or other presuppositions in the process of translation. Certainly no one translation will pass every test; but at the very least readers should be aware, where possible, of the kinds of issues which are likely to have affected what they assume to be an accurate interpretation. I will turn to that more urgent question in a moment; but must first raise a different sort of concern, which is implicit in the processes described both by the NEB and the NIV, but is a problematic of every 'committee-produced' translation. I mean the interaction between individual translators, panels of translators, and panels concerned with style and overall presentation.

These are presumably unavoidable processes, but they introduce serious doubts about the character of the final production. The NIV describes a hierarchical system in which the ultimate publication is authorised by the highest stage. It is worth quoting the relevant passage, since the publishers are evidently proud of this aspect of their work:

> How it was made helps to give the New International Version its distinctiveness. The translation of each book was assigned to a team of scholars. Next, one of the Intermediate Editorial Committees revised the initial translation, with constant reference to the Hebrew, Aramaic or Greek. Their work then went to one of the General Editorial Committees, which checked it in detail and made another thorough revision. This revision in turn was carefully reviewed by the Committee on Bible Translation, which made further changes and then released the final version for publication. In this way the entire Bible underwent three revisions, during each of which the translation was examined for its faithfulness to the original languages and for its English style. All this involved many thousands of hours of research and discussion regarding the meaning of the texts and the precise way of putting them into English. It may well be that no other translation has been made by a more thorough process of review and revision from committee to committee than this one.
>
> (NIV: xi)

The problem is a familiar one to anyone who has seen the progress of a sensitive document through committee procedures: these very processes make room for a wide range of perhaps irrelevant and possibly damaging special interests to be given undue prominence. In the case of the NIV, for example, one might wonder whether the influence of the sponsors – the Christian Reformed Church and the National Association of Evangelicals – and the stated belief in 'the authority and infallibility of the Bible as God's Word in written form' have had any effect. Their influence could explain, for instance, the decision to return to the (now largely discredited) reading 'virgin' for the Hebrew *'almah* in Isaiah 7.14. But no modern translation is free of this kind of reservation: the best we can do is to identify any effect it may have had. Often, indeed, the worst charge is of a certain blandness, with the robust language of the original euphemistically rendered in the interests of a rather antiquated reserve. Hebrew is quite happy to call a spade a spade (or a breast a breast, for that matter), and we do the original a disservice by softening its blunt-ness. Ironically, the KJV is much less prurient than its successors in this respect, though the tide has apparently begun to turn again (compare, for example, Proverbs 5:19 in the KJV, RSV and NRSV; but, contrariwise, look at 1 Kings 21:21 in the same three versions![10]).

One final observation on this first question. Each translation apparently aspires to produce a fluent and clear English version, yet all acknowledge problems (often intractable) with the original. The Preface to the KJV puts it rather charmingly:

> [I]t hath pleased God in his Divine Providence here and there to scatter words and sentences of that difficulty and doubtfulness, not in doctrinal points that concern salvation, (for in such it hath been vouched that the Scriptures are plain,) but in matters of less moment, that fearfulness would better beseem us than confidence. . . .
>
> (7b)

The caginess of this statement is instructive: there is an awareness that to admit that there is some doubt or confusion in the text of scripture could have far-reaching consequences, and so avoiding action is taken in the form of a quite unsupported assertion that none of the dubious passages affects important doctrine. In various ways, all translations recognise the problem;[11] the NEB is the most radical in dealing with it, and is not shy about rearranging the text at many points where it might seem (to the translators? to the committee?) to make more sense.[12] It may be objected that there is a real incom-patibility between the need to render accurately what we have before us, and the need to give the audience a text it can easily follow. I suspect that biblical translations too often err in favour of the audience, and that it would be healthier, as well as more honest, to produce a confusing translation of a confused text. No doubt the system of footnotes can help, but even that is misleading, as we shall see when we turn to my third question.

In so far as the first question helps us to choose, the most serious reservations must be entered against the NEB and the NIV, both of which in my judgement allow quite intrusive features (the former in its extreme freedom with the arrangement of the text, the latter in its committee control by a group with a special interest to pursue) an unnecessary influence in the final translation. We may leave aside the 1966 Jerusalem Bible, since it has been criticised by its own successor (NJB) both for its reliance on its 1956 French predecessor (La Bible de Jérusalem) and for a tendency to paraphrase.[13]

What presuppositions (overt or hidden) might intrude on the translation?

This is not entirely separate from the first question, but is distinct in one important respect: it relates to meta-translational assumptions – beliefs (or prejudices) which have no necessary connection with the text in question, but which are none the less brought to bear on the work in progress. The fact that the Jewish Bible was believed by most if not all of those engaged in the production of our selection of translations to have been divinely inspired, and this belief was certainly officially held by every sponsoring group, cannot be irrelevant. We may assume that it remains a background belief which does not impinge too much upon the quotidian work of translation – though my remarks above on translations of Psalm 82 and Ruth 1 suggest that this may be an overly naive assumption. However, having noted it, there is little we can do, since there seems not to be any complete version which has been produced in a secular context.[14] What does raise cause for concern, however, is that there are degrees of forcefulness with which the doctrine is affirmed. It might be possible, by noting these, to identify relative criteria to guide our choice. Further, there is a closely related assumption (again driven by the very nature of the groups which have in the main initiated and funded the work of translation) that the scriptures (Hebrew and Greek alike) are Christian, and that their readership is made up of those who desire a closer knowledge of Jesus Christ.

The KJV, not surprisingly, is distressingly forthright; though it mercifully lacks that element of pious self-satisfaction in the form of false modesty which is a feature of some more recent efforts.[15] Following an admirable 'desire that the Scripture may speak like itself, as in the language of *Canaan*, that it may be understood even of the very vulgar', we descend to this warning to the 'gentle Reader': 'Ye are brought unto fountains of living water which ye digged not; do not cast earth into them, with the Philistines, neither prefer broken pits before them, with the wicked Jews' (KJV: 8b).

There we have it then: Jews and Philistines are excluded from the circle of readers of the Bible (despite the fact that both of their histories are given in its pages). While the King James Version's baldness might be excused as a consequence of the culture in which it was produced, the more subtle exclusivism which is found in the NIV (see footnote 15), the RSV ('This ecumenical edition has been prepared with the consent and co-operation of the Division of Christian Education of the National Council of the Churches of Christ' – but not, it appears, in consultation with the Jews), the NRSV ('This new version . . . is intended for use in public reading and congregational worship', a formulation which tends to pre-suppose a Christian context[16]) and the REB ('All those who have been concerned with the production of this translation have done their work in the conviction that the Old Testament has contributed vitally to every tradition of Christian worship and culture, and that an accurate understanding of the Bible of the Jews is essential to the full appreciation of Christian doctrine and the events recorded in the New Testament') must inevitably remind us that when we choose our translation of the Psalms we will invariably be reading a version filtered through Christian lenses.[17] The saving grace, such as it is, belongs to those who at least acknowledge a shared inheritance: the NRSV ('In traditional Judaism and Christianity, the Bible . . . is recognised as the unique record of God's dealings with people over the ages') and the REB ('the Bible of the Jews').

I have lingered over this point because I believe it to be the single most intrusive yet least noticed hindrance to a proper understanding of the Jewish Bible. On this ground alone, I would be strongly inclined to exclude the NIV, the KJV and the RSV from further consideration; but the others are only marginally better in this respect. Other presuppositions are also present, more representative of cultural than religious conditioning. Thus masculine gender may be used where neutral (or feminine) would be just as good;[18] though in some recent versions, an explicit intention to avoid this bias is announced.[19] There are problems relating to unrecognised forms of language which are in fact purely biblical, no longer used in modern formal (let alone idiomatic) English, but which persist because of the overwhelming influence of the KJV. One of the most difficult tasks confronting students familiar with traditional biblical expressions is to render passages of Hebrew into idiomatic English. I am therefore sympathetic to the (sadly, failed) attempt made by the NEB to grasp this particular nettle.[20] Oddly enough, for all its undoubted anachronisms, the KJV frequently contains idiomatic translations which have not been bettered. This not to say that we can simply cut the Gordian knot and go back to 1611; but it might be an indication that there is something to be said for those modern versions which trace their ancestry explicitly to the King James – and here the obvious candidates must be the RSV or the NRSV and the NIV.

How honest is the process of translation?

This may seem a strange criterion to impose, but experience has shown that in most versions there are hidden changes and un-acknowledged resolutions of ambiguities which make a material difference to the understanding of the text. As a result the English text sometimes reads much more smoothly and coherently than the Hebrew, thus deceiving the reader into thinking that it is problem-free and uncontroversial, where the reverse is the case. Perhaps the reason lies in the need to be economical with footnotes; even so, some are worse than others, and it is worth identifying the culprits!

The KJV sets an honourable precedent in its insistence on the use of proper marginal notes. It is worth recording that the marginal notes we now take for granted in every reputable edition of the Bible were once the subject of controversy precisely because they make public the fact of uncertainties and differences of opinion about the original texts. The translators of 1611 had this to say in their defence:

> Some peradventure would have no variety of senses to be set in the margin, lest the authority of the Scriptures for deciding of controversies by that show of uncertainty should somewhat be shaken. But we hold their judgement not to be so sound in this point. . . . There be many words in the Scriptures, which be never found there but once . . . so that we cannot be holpen by conference of places. . . . Now in such a case doth not a margin do well to admonish the Reader to seek further, and not to conclude or dogmatize upon this or that peremptorily? For as it is a fault of incredulity, to doubt of those things that are evident; so to determine of such things as the Spirit of God hath left (even in the judgement of the judicious) questionable, can be no less than presumption.
>
> (KJV: 7b, 8a)

The problem with footnotes (or marginal notes) is that the margins quickly become full, and decisions have to be taken as to what needs to be communicated to the 'very vulgar' – or, in modern terms, the lay reader. Some of the questionable decisions taken are unacknowl-edged – yet many editions carry between passages of scripture a system of cross-reference which is irrelevant to translation, but a significant indicator of the theological interests of the translators. While the use of cross-references to show where one text quotes another may seem innocent, it has the effect of creating an organic whole out of the combination of Old and New Testaments, not just on the general principle that for Christianity this is a given, but in significant detail. Thus the seemingly innocuous cross-reference between Isaiah 7:14 and Matthew 1:23 is more than a mere factual note, for it has the effect of lending apparent authority to Matthew's misreading of Isaiah 7:14, and endorsing in consequence a very specific ideology of prophecy.[21] More strikingly, it is common to find Genesis 3:15 linked to several New Testament verses – though none actually quotes it: thus the KJV (Romans 16:20; Hebrews 2:14; 1 John 3:8); the NIV (Matthew 1:23; Luke 1:31; Galatians 4:4; Revelation 12:17; Romans 16:20; Hebrews 2:14); RSV (Revelation 12:9; 20:2); the JB and NJB (Revelation 12:17). The diversity of links gives the game away; and it is made perfectly explicit by the footnote commentary provided in the (N)JB: this is a theological interpretation of the Genesis verse as a messianic prophecy, an interpretation first made by the Christian Fathers. These are not isolated cases, and they make it clear that the purpose of footnotes is to sustain a systematic hermeneutic which effectively pre-empts many alternative readings. It is encouraging, therefore, that the NEB, the REB and the NRSV do not include cross-references, while the extensive commentary provided by both Jerusalem Bibles must, on the contrary, render them less useful for the kind of reading which a literary approach envisages. In effect, space which could have been devoted to a greater openness and clarity of translation is given over to a system of secondary interpretation which, though at times helpful, is as often misleading, and is strictly speaking irrelevant.

Given that the RSV uses cross-references of this kind, its approach to emendation is somewhat unsatisfactory:

> The present revision is based on the consonantal Hebrew and Aramaic text as fixed early in the Christian era and revised by Jewish scholars (the 'Masoretes') of the sixth to the ninth centuries. The vowel signs also, which were added by the Masoretes, are accepted in the main, but where a more probable and convincing reading can be obtained by supplying different vowels, this reading has been adopted. No notes are given in such cases, because the vowel points are less ancient and reliable than the consonants.

Departures from the consonantal text of the best manuscripts have been made only where it seems clear that errors in copying had occurred before the text was standardized. . . . In every such instance a footnote specifies the version or versions from which the correction has been derived, and also gives a translation of the Masoretic Text.

Sometimes it is evident that the text has suffered in transmission, but none of the versions provides a satisfactory restoration. Here we can only follow the best judgement of competent scholars as to the most probable reconstruction of the original text. Such corrections are indicated in the footnotes by the abbreviation Cn, and a translation of the Masoretic Text is added.

(RSV: vi)

There are two problems with this account (I have no quarrel with the middle paragraph). The failure to record departures from the traditional vowels is unacceptable, since these are just as significant as the changes indicated in the first and third paragraphs, and the reader ought to know where they occur. The other problem is lesser, but still significant. The use of the abbreviation 'Cn' is at times an invitation to a less than sympathetic approach to the text, for on occasions it is used where the text is not in fact intractable, but simply difficult or obscure. Translatable obscurities should be left to the reader to resolve. Thus, for example, the emendation of Psalm 2:11–12 is labelled 'Cn' in both the RSV and the NRSV. The text, however, can be translated – as 'rejoice with trembling; kiss the son' – with the last word oddly, but not untranslatably, in Aramaic rather than Hebrew (see Chapter 5, pp. 64f.). There is a similar case in Proverbs 3:35, where the Hebrew reads 'fools exalt shame or disgrace'. Most versions offer 'fools get or inherit disgrace', or something similar; the RSV denotes it by 'Cn', and the NRSV passes over the change in silence. Surely it is not so strange to imagine fools taking pride in that which, for wiser folk, would be a cause for shame? The translator here, it seems, is trespassing firmly on the territory of the interpreter.

The NEB, as has already been noted, shifts whole passages in the interests of what the translators take to be a more coherent text;[22] and it is famous (if not notorious) for having introduced a considerable number of what can best be described as idiosyncratic readings of individual words and phrases, based on a comparative philological approach to cognate languages such as Babylonian, Assyrian, Arabic,

Syrian, Aramaic, Ethiopic and others. Many of the most eccentric of these have been amended in the REB.[23]

Which version shall we choose? With some regrets, I rule out the Authorised Version, on the simple grounds that for today's readers it requires itself to be translated. I would, however, strongly recommend that a copy be kept close at hand for consultation. If translators are ever inspired, the KJV's surely were. The RSV, a sturdy workhorse of a version, is now ready for retirement. Its weaknesses are too well known, and its age is showing, in that it bears the marks of its time. Both the NIV and the NEB are too specialised, too eccentric to serve our purposes, which are to have a good, reliable, reasonably 'objective' and 'unbiased' version which will at least have the negative virtue of not alienating certain readers from the outset. The (admirably open) evangelical allegiance of the NIV, which certainly colours its readings at various points, makes it more of a sectarian than a public translation. And the oddities of the NEB, and its (courageous?) failure to find the holy grail of a contemporary idiom which is both convincing and of some permanence make it more of a curiosity than a viable translation. Similar problems attend the JB and NJB. They are too explicitly and intimately identified as study Bibles for the use of the Christian community, and their apparatus too directive, for them to serve a literary approach which ought to be open to a wide readership.

Only the REB and the NRSV remain in the field.[24] Though it retains some of the faults of the RSV, the latter has many virtues, its one great virtue being a very wide availability, which probably gives it a pragmatic advantage over the REB. I will, therefore, regard it as my source text for the discussion of the Psalms in this book. But keep the KJV to hand – we may yet need it! In the meantime, as an illustration of the issues involved, I will examine in detail the differences between the versions as they approach the translation of a particular Psalm.

Translating Psalm 29

One of the most interesting compositions in the Psalter is Psalm 29. There is a broad consensus that if any of the Psalms has a claim to belong to the Canaanite world, which is assumed to be the wider cultural and religious context of Israel, it is this one. From what we know of Ugaritic liturgical compositions, there are very clear affinities; and the simple substitution of Baal for 'LORD' throughout Psalm 29 would convert it to a piece which could immediately be associated with the Ras Shamra texts. This is not to say that Psalm 29 was composed for a Canaanite celebration; the point is that we see in this example the way that Hebrew (or Israelite) and Canaanite traditions significantly overlap.

One of the signs of this is the picture of the divine council which lies behind verse 1; another is the fact that at a number of points the text is peculiarly difficult to interpret. The KJV has no fewer than nine marginal notes on the text; the others have fewer, but the different translations make it clear that we are dealing with a particularly problematic case. I will provide an interpretative reading of this Psalm in Chapters 5 and 6; my immediate interest is to set out comparatively the way the six versions I have considered deal with the task of making an English version where no single agreed line is available.

Verse 1

The first line of this verse contains a phrase, *bene 'elim*, which almost certainly is a reference to a gathering of gods – its most likely literal meaning is 'sons of the gods' or 'sons of El'.[25]

KJV	Give unto the LORD, O ye mighty	NIV	Ascribe to the LORD, O mighty ones
RSV	Ascribe to the LORD, O heavenly beings	NRSV	Ascribe to the LORD, O heavenly beings
NEB	Ascribe to the LORD, you gods	REB	Ascribe to the LORD, you angelic powers
JB	Pay tribute to Yahweh, you sons of God	NJB	Give Yahweh his due, sons of God

Only the NEB, the JB and the NJB face up to the full implication of the Hebrew. The REB's 'angelic powers' is a straightforward anachronistic misrepresentation, introducing a concept from (at the earliest) the third century BCE to a text hundreds of years older, and invoking, for Christian readers at least, wholly inappropriate imagery.[26] The KJV and the NIV remove the phrase entirely from the supernatural realm, perhaps under pressure from the theological problems presented by the idea of the Lord being surrounded by a group of minor deities. 'Heavenly beings' is weak; but at least both the RSV and NRSV give the stronger alternative in their footnotes.

Verse 2

KJV	in the beauty of holiness	*NIV*	in the splendour of his holiness
RSV	in holy array	*NRSV*	in holy splendour
NEB	in the splendour of holiness	*REB*	in holy attire
JB	in his sacred court	NJB	in the splendour of holiness

At the end of this verse there is a phrase – *behadrat qodesh* – which resists any clear interpretation. The phrase is found just four times in the Hebrew scriptures, in three of which (Psalms 29:2 and 96:9; 1 Chronicles 16:29) exactly the same context is found. The remaining instance is in 2 Chronicles 20:21. The first word is related to a root meaning 'splendour'; perhaps the form we have (which is feminine) means 'a fine garment'. The second word means 'holy' or 'holiness', and can be used metonymically to refer to the temple (the place of God's holiness). I do not propose to enter here into the even more vexed question as to what 'holy' might mean either in Israel or in our own discourse!

This is an instance where the mystifyingly apt phrasing of the KJV can hardly be bettered; however, if we must choose another, the NRSV seems closest to the Hebrew. The NIV introduces an unsupported possessive form ('his' holiness), which I believe is simply a misreading. The RSV and the REB adopt the somewhat speculative suggestion that a garment is implied.

One other suggestion, followed by the JB and hinted at by the Septuagint, is to see here a reference to the temple. This would have the effect of providing a parallel to the explicit reference to the temple in verse 9. Since, as we shall see in due course, this Psalm exhibits powerful symmetry, that is not an inappropriate point. I am tempted, therefore, to suggest a translation based on the JB: 'Worship the LORD in the splendour of his holy place.'

Verse 3

The only variation in this verse is between 'many waters' and 'mighty waters', arising from the fact that the Hebrew adjective can have either meaning. Otherwise, the NEB (inexplicably) reverses the first two lines.

Verse 6

There is near-unanimity among the versions, with the exception of the KJV. Apart from its discovery of a unicorn (which, sadly, becomes 'a young wild ox' in the other versions), there is a curious word order which is worth noting. All the others provide a symmetric parallel: 'He makes Lebanon skip like a calf, Sirion like a young wild ox' (NEB); but the KJV reads:

> He maketh them also to skip like a calf;
> Lebanon and Sirion
> like a young unicorn.

As it happens, this is the most literal representation of the form of the Hebrew syntax of this verse, though it seems strange in English. A common poetic device in Hebrew is to place a word or phrase common to both halves (hemistichs, to use the technical term) in the middle of the line; the reader is then to understand that phrase as the subject of each hemistich. In the example before us, there is a single verb ('he makes [them] skip') which also refers to both halves. The most accurate translation (somewhat pedantically) would thus be:

> He makes Lebanon and Sirion skip like a calf,
> he makes them skip like a young wild ox.

Verse 7

The verb in this verse undoubtedly means 'to divide' or 'to cut out'. The KJV uses this meaning, which unfortunately does not seem to make much sense in English ('the voice of the LORD cuts out flames of fire'). The JB has 'The voice of Yahweh sharpens lightning shafts' and the NJB has 'carves out'. These suggest that Yahweh is engaged in the preparation of sharp weapons – a not inappropriate reading in the context of the Psalm. All of the other versions commit one of the offences noted in Chapter 2 – that of a hidden and unexplained emendation in the interests (presumably) of a (relatively) coherent English translation.

Verses 8–9

The verb *ḥil* (found in both hemistichs of verse 8 and in the first of verse 9) is somewhat puzzling. The most obvious meaning of the root is 'to give birth', though the sense of 'tremble' or 'writhe' is also found, and the problem all the versions face is that of deciding which is the appropriate sense in the context. This problem is exacerbated by the fact that the object of this verb in 9a is also ambiguous – it is a word meaning either 'hinds' or, with a small change (suggested by the reference to 'forest' in 9b) it could mean 'oak trees'. Almost certainly the psalmist is playing with words in these verses, possibly linking the ideas of verses 8 and 9 with the thought in verse 6. There is no way to resolve this quandary, and most of the versions have recourse to footnotes to indicate the ambiguity.

KJV	The voice of the LORD shaketh the wilderness; the LORD shaketh the wilderness of Kadesh. The voice of the LORD maketh the hinds to calve.	NIV	The voice of the LORD shakes the desert; the LORD shakes the Desert of Kadesh. The voice of the LORD twists the oaks.
RSV	The voice of the LORD shakes the wilderness, the LORD shakes the wilderness of Kadesh. The voice of the LORD makes the oaks to whirl.	NRSV	The voice of the LORD shakes the wilderness; the LORD shakes the wilderness of Kadesh. The voice of the LORD causes the oaks to whirl.
NEB	The voice of the LORD makes the wilderness writhe in travail; the LORD makes the wilderness of Kadesh writhe. The voice of the LORD makes the hinds calve *and brings kids early to birth.*	REB	The voice of the LORD makes the wilderness writhe in travail; the LORD makes the wilderness of Kadesh writhe. The voice of the LORD makes the hinds calve.
JB	The voice of Yahweh sets the wilderness shaking. Yahweh shakes the wilderness of Kadesh. The voice of Yahweh sets the terebinths shuddering.	NJB	Yahweh's voice convulses the desert, Yahweh convulses the desert of Kadesh, Yahweh's voice convulses terebinths.

The NEB, true to its determination to stand out from the crowd, goes even further in pursuit of the birthing metaphor and replaces an unusual plural form of the word 'forest' in 9b with another designating an animal, thus introducing complete consistency in the opposite direction to the others'. But the essence of this passage is a mixing of metaphors – God with equal ease strips forests bare and causes premature births in the animal world. Again, the KJV is closest to the spirit of the Hebrew.

Verse 11

The Psalm ends with a prayer, a promise, or an affirmation, depending upon the interpretation of the verb forms in verse 11. The KJV, the NEB and REB, by using the future tense ('The LORD will . . .'), leave us with a promise of blessings to come. The RSV and NRSV use a precative form of the verb ('May the LORD . . . ') and so leave the Psalm as it began, in the form of a prayer. The NIV, the JB and NJB take the verse to be in the present tense ('The LORD gives . . . '), indicating a promise fulfilled, a present reality of blessing.

It is well known that the Hebrew verb is poorly endowed with formal indications of tense and mood, so that the translator frequently has to determine from the context which of the much richer variety of English forms is the most appropriate. The verbs in verse 11 are in the imperfect form, which is indeed associated with present and future tenses, and with the jussive or cohortative moods required for prayer. The choice, in short, is the translator's. I prefer here the precative used by the RSV and the NRSV; my preference is related to a point I have already made about the symmetries of the Psalm: the exhortation forms with which the Psalm begins are, in my judgement, well matched by the use of a prayer formula at the end.

It will be apparent from this detailed examination of Psalm 29 that there are many difficulties facing translators and affecting the selection of a standard version. I believe that the conclusion of Chapter 2 is broadly supported by this exercise, namely, that we will be best served by the NRSV, so long as we keep within our reach a copy of the Authorised Version.

3

READERS AND READING

This book assumes a literary approach to the Psalms. In Chapter 1 I examined briefly a number of familiar forms of reading which address concerns other than those of a literary character. I want now to make explicit what was tacit there: that we are not engaged upon a theological, spiritual or pious quest for meaning. At the end of Chapter 1 I identified certain assumptions necessary to our project of reading the Psalms in general, and any psalm in particular, in such a way as to attend specifically to their character as text, literary composition, or poetry (albeit of a rather specific kind). In Chapter 2 I considered the first of those assumptions – the choice of a suitable translation; the next step is to define the set of readers. Clearly that is in general an impossible requirement, since anyone with the necessary language and the ability to read is free to pick up a text of the Psalms and 'read' it. I have, however, defined a joint enterprise in this particular instance, and so it is reasonable to hope that a 'reader' will have those qualities which will enable her or him to be willing to read in company with us, to be prepared to allow our chosen approach, and to agree to the bracketing out of certain alternative agendas.

Despite its apparent naivety, this definition is apt in that it is precisely in being conscious of ourselves as readers that we enter into the kind of engagement with the text which a literary approach entails. We are not independent subjects scanning an object, 'the text': as readers we relate to and are shaped by what we read. Lack of such self-consciousness indicates a certain blindness to the fact that reading is not an objective exercise. It is a dialogical process in which the baggage of experiences and prior assumptions which we carry with us is both modified by what we read and indicates how we read it. Only by abdicating our own right of interpretation to some other authority can we withdraw from this interactive event; and in that case we would be as well going directly to the authority and leaving the text alone.

Having thus characterised a potential readership, it is important to recognise the basis upon which our reading is founded; and, most importantly, to be aware that we are experienced in the business of reading, that textuality is our natural *modus operandi*. This has several aspects, which I will attempt to set out briefly. First, we have certainly read many other texts before, covering a wide range of genres: we are therefore (whether we know it or not) considerable experts in the business. We can distinguish a love song from a car manual, a chapter of history from a folk tale, a theological proposition from an indecent one, a prayer from a political soundbite. We are, in short, not novices, and not naive, and so we need not leave our minds at the door when we open the Psalter. Second, we will in all probability have read the Book of Psalms, or at least parts of it, and must therefore have a number of opinions and thoughts about it which will either collide with or cohere with the direction my arguments take. Third, we have an everyday *parole*[1] which relates to, but does not exactly overlap with, that of either the NRSV Psalter or of the author of this book. How any reader approaches a text will be in part controlled by his or her *idiolect* (personal dialect), a reality which contributes equally to the creativity of language in use and the frustrations of trying to communicate. Fourth, there is a diachronic aspect to reading, related to the fact that we change and develop through time as individuals. Returning to what one thought was a familiar text after a significant gap in time can be a salutary or a surprising event, not because the text as object has changed (the same dog-eared book you carried around with you that summer long ago is still on your shelves), but because the 'I' who now reads is not the 'I' of that ancient summer. And, finally, a significant part of our identity as individuals (unless we subscribe to the idea of an ontically given personality which, being our birthright, remains fixed and unchangeable) is one of change – and change, moreover, mediated through a community of language which is both our inheritance and our creative hermeneutic. That is, almost before we are aware of ourselves as selves we have acquired language (an inheritance); but that acquired language then provides us with the most powerful tool for self-development (a creative hermeneutic), a tool which is arguably the fundamental distinction between the human species and other animals. These principles carry important consequences, which I will attempt to clarify.

Open reading

No reading is final; and by the same token, no reading bears the mark of irresistible authority. That is not to say that readings are purely tentative, or that they routinely fail to persuade. The eye-opening insight provided by this reading now has a momentary finality which, even as it fades, is persuasive; and, like Wordsworth's 'inner eye' experience, may return in future to speak to us even as we uncover further (and perhaps contradictory) meanings. The caveat concerning *irresistible* authority is particularly necessary in the case of religious literature and canonical texts which have for so long and in so many places been regarded as incontrovertible (not to mention incorrigible). Even after more than 200 years of the disciplines associated with biblical criticism it is still quite common to encounter naive assumptions about the inerrancy of the biblical text and its infallible authority. Much ink has been spilled in other places on this subject;[2] I refer to it here only to clear the ground of ancient debris, not to reopen an archaeological site.

Reading in context

The readings we uncover and the sense we make of the texts we read are unavoidably part of the nexus of textuality and linguistic usage which we all share in the synchronicity of the present tense. Even our *soi-disant* 'historical' conclusions are statements within and about us and our contemporary world every bit as much as they are accounts of the past. Collingwood's thesis, in *The Idea of History* (1993), that the past can be recovered only by a contemporary rethinking of the motivations of past protagonists, is a good expression of this reality; as is the fact that what we find in an archaeological site is material evidence in the present. The 'past' is an imaginative creation prompted by surviving artefacts – a truth unfortunately unrecognised by too many eager inventors of ancient Israel who seem to believe that their reconstructions have some mysterious scientific validity conveyed by the mantra 'Archaeology proves . . . '.[3] Thus our narratives of the past confirm our present values. When monarchs have real power, history deals with kings, queens and dynasties. While patriarchy rules, historians tell us of the epoch-making endeavours of great *men*. Societies in which the narration of myth, of story-with-meaning, has a formative function predominantly offer their history in episodic narrative form. The social-democratic movements of the 1960s in the West led to a new interest in the forgotten voices of the past – the masses, the individual poor, the emerging bourgeoisie – and so the French *Annaliste* School came to the fore, together with the sociological treatment of history now common in the USA and the UK. It would not surprise me if nationalism were to turn out to be the shaping idea of not a few histories in the next decade or so. What is unusual about our modern situation is that these various modes (and others) of doing history co-exist – or compete – in the same bookshops, in the pages of the same literary magazines, and in the same college and university curricula. The important point is that it is perfectly commonplace to find a wide diversity of readings, all claiming the generic title 'history'; and this is not even to consider the deconstructionist version of history deprived of the concept of objective event. 'The past', however it is to be defined, is simply too complex to admit of just one convincing reading; moreover, the past is *our* past, not some mythical 'present–past' which would be recognised by those who were alive then.

This digression into history is not as inappropriate as it might seem. The texts of the Psalms which are our concern are outcroppings into our present of material with a long and varied history: they are in themselves a form of historical evidence, and the historical question is one we will wish to put to them. Nevertheless, the discourse (whether historical or literary) is ours, and will therefore be couched in contemporary linguistic idioms, in the natural interplay of phrases and concepts within that network of syntax and paradigm which is the everyday argot of our conversation. If, for example, I say to someone in Britain, 'The Lord is my shepherd', images of green fields and northern fells, of rugged men (in the main) with faithful dogs, and a whole industry of kitsch cards, poems and illustrations will be called to mind. How this relates (for example) either to a vastly different tradition of sheep-rearing in the Australian outback, or to lean animals foraging in the pitiless near-barren hillsides around Jerusalem, is hard to ascertain.

This sense of remoteness in what we commonly 'feel' to be a most familiar Psalm becomes almost intolerable if we recognise that in Hebrew the metaphor 'shepherd' belongs to a well-attested ancient near-eastern trope for kingship:[4] thus Psalm 23 may 'really' be (that is, in a certain historical context) a royal Psalm[5] in which the king of Israel expresses his confidence in King Yahweh. If so, this would help to explain both the triumphalist verse 5 ('You prepare a table before me in the presence of my enemies; you anoint my head with oil;[6] my cup overflows') and the concluding reference to the temple ('I shall dwell in the house of the LORD my whole life long'). The temple was, in monarchic times, almost the royal chapel of the Davidic dynasty. Clearly our familiar and long-established reading of Psalm 23 is at odds with at least one probable historical explanation of its meaning. I make this point not to call in question the long Christian tradition of interpretation, but to illustrate my historical argument, and to emphasise that the process of reading, which is the subject of this study, is not in fact unfamiliar. The essential point is that the discourse is plural and has to be couched in terms which can be mutually understood – or rather, has to recognise that terms *we* take to be clear and univocal will turn out more often than not to be polysemic. We have always found ways of appropriating ancient texts, whether sacred or not, and finding for them a contemporary relevance; the challenge is both to recognise this process, and by being aware, to be enabled to apply it more powerfully.

Critical reading

An element of critical response is built into literary approaches. It is often said, though less often allowed in practice, that the essence of the scholarly tradition is to be constantly questioning, and to expect in return to be questioned. Students are regularly told at the outset of their studies that, particularly in the humanities, critical questioning is essential to learning. Hollow laughter is likely to be the experienced student's response to this claim, which is commonly observed in the breach; but in a system of interpretation, where polysemic discourse is vital to the health of the discipline, the questioning, critical and interrogatory mode is not an optional extra. Where there are no 'correct' interpretations there can be no unthinking acceptance of approved answers. This can be disconcerting, since it places greater responsibility on the individual reader than he or she would normally acknowledge (the responsibility is, I would argue, always in fact present, but not admitted). But it is certainly not a recipe for irrationalism, or for a wilful disregard of shared meaning. Psalm 23 uses the Hebrew word 'shepherd', and does not mention 'king'; we can connect the two because of other shared information about the use of language. Neither, of course, does Psalm 23 mention 'Jesus' or 'messiah' (the word translated 'anointed' in verse 5 is not the common word from which *messiah* is derived), yet these are both acceptable reference points in certain traditional Christian discourses about the Psalms. Polysemy is not arbitrariness. Black is black and white is white (and a rose is a rose is a rose); but there may be contexts and occasions when black signifies white, or a rose-garden has no horticultural reference (as in, 'I never promised you a rose-garden').

Two special cases call for comment. The first is that, where the Hebrew itself is ambiguous or obscure, particular attention needs to be paid to the broader context, since the translation chosen will depend upon the way ambiguity is resolved in that context. This issue remains to be dealt with in specific cases, notwithstanding the overall choice of version which we have made. It will not in general be possible for us to deal with these situations, since they relate to the Hebrew original. However, the following relatively straightforward example from Psalm 73 might help to illustrate the problem. A comparison of the King James Version with the NRSV of Psalm 73:1 reveals a difference of some substance:

KJ	Truly God is good to Israel, even to such as are of a clean heart.	NRSV	Truly God is good to the upright, to those who are pure in heart.

This variation reflects a problem with the underlying Hebrew text, of which the following is a literal translation:

How   good   to-Israel [*leyisra'el*]
God   [*'elohim*]   to-the-pure-in-heart

Effectively, the KJV assumes that the word for God is to be distributed over both 'Israel' and 'the pure in heart'. In fact, I would go further, and regard the phrase 'how good' as also referring to both objects. We thus have two parallel distributors, and two objects in parallel.

How good	[is God]	to Israel	a {b} c
[how good]	is God	to the pure in heart	{a} b c

Why then does the NRSV adopt a quite different interpretation? It would be fair to say that the Hebrew as it stands is strange, and presents difficulties of syntax which are perhaps only masked by the solution just offered – for example, the position of *'elohim* is not really a natural one. However, it is noteworthy that the consonants which make up the phrase 'to Israel' may be divided differently to give two words: *layyashar 'el*, which means 'to the upright, God'. The grounds for such a suggestion lie in the fact that originally the Hebrew text had no representation for vowel sounds, and was often written without spaces for word divisions. It is this proposal which lies behind the translation in the NRSV. It remains inconsistent, however, for it does not repeat the divine name. We should have:

| How good | to the upright | El | | a b c |
| | God | to the pure in heart | | c B |

Note that now we have a chiastic[7] parallel, with a much more natural appeal to the distributive effect of just one phrase; moreover the Hebrew is syntactically more satisfying. We can offer one more refinement which might at the same time help us to see how the (hypothetical) original came to have the form we now have. There is evidence to suggest that in Psalms 42–83 there has been an editorial tendency to replace the divine proper name *YHWH* with the generic *'elohim*.[8] The name *El* itself is the proper name of the head of the Canaanite pantheon, but was one of the words used by Israel to designate God. We might, then, guess that originally the Hebrew had Yahweh, not Elohim, so that a still better parallel existed:

| How good | to the upright | El |
| | Yahweh | to the pure in heart |

If this is correct, the first change would have been theological, replacing Yahweh with Elohim. Then at a later stage we may guess that a scribe copying out the text, and seeing the word for God already present, read the preceding group of letters not as 'to the upright El' but as 'to Israel'. The end result is a theological statement of a nationalist nature, in which Israel is identified with 'the pure in heart', whereas the original could be read as a statement about the faithful within Israel. At the end of the day, the choice of translation must be left open – there are arguments in favour of either – but the subsequent reading of the Psalm will clearly be different, depending upon that choice.

The second special case is that where the Hebrew yields an agreed English version, but no obviously coherent sense. A nice example, because it is so familiar, is to be found in Psalm 127:2, 'He gives sleep to his beloved'. That seems to be a straightforward statement, but its meaning in the context of the Psalm is far from apparent. Are we to assume that God sends those whom God loves to sleep? Or is it (in context) a promise that while everyone else is working their fingers to the bone, God's beloved can stay in bed? The word 'beloved' is from a root which is also used as one of the names of Solomon,[9] and it may be significant that, alone of all the Psalms of Ascents, the group to which this Psalm belongs, 127 bears the superscription 'Of Solomon'. If these observations are pertinent to our interpretation, they may point to a royal context, with the king at ease and confident in the temple ('house', verse 1) built by Yahweh and the city guarded by him. If we do not find it appropriate to make this very particular connection, should we take the phrase to have contemporary resonances? In today's English context 'beloved' is a word charged with erotic, romantic or connubial significance, reminding us of what is in fact a powerful biblical tradition: the metaphor of God as lover. Obviously this line of thought could be pursued; for now, I hope that I have done enough to show that at every level the questioning critique of readings is a positive and creative activity.

Dialogue between readers and readings

There is a need for three kinds of dialogue: between sets of readers; between types of reading; and between translations and 'the text'. The last of these has effectively been covered by the discussion in Chapter 2 and in the treatment of Psalms 73:1 and 127:2, above. That there is an ongoing dialogue between translation and the Hebrew text can hardly now be doubted.

The debate between different sets of readers is much more problematic, not least because of the natural tendency to imagine that one's own preferred approach is specially privileged and carries a clear mark of authenticity. Certain forms of such dialogue are probably to be ruled out *tout court*: an evangelical group convinced of the Christological significance of the whole of scripture may find it rather hard to countenance (say) a historical-critical reading in which no such anticipatory theology can be admitted. Indeed, the latter-day collapse of historical criticism into a kind of scholastic pedantry[10] was in part due to the absence of such dialogue, and its perceived failure has encouraged the return of a form of neo-conservatism which (it has to be said) has not eschewed the opportunity to say, 'I told you so'! I refer, for example, to the alacrity with which the demise of the Wellhausen Hypothesis in its documentary sources[11] form has been seized upon as evidence of the impropriety of the historical–critical method as a whole.

What is rather interesting is that structuralist and deconstructive approaches have found a cautious welcome in both evangelical and rabbinic circles, precisely because the historical question is not put, and so cherished assumptions are not challenged. For this reason, some observers have expressed unease with these and similar hermeneutical tools, arguing that they open the door to an apparent legitimation of obscurantist views in the name of a plurality of readings.[12] Whatever the risks (and risk, of course, is in the eye of the beholder) it is more significant that a hermeneutic is able to cross previously embattled lines than that it should be suspected of betraying one particular standpoint. No law compels a reader to endorse an unacceptable case simply because its proponents share common ground with that reader at other points. Or, to put it in more specific terms, I (as a convinced historical sceptic) have no difficulty in relishing a good deconstructive analysis carried out by someone who believes that Moses wrote the Torah:[13] my scepticism (like his or her conviction) is a separate matter.

Finally – the dialogue between readings. Naturally, this is to some extent the same issue as that of dialogue between sets of readers. But it is a distinct matter, in that a single reader may well, in the process of reading, employ a range of interpretative techniques which will sometimes reinforce, but more often undermine, each other. This is in itself a kind of deconstructive process: deconstruction, at a commonplace level, is simply the recognition that we regularly (and without imagining that we are being controversial) upset our own and others' cherished or received opinions without feeling that the world has ended or that the canons of literature or religion have been blown apart. Postmodernism becomes a problem when this natural process is given formal theoretical and philosophical status, and when the exercise itself becomes the point of the hermeneutic. I will return to this matter in Chapter 6; in the meantime, I would like to illustrate this point, and conclude this chapter, by setting out a deconstructive reading of Psalm 121 which will, I trust, make somewhat clearer what I mean by this question of dialogue between readings.

Psalm 121 occupies a place of particular affection in Scottish religious tradition. It is one of the best-loved of the Metrical Psalms, and serves as a kind of affirmation of the religious significance of the hills in that mountainous country. Prothero gives us a description of the Covenanters which seems to combine rather effectively these features: 'The hills were crowded with ghostly worshippers, who were singing Psalm 121.'[14] Yet, ironically, the belief that the Psalm endorses a native Scottish worship of mountains is based on a misinterpretation in the KJV, which gives for verse 1: 'I will lift up mine eyes unto the hills, from whence cometh my help.' What the Hebrew actually suggests is a question, which is clearly put in the NRSV: 'I lift up my eyes to the hills – from where will my help come?' The answer, of course, lies in verse 2: 'My help comes from the LORD, who made heaven and earth.' Thus it appears that we should rather read a contrast between the hills and the place of security than any identification of the one with the other. The Scots had better rethink their theology, it seems!

Let us consider the shape of the Psalm as a whole. It consists of a question and an answer, followed by an affirmation of the protective power of God. It is the second of the Psalms of Ascents, which I will examine as a group in Chapter 12. The title has various possible meanings, but in the light of the journey implied by verse 3, the context of a pilgrimage is appropriate. Since both the question *and* the answer are in first person, while verses 3–8 use the second-person address, the division should reflect that difference. A conventional way to express this is to posit different speakers – one who poses and answers his or her own question, and a second voice to provide the assurance required. It is often further supposed that verses 1 and 2 are spoken by a representative of the pilgrims. With this in mind, the text of the Psalm may be set out:

1 I lift up my eyes to the hills – from where will my help come?
2 My help comes from the LORD, who made heaven and earth.
3 He will not let your foot be moved; he who keeps you will not slumber.
4 He who keeps Israel will neither slumber nor sleep.
5 The LORD is your keeper; the LORD is your shade at your right hand.
6 The sun shall not strike you by day, nor the moon by night.
7 The LORD will keep you from all evil; he will keep your life.
8 The LORD will keep your going out and your coming in from this time on and for evermore.

If this division of labour is correctly defined, it is immediately notable that there is no clear contrast in tone between the two sections; and it is of interest that two commentators, in different ways, seek to introduce an element of tension. Anderson (1972) does so by suggesting that the first phrase could be translated as 'I look anxiously to the hills', and Weiser (1962) wants to change the Hebrew of the second line from 'my help' to 'help'. Both, in short, want to deconstruct the text!

We should interrogate the idea of 'hills' more sharply, since this is clearly a cause of some concern to the poet: it is the vague threat or promise implied by that word which sets the Psalm in motion. There are several possible readings: they could be, quite literally, the hills upon which Jerusalem is built, and which surround the city (compare Psalm 125:1–2) – a sign of security; they might represent the dangers of the journey, whether to or from Jerusalem (a thought which those familiar with the New Testament will find reflected in Luke's parable of the Good Samaritan (Luke 10:29–37)); if, as seems likely, religious cults in Canaan were accustomed to place their altars and symbolic monuments on hilltops, 'the hills' might convey a confused message, at one and the same time the place of God's dwelling and the focus of the worship of Baal, Asherah, and others.[15]

The very ambiguity which we have identified as a feature of 'the hills' affords us a reading which separates the two sections nicely. The first two verses resolve uncertainty by the specific content of the response to the question. The 'LORD who made heaven and earth' is not a cliche: it answers the question precisely, since it assures the speaker that, whatever the hills are in themselves, or represent metaphorically, they are after all a part of creation and so inevitably under God's power. With this assurance to hand, the directly confident speech of verses 3–8 can proceed.

Turning to the main body of the text, we can identify three sections, each building within itself to a climax, and the three together forming a progressive movement culminating in the boldest affirmation of all. Thus, verse 3 begins with an anonymous reference to an unspecified 'he' who will provide unsleeping protection; in verse 4 'he' is revealed to be 'he who keeps Israel'. Verses 5 and 6 build tension in a different fashion – by first of all guaranteeing the presence of Yahweh (the LORD) as protector, and then in verse 6 setting out in all its horror the cosmic nature of the dangers to be faced. The Hebrew here is so specific and so tightly organised that (as one of the exceptions to my own rubric) I intend to give it some attention by setting out an English translation which matches (at the expense of fluency) the actual form of the Hebrew:

Daily the sun // shall not smite you // nor moon by night

The balance is perfect: the centrally placed verb covers both threats;

the adverbial form 'daily' reflects the Hebrew use of a suffix to create the adverb; similarly 'by night' matches here the Hebrew use of a prefix. We have a virtually perfect palinstrophe[16] which begins in the day and ends at night and sums up the dual threat of madness through sunstroke and illness, or insanity caused by 'moonstroke' (Weiser 1962: 749, note 20), remarks that the moon was in antiquity regarded as the cause of diseases). Of course the idea of God as creator and the familiar notion that the heavenly bodies are deities combine to give this powerful line a cosmic reference – a hint that the pilgrim is in danger not just from physical phenomena but from supernatural forces, against whom the only secure protection is 'the LORD who made heaven and earth'.

The final verses provide a list of three forms of protection – from evil, from threat to life, and during journeys – but it is the last word which is the most resonant: 'from this time on and *for evermore*' (a promise which returns at the conclusion of another two of the Psalms of Ascents – 131 and 133). This provides in addition the climax to the three 'movements'. The first makes no mention of Yahweh, is somewhat low-key; the second brings Yahweh on-stage, and deals with the journey itself; but in the third we learn that the journey, which we (and the pilgrims?) took to be a festival event, has become nothing less than the journey of life. The God, in short, from whom was sought some reassurance regarding a particular danger, has guaranteed more than was asked, more than could have been expected or imagined.

A neat interpretation, which might even allow the Scots to climb their mountains safe again in the knowledge that they are within the realm of the creator.

Too safe, perhaps. Too restricted. Look again at the fundamental thought of this Psalm, and the language of control that it employs. Read verse 1 again – a plea for confirmation of a genuine belief: 'I lift up my eyes to the hills – from where will my help come?' Answer – 'from the hills'. But no; there is a disjunctive disconfirmation, and suddenly the mountain tops (the place of the gods in so many religions, *including that of Israel*) are demonised, ruled out of bounds. Keep off! They're dangerous; you must trust yourself to 'the LORD who made heaven and earth'. Now we become nervous, like children who have been told a ghost story and can't sleep because the comforting darkness has been transformed into a hiding place for monsters. Our feet are in danger of slipping on the hills (verse 3) – the hills which surround Jerusalem and which we are accustomed to regard as a symbol of God's power on our behalf (Psalm 125:1–2); we are assaulted by the sun and the moon. And who is responsible? Surely God, who made the heavens (the sun and the moon) and the earth (the hills). Thus, not only has our source of comfort been taken from us, but we are humiliatingly forced to trust ourselves to the very God who made that which puts us in danger; a God moreover who (sinisterly?) never sleeps, watches us all the time.

And what of the language used – the language of control? It is everywhere: 'he will not let', 'he who keeps you', 'he who keeps Israel', 'the LORD is your keeper', 'the LORD will keep you', 'he will keep your life', 'the LORD will keep your going out and your coming in'. And there is no relief, no promise of parole: 'from this time on and for evermore'! By now you might think that lifting up your eyes to the hills is an innocent enough activity, compared with this obsessive deity who can't keep his eyes off of us, and has the gall to claim 'The LORD will keep you from all evil'. But what evil threatens us? Discomfort? Danger? Adventure? Notice that in the Psalm 'evil' is identified in terms of 'hills', 'sun' and 'moon', yet it was God who made these things – God stands condemned *out of God's own mouth* as the source of evil.

This deconstruction is, of course, not a definitive reading.[17] Many may find it a wholly objectionable reading, an insult to scripture. But it is one which (at least implicitly) has the backing of a staunch religious tradition – for the Metrical Psalms as they have been understood in Scottish worship have already performed this deconstruction! 'The hills' is a positive concept!

4

THE LANGUAGE OF POETRY

What is poetry?

The separation of language into poetry and prose is a familiar convention, and is in many ways a useful distinction. Yet, despite its familiarity, there are serious practical and theoretical difficulties in the way of any attempt to say precisely what the difference is.

There are, on the one hand, differences of form – how the text is laid out on the page, whether rhyme is present, what sort of rhythm can be identified, how densely packed with figures of speech is the language. And, on the other hand, there may be differences of substance. Poetry is always many-layered: its apparent subject matter never exhausts the meaning of what is written; it is full of allusion and the possibility of surprise. But these simple observations hardly provide a definition; and the perceptive reader will already have registered the problems. For a start, that which has 'poetic form' may well not be poetry in any sense which practised readers would accept. Doggerel and advertising jingles are so profoundly lacking in substance that their formal features become those of pastiche or parody rather than of poetry. And, just to confuse matters, much twentieth-century poetry is apparently devoid of rhyme, and its rhythms can be obscure to all but the expert reader, so that the only obvious formal characteristic left is the seemingly arbitrary one of typographical setting.

The problems are just as acute if we try to make substance the deciding factor. Who could deny to Joyce's *Ulysses* the characteristics which are set out above – inexhaustible levels of meaning, rich allusiveness, constant surprise! It seems that we are forced to conclude that the only difference is typographical or conventional. It is a poem if more than 50 per cent of the page is white! Or, as a character in a novel by Jan Mark (1987: 8) discovers when he asks

46

a class how we recognise a poem, it is a poem because 'it says Ted Hughes at the bottom'.

The problem is not academic. What we perceive a text to be may well affect how we read it, just as who we are – our experience as readers, our cultural location, our personal hopes and fears – will make that text seem freshly written each time we confront it. So the prior decision, whether conscious or not, 'this is prose' or 'this is poetry' is important. A perhaps apocryphal experiment illustrates this point. Two tutorial groups were each given the same text to study, with no commentary provided. One group, given the text in the form of a prose narrative, disposed of it in twenty minutes and lapsed into awkward silence. The other, for whom the same text had been cast in verse form, took two hours to explore the many levels of meaning and subtle interpretation which it offered.[1] This example is not designed to poke fun at college students. It serves rather to indicate two vital points: first that poetry and prose are not sharply divided genres, but rather belong to the same spectrum of language; and, second, that naming a passage 'poetry' triggers reader responses[2] which would otherwise remain dormant.

This last point touches on what I believe to be a central feature of poetic language: the distinction between primary reference and concern with and for the language itself as the principal focus of interest.[3] When confronted with a passage which we take to be prose we are led to place a major emphasis on that to which the language apparently refers. Conversely, poetry (or poetic form) sends us a signal that we should look elsewhere for significance. To take a somewhat light-hearted example, no-one who hears the words 'Ding dong bell, pussy's in the well' is likely to respond by calling the fire brigade, looking for a stout rope, or bursting into tears. But were someone to cry out, 'My God! The cat's fallen down the well!', any or all of these responses might reasonably be expected. I do not for a moment propose that 'Ding dong bell' is other than doggerel; the point is simply that form makes a difference to interpretation.

Henry Reed's famous poem *Naming of Parts* (1991: 49) provides an interesting comparison. The poem makes reference to various technical aspects of the soldier's equipment:

> Today we have naming of parts. Yesterday,
> We had daily cleaning. And tomorrow morning,
> We shall have what to do after firing. But today,
> Today we have naming of parts. Japonica
> Glistens like coral in all of the neighbouring gardens,

And today we have naming of parts.
This is the lower sling swivel. And this
Is the upper sling swivel, whose use you will see,
When you are given your slings. And this is the piling swivel,
Which in your case you have not got. The branches
Hold in the gardens their silent, eloquent gestures,
    Which in our case we have not got.

It is clearly of no moment whether the reader is familiar with the technology involved, for the poem is not 'about' guns and how to maintain them. But a passage like the following, from an old computer handbook, will be seriously misunderstood by the technologically challenged, because it matters that its primary reference be clear and unmistakable:

The SETEMS program performs two tasks. Firstly, it programs the NEAT CMOS configuration to change to hardware handling of the memory on the motherboard from Extended to paged EMS.
    Secondly, it adds the line DEVICE = C:\UTILS\EMMS.SYS to the CONFIG.SYS file. Hence, when the system starts up, the EMM.SYS driver allocates the Expanded Memory Pages according to the LIM 4 specification.

We are of course at two extremes of prose and poetry here. The functional character of the second passage and its complete lack of any poetic features leave the reader in no doubt as to its proper mode of interpretation.
    I turn now to a case-study from one of the most famous literary partnerships in the history of English Literature. On 15 April 1802, Dorothy and William Wordsworth took a stroll round Ullswater. Some 10 kilometres into the walk (the Wordsworths were no slouches when it came to exercise) they came upon a bank of daffodils. Dorothy recorded the scene in her journal (1978: 192):

When we were in the woods beyond Gowbarrow Park we saw a few daffodils close to the water-side. We fancied that the lake had floated the seeds ashore, and that the little colony had so sprung up. But as we went along there were more and yet more; and at last, under the boughs of the trees, we saw that there was a long belt of them along the shore, about the breadth of a country turnpike road. I never saw daffodils so beautiful. They grew among the mossy stones about and about them, some rested their heads upon these stones as on a pillow for weariness; and the rest tossed and reeled and danced, and seemed as if they verily laughed with the wind, that blew upon them over the lake; they looked so gay, ever glancing, ever changing.

William subsequently composed a poem (1804) which must be one of the best-known in the English language. It has been sadly over-exposed, but still reads powerfully:

> I wandered lonely as a cloud
> That floats on high o'er vales and hills,
> When all at once I saw a crowd,
> A host of golden daffodils;
> Beside the lake, beneath the trees,
> Fluttering and dancing in the breeze.
>
> Continuous as the stars that shine
> And twinkle on the milky way,
> They stretched in never-ending line
> Along the margin of a bay:
> Ten thousand saw I at a glance,
> Tossing their heads in sprightly dance.
>
> The waves beside them danced; but they
> Out-did the sparkling waves in glee:
> A poet could not but be gay,
> In such a jocund company;
> I gazed – and gazed – but little thought
> What wealth the show to me had brought:
>
> For oft, when on my couch I lie
> In vacant or in pensive mood,
> They flash upon that inward eye
> Which is the bliss of solitude;
> And then my heart with pleasure fills,
> And dances with the daffodils.[4]

These two compositions – the journal entry and the poem – present us with a serious test-case for our ability to distinguish prose from poetry and the criteria we might use to make the distinction. There is no question here of one being inferior to the other: Dorothy's account is a superb piece of work, replete with the heightened metaphoric language which distinguishes poetry at its best. Such is her skill that many of the linguistic features familiar from poetic work are found here: metaphor in 'some rested their heads upon these stones as on a pillow for weariness'; metonymy when she writes 'the lake had floated the seeds ashore'; rhyme in such phrases as 'more and more [.] along the shore'. We are, in Dorothy's passage, close to the point on the spectrum of language where poetry and prose are almost indistinguishable. Indeed, the matter may be precisely one of choice: how we decide to read her journal is what makes the difference, what removes the piece from the category of prose to that of poetry. It is interesting to speculate on the likely effects of re-casting the prose account typographically so that the reader's first instinct would be to take it as a poem, thus pushing to the fore those elements of rhythm, rhyme and heightened language which we have already noted. What follows is an attempt at such a formal re-presentation. Let the reader decide whether it successfully functions as a poem.

> We fancied that the lake
> had floated the seeds ashore,
> and that the little colony
> had so sprung up.
> But as we went along
> there were more, and yet more
> and at last, under the boughs of the trees
> we saw
> that there was a long belt of them
> along the shore
> about the breadth
> of a country turnpike road.

Note the rhymes or half-rhymes at the end of several lines (*ashore, more, saw, shore, road*) which are echoed internally in lines 2, 4 and 6 (*floated, so, more*). These serve usefully to interconnect the poem as it meanders (like the walkers) along the path. Alliteration is employed effectively in *fancied / floated* and *seeds ashore* in lines 1 and 2, and even more intensively in the next two lines (*that the, little colony, so sprung up*). The writer plays on various nuances of 'along' (indicating the somewhat aimless journey in line 5), contrasted with 'a long' in line 9 and 'along' in line 10 (describing the dense and determined colonising of the area by the daffodils). In line 11 the word 'about' is pleasingly ambiguous – does it indicate that the daffodils covered the turnpike road on which they walked, or is it by way of comparison? The uneven length of the lines might be a mimetic effect for the irregular pattern of daffodils by the shore, or for the rambling character of the Wordsworths' walk. The rhythm of the first three lines is regular, in fact quite jaunty, reflecting perhaps the rhythm of the walk (iambic tetrameters, with the last foot omitted in lines 1 and 2 – the second foot in line 2 is anapaestic – followed in line 4 by a dimeter of one iamb followed by a spondee). Thus line 4 breaks the regularity, and the second part of the 'poem' is very irregular metrically. These structural observations might lead us to an interpretation of the 'poem' in terms of the way that neat and convenient theoretical explanations are so often undermined, confused, deconstructed, by the discovery of more evidence 'as we go along'. Thus the simple, confined 'little colony' becomes a wide, rambling, endless 'country turnpike road'. The first admits of finite boundaries; the second has no apparent limits. But there are, of course, connections. The persistence of a single rhyme based on the vowel 'o' hints at a resolution despite the apparent confusion – a belief which underpins all human intellectual attempts to understand the seeming chaos of life; perhaps even an onomatopoeic 'O!' representing wonder both at the particularity of the swathe of daffodils and at the generally astonishing character of nature as a whole.

The above analysis suggests that the crucial distinction is that implied by the decision to read 'prose' rather than 'poetry'. We are compelled by its form to take *The Daffodils* by William Wordsworth as a poem, and in so doing we put the descriptive aspect of the writing in a less prominent position. We attend to the formal features of the language and enjoy them in themselves, and we share the insights which the poem offers into the process by which the 'raw material' of nature becomes a part of the romantic imagination. The hyperbolic loneliness of the poet is a metaphor for the private nature of that process; yet the poem is public, and so we appear to be privileged to share in that private moment. And, of course, the poem itself is an example of what it is about: the transformation of an experience of nature into a contemplation of the nature of that experience. None of this is to deny that the poem in some sense describes the daffodils; the point is that this is perhaps the least of what the poem does.

'[April] 15th, Thursday' by Dorothy Wordsworth, on the other hand, when taken as prose makes it possible for us to be vividly present by the shores of Ullswater. Of course, that vividness is an illusion; of course the attempt to identify the exact spot and plans to visit the place will lead to disappointment. The power of poetic prose

– as of poetry – is to grant us an imaginative entry to a world we do not possess. That prose will certainly then have harmonics of meaning which we can hear when our ear is properly attuned. But when it is read as prose, the formal aspects of the writing remain secondary. They 'help us to see' what the writing refers to. *The Daffodils*, on the other hand, while sharing at one level the descriptive concerns of the journal, arguably does not ask us to return to the shores of Ullswater. If anything, it prompts us to wonder about the experience of reliving the scene on the lakeside: a quite different matter. But even this is not the commanding feature; for what draws our attention is the rhythm and rhyme, the assonance and imagery, which in a profoundly important sense constitute the poem.

There is almost certainly no final word to be said on these questions. At the margins of literary theory the element of individual experience has a controlling effect; subjectivity cannot be eliminated, for we are not concerned with scientific or quasi-scientific evidence, but with the living and lively interaction between text and reader which is at the heart of all communication. Thus the distinction I have tried to make – between primary reference and concern with and for the language itself as the principal focus of interest – may well prove unsatisfactory where prose merges into poetry.

Another problematic case is that of poetry which seems to mimic the narrative forms of prose. Are not the *Odyssey*, the *Song of the Sea* (Exodus 15) and *Beowulf* analogous to prose in that they 'tell a story' in a chronological fashion? Are not the plays of Shakespeare poetry, despite their narrative thrust? And conversely, how can we possibly say that a prose fiction is characterised by 'primary reference'? To these rhetorical questions we are forced to answer 'Yes! But . . . ', and it is in that answer that our tenacious hold on the difference is located. At the risk of entering territory usually avoided by angels, let me reaffirm that irrespective of the problem cases the perception that a composition is prose encourages us to read it 'as if' it referred: the form persuades us to suspend disbelief and enter a created world which, at its best, captures our imagination. We recognise the lie, but enjoy the story none the less. Poetry, on the other hand, finds us with our eyes open and our critical faculties alert. Because we do not have to 'believe' it in the prime-reference sense, we hear it all the more clearly. This is why bad poetry is so disappointing, either when (like 'Ding dong bell') the poetic form is at the service of hollow parody, or when, having initially taken the typesetter on trust, we become convinced that nothing but dull prose is here before us. That is when poetry lies – when it denies its own true nature.[5]

The power of prose to compel its readers to look for primary reference is seen in the phenomenon of identification with the characters of TV soaps. While it is doubtless only a small minority who come to believe in the real existence of the characters involved, the extent of popular interest in the *rites de passage* of these figures suggests that a great many more people have suspended disbelief to a significant degree. Or, to take a (possibly) more reputable example, for all its poetic qualities, there is a considerable industry dedicated to the re-enactment of Bloom's peregrinations in *Ulysses*, and to the identification of its characters with 'real' people of 'Joyce's' Dublin (scare quotes intended!). The Hebrew scriptures offer an instructive instance. The poem-form *Song of the Sea* in Exodus 15 is preceded by a prose chapter which reports some of the same material, and introduces various miraculous elements. Both chapters pose historical problems; neither can easily be conformed to any likely event which might be thought to lie behind the biblical material. But the prose of Chapter 14 has been subject to much more rigorous historical scrutiny than has the poem. It is precisely the expectations raised by the respective forms of the two chapters which determine how many have responded to them. The likelihood that Exodus 14 is not historically accurate is much more disturbing than would be a similar observation about Chapter 15.

The constituent features of poetry

I turn now to the task of identifying and describing those features of language which characterise poetry. Since our concern is with the poetry of Israel, and in particular the Psalms, I will exercise a certain restraint in what I say. And further, in view of our aim to discuss mainly those features which do not depend upon a knowledge of Hebrew, the greater emphasis is to be placed on those things which survive the process of translation. That does not mean that no reference will be made to the originals of those Psalms with which we shall be dealing; but clearly there is little point in offering detailed analyses of Hebrew word-play and stress or rhythm in such a study. It ought further to be made clear that what follows in no way implies any claim that these characteristics are exclusive to forms typographically denoted as 'poetic'. What has already been said should make this clear; but let it be stated quite explicitly, in agreement with the greater part of recent opinion, that the characteristics which are described below are noticeable in poetry for their density and frequency of occurrence. It is a matter of degree, not of kind.

I make a preliminary distinction of poetic modes into two broad categories: semantic (that is, to do directly with the meaning of the language used) and formal (that is, dealing with the structures and sounds of the language). In each case attention is drawn to those aspects which are preserved in translation and those which are lost.

Semantic features

The semantic or non-formal aspects of poetic language which are to a great extent preserved are metaphor and its related figures, metonymy (including synecdoche) and hyperbole. The use of metaphor, where one thing is substituted for another in order to say something about the latter by analogy, transcends language difference. So too does metonymy, whereby an aspect or part of something is made to stand for the thing itself (e.g. Psalm 125:3: 'The sceptre of wickedness shall not rest upon the land allotted to the righteous'). Figures which are partly or wholly lost are word-play and ambiguity. Both are constant features of poetry, though the specifics are usually destroyed in translation. A good example of lost word-play may be found in Genesis 2:7, where we read in English: 'the LORD God formed man of dust from the ground'. This completely conceals the fact that the Hebrew words for man (*'adam*) and earth (*'adamah*) make the statement 'man is made from earth' literally true as well as theologically meaningful. Similarly the ambiguity in the Hebrew word *beth* used for 'house' in Psalm 127:1 is difficult to convey: it can mean 'house' as in building, household, or even temple – and each can be argued for in the context of the Psalm.

Formal features

The formal features of poetry are in the main lost in translation. Rhyme and other forms of morphological repetition (alliteration, assonance, consonance, onomatopoeia) are almost inevitably destroyed. Rhythm can be preserved only with difficulty, assuming that the cadences of the receptor language can be made to fit the rhythmic pattern of the original. In the case of classical Hebrew a further difficulty presents itself, in that scholars disagree about the form of poetic rhythm. The accents which have been handed down are seemingly much later than the compositions. Recent work by Haik-Vantoura (1991) and Weil (1995) has opened up the possibility that these markings do in fact record the singing of the Psalms from earlier times, and so give us accurate information on the vexed question of rhythm. These are, however, highly specialised issues, and cannot delay us here: whatever rhythmic element we deal with will be that of the English translation.

In discussing individual compositions these features should be identified and their significance elucidated. But they must be considered in the broader context of a poetic device whose significance transcends any one of these particular characteristics. I refer to *parallelism*, a phenomenon which has been exhaustively described in the literature on the Psalms, but which has arguably been misunderstood nearly as often as it has been analysed. It is complicated by the fact that it finds expression in both semantic and formal ways, and so does not fit neatly into the division set out above.

Hebrew poetry has sometimes been presented as though parallelism were the only characteristic feature it possessed; furthermore, the false impression has been given that parallelism is somehow unique to Hebrew (or Semitic) poetry. This is of course a travesty, made the worse by a tendency to reduce the phenomenon to a few basic types which are then used as a straitjacket in which to imprison the Psalms. It is important therefore to describe this phenomenon in some detail as a characteristic of all language. It can take the form of semantic parallelism, where meanings of words, phrases and lines are paired; or it can be a matter of morphology (rhyme is essentially a kind of parallelism) or of grammar. The first of these can readily survive translation, the second rarely, the third occasionally.

Parallelism is in effect a kind of repetition, and repetition in all its forms is particularly important to poetry. Jakobson (1987: 117) is quoted by his editors as saying that 'on every level of language the essence of poetic artifice consists in recurrent returns', and even if we qualify that claim, it none the less remains clear that repetition contributes significantly to poetry, as the verses from *Naming of Parts* quoted at the beginning of this chapter demonstrate. Parallelism must therefore be understood not as a limited set of formal possibilities but as repetition within a limited context – it is the placing in close proximity of pairs of words, phrases, sentences or sounds in such a way that they are made to inform or illuminate each other.

Parallelism involves two simple processes which turn out to have profound consequences: selection and combination. On the one hand, the repetitions which reveal parallelism are constructed by the substitution of one element for another from a set of possibilities (selection). This produces an echo effect in which each member of the pair influences the interpretation of the other in the context of the poem. And on the other hand the bringing together of elements in close proximity (combination) produces a different kind of resonance.

Before proceeding to consider in more detail the theory of selection and combination, it will be helpful to look at how they function in a particular case. I have chosen Psalm 120 because, being less obviously provided with the traditional forms of parallelism, it constitutes something of a test-case for a broader view of the subject (see the text of Psalm 120). Two themes run through this poem like threads in a garment: the contrast between truth and lies (the theme of speech: *I cried – he answered – lips – tongue* (repeated); *I speak – they cry*) and the contrast between war and peace (the theme of conflict: *my distress – deliver me – warrior's sharp arrows – glowing coals – those who hate peace – I am for peace – 'To battle'*). The intertwining of these in the composition ('combination') sets up a comparison and alerts us to a metaphoric process whereby the opposition of truth and lies is (by 'selection') equivalent to the opposition of peace and war.

		PSALM 120 NRSV (modified)[6]
LINE	VERSE	
1	1	*To Yahweh in my distress I cried*
		and he answered me.
	2	*'O Yahweh, deliver me,*[7]
		from lying lips,
5		from a deceitful tongue.'
	3	*What shall he give to you?*
		And what more shall he do to you,[8]
		you deceitful tongue?
	4	A warrior's sharp arrows,
10		with glowing coals of the broom tree!
	5	Woe is me that I am an alien in Meshech,
		That I have lived among the tents of Kedar.[9]
	6	Too long have I had my dwelling
		among those who hate peace
15	7	I am for peace;
		but when I speak,
		they cry, 'To battle!'[10]

The metaphoric pairing of *war* with *lies* is in fact directly linked in the middle section of the Psalm (lines 8 and 9), in a juxtaposition which is profoundly ambiguous. Do lines 8 and 9 represent the punishment accorded to the deceitful tongue or a description of it? Undoubtedly the substitution *sharp arrows—deceitful tongue* is an appropriate one, and the explicit equation is made elsewhere (Psalms 64:2–3 and 140:1–3; Proverbs 25:18; Jeremiah 9:8); but the arrow also figures in many places as an instrument of God's punishment (eg Psalms 18:14 and 64:7) and, in Isaiah 49:2, as a symbol of the powerful speech of the servant! Perhaps the combination of *arrows* with *glowing coals* might be more explicit – yet here too we find the same ambiguity. Burning coals are associated with the speech of the wicked in Proverbs 26:18–21 and as their punishment in Psalms 18:12–13 and 140:11. Even within the Psalter, virtually every combination is found: In Psalm 18 both arrows and coals are a form of punishment; in Psalm 64 arrows figure both as the speech of the wicked and as their punishment; and in Psalm 140 we find arrows standing for wicked speech, while hot coals are their punishment!

These few comments clearly show the importance of combination and selection in Psalm 120, and should encourage the reader to explore its explicit and implicit parallelism. The opening section is intriguing: the poet begins by referring to an unspecified past experience of suffering and distress which was resolved by the receipt of an answer from Yahweh. This is in fact a standard opening move in many psalms; what makes the present example distinctive is that there is a repetition of the normally conventional speaking motif in a substantive way in lines 3 and 4. Form has become content – the Psalm is an utterance, and it deals with the problematic nature of utterance. Thus the juxtaposing of 1–2 with 3–4 has metaphoric value: 'O Yahweh' in line 3 answers to 'To Yahweh' in line 1; 'deliver me' to 'I cried'; and hence 'lying lips' are the substance of 'my distress'. We are left with two phrases which at first sight appear unrelated – 'and he answered me' and '[from a] deceitful tongue'. The latter phrase, of course, serves as a repetition which reinforces 'lying lips' in line 4, and its repetition in turn in the middle section (line 8) marks it out as a most important motif.

We are thus pushed to examine whether the repetition and parallelism already identified (and they are considerable) create a metaphorical meaning from the combination of lines 2 and 5. We may note the following: the past-tense speech of 1–2 leads to a closure in the form of the entirely satisfactory response 'he answered me'; by contrast, the present-tense situation of 3–5 issues not in a satisfactory answer but in a deeply disturbing reinforcement of the lie which constitutes the problem. There is no closure, and so the poem proceeds to open out into an exploration of the alienation which the experience of deceit creates. At the same time, this uncertainty reflects back on to the confidence of 1–2. Was the past answer really as satisfactory as it seemed? Is there not always some kind of doubt about the response of God to prayer, which makes the thought of 'a deceitful tongue' a surprising but not improper choice to pair with 'God answered me'?

This is not the place to give a fuller account of Psalm 120, and I shall for the moment make only one further point. The parallelism of the poem forces together rather awkward companions, as we have pointed out. The central metaphors are to do with contrasting positions (truth and lies, war and peace). There is, in short, a sense of unease, of conflict about this Psalm, a feeling of alienation. And indeed this is found in a remarkable couplet in lines 11–12, where geographical estrangement serves as a metaphor for the situation of the psalmist. Just as truth can barely live with lies, peace with war, so the poet speaks bitterly of being a stranger in Mesech and of being forced to live in Kedar. It is of no importance where these places are: what signifies is the poet's feeling of alienation. And just as 'from a deceitful tongue,' in line 5, is both a repetitive echo and a significant parallel, so 'too long have I had my dwelling', in line 13, both repeats the verb of line 12 and creates a parallel between the physical alienation of lines 11–12 and the existential alienation of lines 13–17 in which the central metaphors are finally combined.

The importance of parallelism is strikingly expressed in a passage written by the poet Gerard Manley Hopkins in 1865, and quoted by Jakobson (1987: 82f.):

The artificial part of poetry, perhaps we shall be right to say all artifice, reduces itself to the principle of parallelism. The structure of poetry is that of continuous parallelism, ranging from the technical so-called Parallelism of Hebrew poetry and the antiphons of Church music up to the intricacy of Greek or Italian or English verse. But parallelism is of two kinds necessarily – where the opposition is clearly marked, and where it is transitional rather or chromatic. Only the first kind, that of marked parallelism, is concerned with the structure of verse – in rhythm, the recurrence of a certain sequence of syllables, in metre, the recurrence of a certain sequence of rhythm, in alliteration, in assonance and in rhyme. Now the force of this recurrence is to beget a recurrence of parallelism answering to it in the words or thought and, speaking roughly and rather for the tendency than the invariable result, the more marked parallelism in structure . . . begets more marked parallelism in the words and sense. . . . To the marked or abrupt kind of parallelism belong metaphor, simile, parable and so on, where the effect is sought in likeness of things, and antithesis, contrast and so on, where it is sought in unlikeness.

The levels of possible parallelism which are indicated in this passage are:

1 rhythm, metre
2 alliteration, assonance, rhyme
3 meaning (semantic level).

As already noted, rhythm and metre are problematic in Hebrew,[11] and alliteration, rhyme and so on nearly always disappear in translation. Therefore our main concern will be with the semantic level. Although it appears that much is thus closed to us, there remains much to be said; and, where appropriate, Hopkins' first two levels as they appear in translation can be analysed. In any case, Hopkins offers us an understanding of parallelism which goes far beyond the simple account given by Lowth in 1753 and followed somewhat uncritically in a host of subsequent introductions to the Psalter. There is more to poetry than synonymous, antithetic and synthetic parallelism![12]

Turning to a more theoretical examination of parallelism, it may be observed, first, that it is essential to consider the two related phenomena, selection and combination, to which I drew attention above. In a somewhat cryptic passage, Jakobson (1987: 71) reminds us that the 'poetic function projects the principle of equivalence from the axis of selection into the axis of combination'. That is to say, when we recognise poetry, the pervasive character of parallelism prompts us to seek for metaphoric connections between adjacent phrases. The essentially formalist position which Jakobson holds provides a helpful pointer to the understanding of parallelism in which the key technical expressions, set out in two related groups, are

(a) selection *or* similarity *or* paradigmatic option *or* metaphor; and
(b) combination *or* contiguity *or* syntagmatic option *or* metonymy.

While the meaning of some of these terms may not at first sight be entirely clear, the basic pattern is simple enough. It recognises, as Jakobson's editor (1987: 17) comments, that 'our entire linguistic activity gravitates around the axes of selection and combination'.

When we create a sentence we select words and we combine them. The syntax of a sentence relates to how we combine the elements to form a meaningful unit; a paradigm provides a class of choices from which we select the words or phrases which are then combined. To illustrate, consider the following sentences:

> The young boy ran swiftly to school.

> The old man shuffled slowly along the road.

The syntax of each is the same:

ADJECTIVE + NOUN   VERB + ADVERB   PREPOSITIONAL
PHRASE

but the paradigmatic choices are different ('young' and 'old', 'boy' and 'man', etc.). Thus the same underlying structure gives rise to different but related sentences. Formalism as we have understood it proposes that these two operations extend to the way literary or poetic language is shaped. On the one hand, units are deliberately paralleled so that a comparison is set up, just as metaphor uses the principle of similarity (or induced similarity[13]) to create its effect. On the other hand, the juxtaposition of units sets up a relationship between them, just as metonymy makes use of the relationship between one thing and that for which it stands. To return briefly to Psalm 120, parallelism promotes the metaphoric interpretation war is *like* lies; juxtaposition induces the further thought that war is intimately related to lies.

Parallelism may be found at five levels of linguistic analysis: the phonological, the morphological, the syntactic, the lexical and the semantic.[14] Berlin (1985: 29) makes a further distinction which has some practical value – between parallelism at the level of the word and at the level of the line or phrase. There are, of course, problems attached to the idea of a single 'word',[15] but for the purposes of an introductory study such as this we may assume that we can perceive adequately what a 'word' is in a given situation. With this further division, some refinement of the five levels can be carried out. Thus phonological equivalence refers either to pairs of words of similar sound, or to phrases in which a series of sounds is repeated. Morphological equivalence at the level of individual words implies that both members of the pair perform the same grammatical function – both are nouns which are the subjects of verbs, for example, or

Table 4.1 Levels of morphological, semantic and phonological equivalence

	Grammatical/ morphological	*Lexical/ semantic*	*Phonological*
Word	Morphological equivalence and/ or contrast	Word pairs	Sound pairs
Line or clause	Syntactic equivalence and/ or contrast	Semantic relationship between lines	Phonological equivalence of lines

Source: adapted from Berlin (1985: 29).

both are adjectives. At the level of the phrase or line, we would expect the underlying grammatical structure to be the same – that is, we would have syntactic equivalence. Lexical and semantic equivalence can be related respectively to the word and to the line or phrase. Table 4.1 may clarify these relationships.

I have tried to give some sense both of the subtlety and complexity of parallelism, on the one hand, and its spontaneity and simplicity, on the other. It forms the natural mode of poetic expression; it persuades us into new insights by the bringing together of terms which then become metaphorically linked; and it provides those purely enjoyable formal resonances which give poetic language at its best a musical character. These things are relatively easy to understand; but the analysis of them can become complex, and the theoretical structures somewhat daunting. It is hoped that those who use this book will find that, even if the theory seems at times obscure, its practical application will offer a way into the strange but strangely familiar world of Hebrew poetry.

5

A FRAMEWORK FOR READING

I Traditional moves

In the first four chapters of this book I have tried to spell out – and to a limited extent resolve – some of the problems and ambiguities which confront any effort to make sense of the Psalms in translation. I now turn to discuss a framework within which to work, and which will provide a rough guide to our reading. It contains seven aspects (I prefer not to think of these as stages, since that would seem to imply a kind of chronological ordering, which could be misleading), not all of which will necessarily apply in every case. Moreover, the results of the application of one aspect may well stand in tension with, or contradict, those of another – a point which is implicit in the analysis of Psalm 121 which concluded Chapter 3. It is worth saying again, because it is a point which the Enlightenment notion of singularity of coherence finds hard to tolerate, that meaning is plural, and not infrequently so in a starkly contradictory fashion. Whether at some profoundly metaphysical level there is an ultimate reconciliation of competing interpretations is a moot point (though I personally doubt it); but in the mundane world of our everyday experience, a historical reading of Psalm 2 which presents it as an accurate description of the Israelite monarchy in the time of David would be hard to square with the view that it is a post-exilic fantasy based on an exaggerated sense of the importance of a long-vanished kingdom. My programme is to allow both to be considered, without demanding a closure of the problem of relative probability.

In order to reduce the level of unnecessary abstraction, I propose to illustrate my framework by referring in detail at each stage to the specifics of Psalm 29, in respect of which I have already made a number of comments in Chapter 2 (see pp. 27–32). Thus the theoretical discussion will be followed at each point by a consideration of what it might mean to read Psalm 29 under the rubric in question.

This is a rather long discussion; but it is central to the whole approach, and therefore it is vital that the issues be covered in sufficient depth and detail. I treat it in two parts, with the analysis of postmodern approaches being covered in Chapter 6.

The aspects of my framework are:

1   implications arising from any linguistic or text-critical points;
2   comparisons with similar material from other ancient near-eastern cultures;
3   readings of a historical, cultic/liturgical and sociological character;
4   reflections on the poetic and rhetorical structures of the psalm;
5   first-level readings which may take into account the results of aspects 1–4;
6   specific applications of modern hermeneutical techniques;
7   an invitation to a personal and subjective appropriation of the psalm.

These aspects are clearly designed to deal best with single psalms, or part-psalms; nevertheless, the recent recognition that there is (or appears to be) purposefulness to the grouping of psalms will also be given some consideration. In particular, I examine in some detail the character of the Psalms of Ascents (120–34), regarded as a coherent collection with an inner dynamic and a plausible function as a group (see Chapters 12–15).

One practical point needs to be made before we proceed. Much work has already been done on the task of interpreting the Psalms, and there is no virtue in repeating such work. Therefore the reader is strongly recommended to have available (when he or she comes to carry out their own work of interpretation) several good critical commentaries. Suggestions are given in the bibliography (1 Standard commentaries and introductions). A competent commentary will provide a good deal of the material needed for aspects 1–3, though it may need to be dug out from introductions as well as the discussions of particular psalms. In addition, individual commentators from time to time introduce stimulating interpretative ideas which can initiate a process of reflection pertinent to 5 and 7. Not many offer much directly by way of the kind of structural analysis envisioned in aspect 4, but passing notes about (for example) parallelism, the existence of refrains, and the recurrence of key terms at various points in a psalm, can all help the reader to develop his or her own structural analysis. Aspect 6 is almost completely absent from the major commentaries, which are effectively rooted in the historical-critical and/or theological-hermeneutical traditions. In Chapter 6 there is an elementary account of modern literary theories as they might apply to the Psalms, and further reading is indicated in the bibliography. But, to be blunt, one of the reasons for the writing of this book is that this subject is notoriously absent from both traditional commentaries and (with a few exceptions) monograph treatments.[1]

Finally, by way of introductory comment I would like to return to the question of the relationship between the seven aspects. The fact that they are numbered as they are could be taken to mean that they ought to be dealt with in that order, and that there is both logical and chronological significance to it. It could be argued that none of the other aspects of interpretation can be undertaken until we have a satisfactory text, so that linguistic and text-critical matters must inevitably come first. However, we have already, on general grounds, chosen our text (the NRSV); thus any other linguistic or textual comment is additional and, strictly speaking, optional. Indeed, aspect 4 (reflections on the poetic and rhetorical structures of the psalm) is strictly speaking independent of any other form of investigation (which is not to say that it could not benefit from other aspects). Moreover, since the hermeneutical process is famously circular, there is every reason to expect that the activity of interpretation will lead to refinements both of our understanding of the original text and of how to explain apparent cruxes. Some seeming textual problems disappear in the light of new ways of reading which may not have been available to earlier generations (no doubt to be matched by the appearance of others where certainty once ruled!). An interesting case in point concerns the famous puzzle, 'kiss the "son" [an Aramaic word]' in Psalm 2:12. Traditionally this has been regarded as a mis-reading, or some kind of cryptic form of another word ('kiss his feet' is the most popular). At least part of the reason for this consensus lies in the belief that the Psalms (especially those in the first book) are largely pre-exilic, and so could not conceivably legitimately contain an Aramaic term for such a common noun as 'son'.[2] I noted in Chapter 1, however, that Psalms 1 and 2 have been recently proposed as introductory to the whole collection and, further, that parts of the Psalter were still apparently in the process of formation as late as the second and first centuries BCE. These developments – based partly on evidence from Qumran, partly on structural observations about the book as a whole – force us to reconsider our hasty rejection of a seeming Aramaism in Psalm 2. For there is little doubt that Aramaic was a strong influence even on religious Hebrew by this period, so that what once seemed (on impeccable textual grounds) an assured position now opens up quite unexpected possibilities.

Aspects 2 and 3, which take up the concerns of comparative and historical studies, perhaps constitute a specialised field, but even they are not immune to interpretative feedback. Whether or not a particular Babylonian hymn (for example) is a true parallel or context for this or that psalm is not exclusively a textual matter. Questions of relative dating in literature like the Psalms, and the identification of sociologically or culturally significant items within them, cannot be resolved purely by some objective shopping-list of points of comparison. Does Psalm 24, for instance, describe an actual ritual procession at a datable point in the Judaean monarchy, or is it an idealised account which was recited but not performed? Do the terms in which it is couched echo songs about a contemporary event, or have they been refined and renewed with the repetition (and copying) of the Psalm by different people in later times? If so, at what point in the wider culture of the ancient Near East should we draw our comparison?

Aspect 5 was defined as 'first-level readings which may take into account the results of aspects 1–4. Here again some clarification is required; for I do not mean to say that these are logically prior – only that they tend to have been the major focus of traditions of interpretation since the introduction of formal biblical criticism. They are more likely, in short, to be found already discussed in existing literature (though typically without much reference to aspect 4). Modern hermeneutical techniques and personal readings could perfectly well form the starting-point of the process of interpretation.

Aspect 1: Implications arising from any linguistic or text-critical points

There are remarkably few Hebrew texts where no textual points require to be noted. Many, of course, are quite trivial, and do not substantially affect the reliability of the translation. But where a word or phrase is obscure, or is ambiguous in such a way that the context gives no clear guidance as to the choice of reading, or where word-play is involved, there is something to be said for these matters being brought to the attention of readers of the English translation. On the other hand, the chosen translation has (one assumes) already considered these and similar features of the text; it would be time-wasting to go through, as a matter of course, all the arguments which will already have informed the process of translation.

PSALM 29: NRSV

VERSE	*Part i*	TEXTUAL NOTES AND STRUCTURE
1	Ascribe to the LORD, O heavenly beings,[a] ascribe to the LORD glory and strength.	[a] Literally, 'sons of gods'
2	Ascribe to the LORD the glory of his name worship the LORD in holy splendour.	Threefold 'ascribe' Fourfold 'LORD' (= Yahweh)

Part ii

3	The voice of the LORD is over the waters; The God of glory thunders, the LORD, over mighty waters.	
4	The voice of the LORD is powerful; the voice of the LORD is full of majesty.	
5	The voice of the LORD breaks the cedars; the LORD breaks the cedars of Lebanon.	
6	He makes Lebanon skip like a calf, and Sirion like a young wild ox.	
7	The voice of the LORD flashes forth flames of fire.	Sevenfold
8	The voice of the LORD shakes the wilderness; the LORD shakes the wilderness of Kadesh.	repetition of the phrase 'The voice
9	The voice of the LORD causes the oaks to whirl, and strips the forest bare;	of the LORD' Tenfold 'LORD'

Intermezzo

	[meanwhile[b]] in his temple all say, 'Glory!'	[b] An admittedly free reading!

Part iii

10	The LORD sits enthroned over the flood; the LORD sits enthroned as king forever.	Fourfold 'LORD' Three 'powerful'
11	May the LORD give strength to his people! May the LORD bless his people with peace!	verbs: 'sits enthroned' (twice), 'gives strength'

In the discussion of Psalm 121 in Chapter 3 (pp. 41–5) I introduced one such example (the detailed structure of verse 6), because I judged that the ability of the reader to appreciate the force of the Psalm would be significantly enhanced by an awareness of the underlying Hebrew syntax. There were other points from the Hebrew that could have been made, but which I judged to be of insufficient importance to the task at hand. Admittedly, these decisions are subjective (necessarily so); this serves only to reinforce the original point that we must by and large stick to our shared version.

The discussion of Psalm 29 in Chapter 2 was in effect a treatment of the issues likely to arise under aspect 1. It was carried out for a particular purpose, as a test-case in relation to our choice of versions, and it will not be necessary to elaborate on that discussion here. However, in keeping with the practice employed in Part II, the NRSV text is displayed with any modifications and some of the more obvious structural points indicated. This can be used as a reference for the more detailed discussion of the Psalm. Strictly speaking, the third column deals with matters to be discussed under aspect 4; they are listed here for convenience.

Aspect 2: Comparisons with similar material from other ancient near-eastern cultures

The rich resources of written materials from Egypt, Mesopotamia, the Hittite lands in what is now Turkey, and to a lesser extent the kingdoms and city-states of Palestine – most significantly, the archives of Ugarit – have greatly enhanced our knowledge of the wider world of Semitic poetry. It is abundantly clear that the forms and conventions found in Hebrew poetry were ubiquitous in the ancient Near East. Collections of comparative materials have been published for the use of biblical readers, usually provided with indexes by means of which possible parallels between particular Hebrew passages and relevant compositions from the wider context can be made. These are noted in the General bibliography, and should be used by anyone interested in this aspect of the process of interpretation. Parallels may also be found in other parts of the Hebrew Bible, for the poetic or psalmic mode of composition is by no means confined to the Psalter; moreover certain literary or cultural conventions are repeated in various places. In practical terms, a concordance can help with this search for parallels, or a cross-referenced Bible (though these indicate supposed theological links, and may not provide the kind of connection relevant to this stage).

In the case of Psalm 29, for anyone familiar with Canaanite traditions there are a number of likely points of connection. Yahweh seems to be described as a thunder-god, which is apt both for Baal and for Hadad (the god of ancient Syria); the power over the 'mighty waters' may well echo the Canaanite myths of conflict between the gods and the waters, including the sea-dragon Lotan

(Hebrew: Leviathan[3]); and the scene set in verse 1, of an assembly of gods, is found several times in the Ugaritic myths, and in several biblical passages (see the discussion of Psalm 82 in Chapter 11). We can demonstrate these putative comparisons by providing specific examples.

First, from *NERTOT* (Beyerlin 1978: 208–9, 221) two general descriptions of Baal/Hadad as god of thunder which have several points of contact with Psalm 29 (the relevant verses of Psalm 29 are given in parentheses within the Canaanite texts below):

> And now Baal will appoint the time of his rain.
> And he will make his voice [3–8, seven times] ring out in the clouds,
> by flashing his lightning [7] to the earth.

> Baal has taken his seat,
> the mountain is like a throne [10].
> Hadad has rested on the mountain,
> like a storm [5–9] in the midst of his mountain,
> the God of Zaphon in a pleasant place,
> on the mountain where he shows his power.
> He sends forth seven lightnings,
> eight bundles of terror,
> the 'tree' of lightning descends [7].

(Note, incidentally, the use of parallelism, and the example in the second extract of the numerical formula 'seven . . . eight' which is a device popular in Wisdom writings in the Hebrew scriptures.[4])

The reference in the first verse to the 'sons of El' (NRSV: 'heavenly beings'), and the striking threefold 'ascribe' leading to a final 'worship the LORD' (Verse 2) can be compared with a dramatic thirteenth-century BCE plea to El for assistance cited by Beyerlin (*NERTOT*: 222), which similarly employs thrice-repeated formulae mounting to a climax:

> O El!
> O sons of El!
> O assembly of the sons of El!
>   O meeting of the sons of El!
> Be gracious, O El!
> Be a support, O El!
> Be salvation, O El!

> O El, hasten, come swiftly!
> To the help of Zaphon,
> to the help of Ugarit.
> Because of the burnt offering, O El!
> because of the appointed sacrifice, O El,
> because of the morning sacrifice, O El.

The idea of the assembly of gods, which might seem at first to be a contradiction of the theological tenets of the Hebrew scriptures, is found also in Psalm 82:1, in the story of Micaiah in 1 Kings 22:19, and in the prologue to the book of Job (1:6 and 2:1). Further, the phrase *bene 'elim* recurs in Psalm 89:6, while Exodus 15:11 asks 'Who is like you, O LORD, among the *'elim?'* Carola Kloos (1986: 19–21) argues cogently that, far from being late metaphorical usages, these testify to a widespread belief among ancient Israelites in a plurality of gods (a point which reinforces my comment in Chapter 2 on the theologically motivated character of translations of Ruth 1:15f.).

One final connection is to be found, hinted at rather than explicitly signalled. The phrase 'The voice of the LORD' occurs exactly seven times in verses 3–9 – in the context of Yahweh's power over the storm, the waters and all the phenomena of nature. The number seven has particular significance both in Canaanite and in Israelite religious traditions, and it may be that this is no accidental feature of Psalm 29, particularly in the context of cosmic control. For the legendary monster of the deep, variously referred to as Lotan, Tanin, and 'the wriggling serpent', is also described as 'the tyrant with seven heads'.[5] It seems probable that the central portion of Psalm 29, by using this numerical device, is providing a symbolic indication of the cosmic battle. This is given further credibility by consideration of Psalm 74:13–17, which explicitly deals with Yahweh's defeat of the sea and his breaking and crushing of 'the heads of Leviathan'. Though they are not explicitly numbered, there is again a hidden enumeration of seven, in the form of the use exactly seven times of the Hebrew personal pronoun *'attah* (you). This is significant because the normal employment of the Hebrew verb does not require an explicit use of the pronoun: when used, it is almost always an indication of special emphasis. *Seven* occurrences in a short passage, then, can hardly be coincidental.

Aspect 3: Readings of a historical, cultic/liturgical or sociological character

Undoubtedly there is nothing to connect Psalm 29 directly to historical events, unless we wish to argue that the weight of connections with Canaanite material implies that this is in origin an 'old' psalm. That does not take us very far, unfortunately, since we know nothing about the extent to which traditional Israelite or Judaean religion continued to use the common materials of the region, or for how long. Thus even those who present Psalm 29 as one which was originally a hymn to Baal in which the name of Baal was replaced by that of Yahweh[6] are no closer to a historical basis. Kloos's conclusion might be as good as we can get. She argues (1986: 12) that a detailed examination of both Psalm 29 and the *Song of the Sea* (Exodus 15:1–21) shows that

> the deity of the Song of the Sea is not less of a Baal than the deity of Psalm 29. The presence of a hymn picturing Yhwh as Baal, and of a tale about Israel's history in which Yhwh functions as Baal, must lead to the conclusion, I think, that the Baal traits were an essential element of Yhwh's character.

These observations bring us neatly to the combined areas of cultic and sociological readings. If Yahweh is indeed capable of being portrayed as Baal-like, we have a powerful example of a canonical socio-religious tradition which gives the lie to much prophetic and Deuteronomistic rhetoric. We glimpse a community which shares religious traditions with its neighbours, makes use of similar liturgies, and defines its God in similar terms. Further, this is not to be understood as a private or idiosyncratic perspective: the Psalm celebrates the high God of Israel, accorded 'glory and strength' by all other gods, acknowledged in his temple (verse 9) and effective on behalf of his people. There are interesting implications for contemporary society in this reading: we too live in a world of shared faiths characterised by a remarkable similarity of language of worship: food, perhaps, for thought.

The strictly sociological or cultural dimension cannot be easily isolated, partly because the religious realm was probably part and parcel of everyday life, and partly because we are not offered any clear information on the subject in this Psalm. Some general observations might be appropriate, but they are hardly specific to this instance. Thus, the concept of kingship which is implied is tyrannical and absolute, with the power to realise every whim regardless of the consequences. Also, the natural order is perceived to be unstable, at the mercy of ineluctable forces which (as the other side of the coin of kingship) are directly controlled by a divine power which requires to be regularly appeased ('in his temple all say, "Glory!"'). But these are little more than truisms of the ancient world, and hardly amount to interesting readings – at least, not as 'raw' information.

Aspect 4: Reflections on the poetic and rhetorical structures of the Psalm

All language is structured. The simplest sentence employs syntactical rules without which speakers would be unable to comprehend one another. Therefore the task of identifying structure within a piece of poetry is, at least in principle, an entirely natural one. Of course, as the detailed treatment in Chapter 4 made clear, poetry employs structure in a comprehensive and deliberate fashion which far transcends the natural organisational framework of language. That said, we should not imagine that these are two sharply differentiated modes, for part of what this is about is a natural instinct for complexity. The speaker who says 'firstly, secondly', etc., is structuring his or her speech. Few pieces of prose are, in fact 'prosaic' – as the consideration of Dorothy Wordsworth's diary entry demonstrated. So we are engaged at this stage upon an analysis of both conscious and unconscious structure, partly formal (rhythm, rhyme, parallelism, etc.) and partly rhetorical (the 'placing' of key words and expressions so as to produce the greatest effect). It is these two aspects of structure to which I apply the respective descriptions 'poetic' and 'rhetorical'.

The task of analysis of structure in this sense[7] is not a scientific one (though some approaches to parallelism, with their gallimaufry of ever-more refined types and arrays of a, b, cs, come close to it) – rules cannot be given. It is to be hoped that the cases presented in this book will provide sufficient examples for the reader to be able to devise and refine his or her own techniques. Nor does it yield a conclusive analysis: most texts are susceptible to a variety of structural analyses, frequently incompatible with each other. The reader has to choose, and to remember that nothing objectively true follows from that choice.

Psalm 29 presents several structures of both kinds. Rhetorically, for example, *part (i)* (verses 1–2) forms a dramatic climax, developing the threefold 'Ascribe to the LORD' to its concluding 'worship the LORD in holy splendour'. This is matched by the equally dramatic scene in *part iii* (verses 10–11) in which, following a single repeated phrase ('The LORD sits enthroned'), the poem moves to a third line – also expressing Yahweh's power – 'May Yahweh give strength', which serves both as the third element of the trio and as a preliminary climax. But the true climax lies in the last line, in which Yahweh's blessing and the gift of peace[8] are combined in the most potent prayer of the psalmic tradition. The subtlety of this paired structure lies in its not being identical; it is entirely possible, indeed, that it was not consciously developed, but flowed from the poetic instinct of the composer.

I have isolated one line in the form of an *intermezzo*, because it seems to me to function as a bridge within the Psalm, linking *part (ii)* to *part (iii)*, but also echoing the conclusion of *part (i)*. I have also taken a small liberty with the translation, interpreting the ubiquitous Hebrew for 'and' (which is in any case tolerant of a wide range of conjunctive meanings) as 'meanwhile'. The resulting interjection – 'Meanwhile in his temple all say, "Glory!"' – serves several purposes. First, it resolves the *Sturm und Drang* of verses 3–9b, as if to say 'Enough!' Second, it announces the presence of the enthroned king-god Yahweh by representing the praise offered by the assembled worshippers. And, third, it resumes one key expression from *part (i)*: the concept of glory as an attribute of the LORD. Indeed, were we to adopt the translation of verse 2b employed in the Jerusalem Bible (following the Septuagint), 'Worship Yahweh in his sacred court', there would be yet another important connection in the form of the identification of 'Yahweh's sacred court' with 'his temple'.

Apart from the general similarity of rhetorical design between *part (i)* and *part (iii)*, it is worth noting the recurrence of certain key words at significant points. I have already referred to the use of the word 'glory' in verses 1, 2 and 9; it occurs also in verse 3, thus providing a motif which effectively traverses the whole Psalm. The word 'strength' in verses 1 and 11 is also important: it is a characteristic attribute of Yahweh, with special associations with the Ark of the Covenant; so the prayer for that strength to be conferred upon the people is no mere convention. Lastly, I note the reference to Elim in verse 1 ('heavenly beings' = sons of Elim) and El in verse 3 ('God' = El), and the fact that the Hebrew terms behind 'splendour' (verse 2) and 'majesty' (verse 4) are derived from the same verb. The significance of these repetitions will be identified in the discussion under aspect 5.

As a matter of poetic structure, we have already noted the sevenfold repetition of 'voice' which characterises verses 3–9; to that enumeration should be added the fact that LORD is found four times in verses 1–2, ten times in verses 3–9, and four times in verses 10–11. It is fairly clear that there is an overall structuring of the Psalm into three parts, each with its own controlling motif. Thus verses 1–2 describe how the pantheon unites in praise of Yahweh; verses 3–9 give an account of Yahweh's supremacy over the natural orders; and verses 10–11 present him enthroned and giving gifts to his people.

Regarding parallelism, several observations are in order. First of all, verses 1 and 2 and verses 10 and 11 exhibit climactic parallelism, in which a similar phrase is repeated in each line, culminating in a summative expression (this is clear in verse 2b; that verse 11b is a similarly conclusive line follows from the familiar observation that peace – *shalom* – is within the Psalter perhaps the highest good a people can aspire to). Second, in the central section verses 4–6 and 8 exhibit a straightforward symmetrical parallelism. Verses 3b, 7 and 9c disrupt this pattern; and, given the signs of structure otherwise present, it is of interest to look at these counter-examples more closely.

Verse 3b interrupts what is otherwise a classic symmetrical parallel describing (as does the rest of *part ii*) the controlling power of Yahweh. Coming, as it does, at the beginning of this section, and containing the only other reference to El, we might well see this as a conscious fracturing of the symmetry. If so, its meaning may lie in the fact of the rupture which could suggest a contrast or conflict rather than a harmonious parallel. In the usual English translations this is concealed by the normal use of 'God' to represent the Hebrew 'El'. This is in most cases unremarkable, since the use in the Hebrew Bible of El as a name for the God of Israel is well attested. However, in Psalm 29 this is the single exception to the use of the divine name 'Yahweh', which occurs eighteen times. Could it be that El is here not to be identified with Yahweh, but contrasted, so that (in effect) the line describes something like El's last attempt to win back from Yahweh the worship offered by the 'heavenly beings' who are, after all, his own progeny – the sons of Elim?

Verse 7 is more puzzling. It does not have a parallel; it is the only reference to fire in the Psalm; and it is (as noted in Chapter 2, p. 30) linguistically somewhat problematical. Perhaps (given the role of the seven voices in *part ii*) it is simply one of a traditional set of functions attributed to the voice of Baal–Hadad–Yahweh.[9] As a singular exclamation it carries a certain force, it stands out dramatically within the Psalm as a whole, and this may be its poetic function.

Overall, the impression is given of a composition whose subject is a resolved conflict: rivals (El and Yahweh) struggle for the allegiance of the gods; Yahweh's superior power prevails, and as a result his people, acknowledging his glory, are endowed by him with that same power, in consequence of which they dwell in *shalom*.

Aspect 5: First-level readings which may take into account the results of the first four aspects

Critical biblical studies has a long history of seeking to interpret passages in what are assumed to be 'original' contexts. Indeed, the whole apparatus of historical criticism, before it became destructively self-referential, was directed towards the elucidation of a historical context which would enable the reader to ascertain the true historical (intended?) meaning of the text. Of course, the practical impossibility of ever arriving at an agreed text (far less the context) led to the project becoming a discipline in its own right, with no requirement to answer to any other criteria, and very few satisfactory interpretative conclusions were reached. The postmodern emergence of the hermeneutic of suspicion raised another kind of doubt about the propriety of what had been the purpose of biblical studies. If meaning is multiple and authorial intention is either irrelevant or inaccessible, the central purpose of the discipline, as traditionally formulated, disappears. In consequence, a three-way split has occurred in which traditional scholars continue to defend their original objective, postmodernists proclaim the end of certainty of interpretation, and neo-conservatives take the resulting divisions within academic discourse as proof of their claim that the truth is to be found in a return to pre-Enlightenment forms of authority. One of the aims of the present study is to propose, if not a reconciliation of these polarised positions, at least a compromise of the 'both–and' rather than 'either–or' variety. Accepting the reality that we cannot return to a unified theory of interpretation, may we not nevertheless explore a range of readings, each appropriate to the questions it with which it begins? I do not envisage a free-for-all: evidence of a historical nature can be found and its reliability estimated on a scale of probability, which will in turn limit the range of possible readings. If, for example, I become convinced that there is compelling evidence for dating the composition of Psalms 73–89 at or immediately after the Babylonian conquest of Jerusalem in 587 BCE, it would be improper for me to offer a psychological reading of them in terms of the supposed character of king David. But, in fact, such restrictions are likely to be rather few and of relatively small importance in the case of the Psalms; unless, of course, the theme of 'prophecy and fulfilment' were to be the hermeneutical model. In that case, historical evidence is crucial and (I wish to maintain) of real impact.

I want to propose, therefore, that a modest degree of such historically contextualised reading is quite proper, and can be illuminating, now that no one is in any danger of imagining that such readings are either specially accurate or specially privileged. Accordingly, I have designated as aspect 5 the endeavour of reflecting on possible readings pertinent to such historical circumstances of the text's likely origins as we can reasonably guess at. These will often be informed by the work carried out in aspects 1–3 (and to some extent 4), but may sometimes be directly deduced from a primary examination of the text. Most readers at all familiar with the historical narratives of the Hebrew Bible would, for example, find it quite easy to 'read' a plausible historical context for Psalm 74 without recourse to any of the other analyses.

In the case of Psalm 29, we have no obvious historical narrative; but the work already carried out suggests several interpretative moves. We might begin, for instance, with the proposal to see it as either an original Baal hymn transformed into a Yahwistic piece, or as a hymn celebrating Yahweh as a god 'like Baal'. In either case, the theme of transformation from one culture, one theological context, to another is significant. Yahweh 'supersedes' Baal (in the most common form of this reading) or, more subtly, like Baal he replaces and humiliates the old high God, El. This is the implication of Kloos's work, and my reading of the middle line of verse 3 and of verse 7 (see under aspect 4, above) further suggests a mimetic effect in which the form of the Psalm embodies in its structure the very contest which is its theme. Taking this as our hermeneutical starting point, we can read the Psalm ironically: while at first sight it appears to be a typically Canaanite composition (Baal–Hadad–Yahweh the 'god of thunder; the divine assembly, etc.), a closer reading shows that Yahweh has defeated and rejected El (and so also the Elim of verse 1). This represents not simply a substitution of Yahweh for Baal in the old myth, but a shift in perspective. Unlike Baal, Yahweh does not need the worship of the heavenly court, because Israel's God commands the worship of Israel's children: 'in his temple all cry "Glory!"' It is (as the Psalm's final prayer makes clear) the nation which stands in the temple and offers praise; the old gods have not only been humiliated, they have been nullified, stripped bare (like the forest, verse 9^{10}). And so, just as Isaiah mocked those who carved their gods from wood (Isaiah 44:9–20), Psalm 29 exemplifies Yahweh's power over the gods as seen in his fearsome power over the great forests and trees of Lebanon, which he hurls around at will and cuts to pieces with his lightning blade.

The Psalm is not only a theological piece; it has a nationalistic aspect also, in its concluding verse, where 'his people' are given the divine strength regularly associated with the power of the Ark of the Covenant, blessing and peace. The conjunction of this idea with the picture of Yahweh enthroned as King over the flood brings echoes of Psalm 24 (particularly verses 1–2 and 7–10, where the procession of the Ark is surely implied); and the confirmation, in verse 9, that the scene is now set in the Jerusalem temple finally overwhelms any remaining Baalistic undertone. Nevertheless, a struggle is involved, and every time the Psalm is sung or chanted or recited the worshippers are reminded of the need for constant vigilance. Other nations have been overwhelmed in the past, their gods forgotten, their children pressed into slavery or the service of new deities. Therefore the Deuteronomistic injunction, 'No other gods before me', forms a constant backdrop to the opening words of this song: 'Ascribe to the LORD, O sons of Elim, ascribe to the LORD glory and strength.' Each informs the other, the Psalm reminding the complacent reciters of the Decalogue that it warns against real dangers; the Decalogue warning the singers not to let themselves be seduced by the cadences of Canaan, which are (perhaps) only marginally under control in this fascinating composition.

6

A FRAMEWORK FOR
READING

II Postmodern moves

The subject of postmodernism is a vast one, to which this section provides only the most rudimentary indicative guide. Suggestions for further reading will be found in the bibliography (see 3 Postmodern and structuralist readings); what is provided here is intended to give the reader some basic currency in the field. The first part of the chapter looks at theory;[1] the second part resumes consideration of Psalm 29, applying the remaining two of the seven aspects which comprise the framework for reading the Psalms.

Literary theory

Structuralism

The starting-point for any survey of modern theory has to be the work of Saussure, whose fundamental insight was that language is based on differences rather than resemblances. It is important to stress that it is difference and not binary opposition which is central, despite the subsequent tendency for the latter to become dominant. Structuralism should ideally not be regarded as a system *per se*, but as a mode of understanding how language works. Thus in this book I do not intend to carry out 'structural*ist*' analyses (though – as Collins (1987) demonstrates – this can be done); rather I invite the reader to take on board what Saussure has to say about the nature of language, while focusing mainly on deconstructive forms of reading.

I have, of course, already indicated that structure is a key part of the process of reading and understanding, and what is done under aspect 5 will frequently take up points which could be regarded as structuralist. I do not, however, wish to deploy the kind of formalist devices associated with Propp and Jakobson (the Russian Formalists), and with Greimas. Let me, therefore, elucidate what I take to be the importance of the Saussurian enterprise.

Two fundamental propositions may be enunciated: the arbitrariness of the sign, on the one hand; and the priority of speech over writing and of abstract language over individual usage, on the other. The first of these may be summed up by noting that 'A linguistic *sign* unites, not a thing and a name, but a concept and a sound image' (LENT: 159). Saussures's terminology for this principle is expressed by, respectively, *signified* and *signifier*. In view of the importance within Derridean philosophy of the primacy of writing over both speech and thought, it is worth emphasising that Saussure retains the principle that concepts are expressed by language, though he does not subscribe to the belief that pristine 'ideas' exist, as it were, in the ether, awaiting our recognition. The following passage perhaps best accounts for his position (1916: 156):

> The characteristic role of a language in relation to thought is not to supply the material phonetic means by which ideas may be expressed. It is to act as intermediary between thought and sound, in such a way that the combination of both necessarily produces a mutually complementary delimitation of units. Thought, chaotic by nature, is made precise by this process of segmentation. But what happens is neither a transformation of thoughts into matter, nor a transformation of sounds into ideas. What takes place, is a somewhat mysterious process by which 'thought–sound' evolves divisions, and a language takes shape with its linguistic units in between those two amorphous masses.

The arbitrariness in structuralism lies at the level of the choice of signs, not necessarily at the level of meaning. 'Language is both *necessary* and *arbitrary*' (SS: 13) is perhaps the neatest summary of this position.

The second proposition is illustrated by the concepts of *langue* and *parole*. The latter refers to the idiosyncratic usage of individual speakers of the language; the former indicates the hypothetical set of all such languages. We can communicate only because our *paroles* approximate sufficiently to the (undefinable) *langue*, which is nevertheless our (unsought) birthright – 'the social part of language, external to the individual, who by himself is powerless either to create it or to modify it. It exists only in virtue of a kind of contract agreed between the members of a community' (Saussure 1916: 31).

We learn to speak as part of our biological development; to an extent, therefore, at least in the early stages of language developments, arbitrariness is not an individual choice. Hence meaning emerges as a function of speech, constrained by the curious un-freedom of the 'contract' to which Saussure refers. As a contract, it is unusual in that 'no one ever gets the chance to evaluate it before signing. The individual absorbs language before he can think for himself: indeed, the absorption of language is the very condition of being able to think for himself' (SS: 12). The seeds of deconstruction are visible here – it is not such a large step from the idea that we learn to speak socially in order to give shape to communicable concepts to the principle that language defines both 'us' and 'our' concepts.

Saussure's field was, of course, linguistics, and what he proposed was a theory applicable to linguistics in which he identified a hierarchy of phonetics (sounds), phonemics (written transcriptions of sounds), syntagmatics (sentence structure) and morphology (rhetorical organisation of larger units).

> Linguistic units derive both their existence and their essence from their inter-relations. Every distinct language is a unique relational structure; and the units which we identify in describing a particular language – sounds, words, meanings, etc. – are but points in the structure, or network of relations.
>
> (Robey 1973: 16)

When applied to literary studies, structure is a heuristic model, something abstract, constructed – even fictional. It is therefore in principle opposed to systems and the systemic view of texts, and thus may be distinguished from New Criticism which tended to regard structure as transcendent. Barthes reminds us that all human activity is constructed, not essential. He criticises mimetic theories of literature – meaning is not an expression of the author (nineteenth-century criticism) or of reality (New Criticism); rather, texts operate through codes and conventions, and it is the business of structuralism to study how these function to limit the possibilities of meaning. (Of course, this notion of limiting meaning is opposed by deconstruction, which undermines all attempts to limit interpretation). The following excerpt (LENT: 35) provides an excellent account of Barthes' understanding of structuralism:

In 'The Structural Activity', one of many essays Roland

Barthes wrote in the 1960s to explain the movement's principles, Barthes defines *structure* as

> a *simulacrum* of the object, but a directed, *interested* simulacrum, since the imitated object makes something appear which remained invisible, or if one prefers, unintelligible in the natural object. Structural man takes the real, decomposes it, then recomposes it.

The result of this *activity* is that

> there occurs *something new*, and what is new is nothing less than the generally intelligible: the simulacrum is intellect added to the object, and this addition has an anthropological value, in that it is man himself, his history, his situation, his freedom and the very resistance which nature offers to his mind.

This is apt both to my approach to the identification of structure already in Psalm 29 and to other psalms in Parts II and III. What we 'find', whether or not it was 'really there', is true to our nature as 'structural man' engaged upon the task of reading. Its reality or integrity belongs to our humanity, not to the text's objectivity.

Polzin (1977: 1–34) in his analysis of structuralism in relation to biblical studies spells out in some detail how it functions heuristically. He first identifies it as a 'self-conscious' discipline (which I take to mean that it does not pretend to be an 'objective' methodology exercising god-like authority, but rather is a methodology which is aware of its involvement in its own findings). He relates this to three categories:

1   the object of analysis – the text is to be seen as a system of transformations which is self-regulating (closed);
2   the nature of the model constructed – what is produced is a hypothetical-deductive interpretation;
3   the subject who is doing the analysing – the structuralist is part of the structure.

1 The text is a structure: and there are 'rules'. (a) 'The soul of a structure consists in this, that it is neither the whole nor its elements that count but rather the relationships between and among its elements.' (b) The structure is a system of transformations. (c) These are self-regulating – that is, only such transformations are permitted

as will keep the structure unchanged. It is, in other words, a closed system. (d) Structural analysis is possible on the plane of content as well as expression, and the latter is not in principle any more secure or less subjective than the former. There is therefore no hierarchy of order of analysis – we can begin anywhere, though with appropriate comparison and interrelation of the analyses on each plane. These points are highly pertinent to my approach, for they ensure that, at both the formal level and that of content, findings are delimited by an understanding of the text under examination as an organic thing whose integrity has a powerful influence on the way the hermeneutic develops. The discussion of the structure of Psalm 29 in Chapter 5 bears this out. We found a pattern of relationships between sections of the Psalm, individual lines, and specific words. These reflected transformations chosen not arbitrarily but because they 'belonged' to the shape of the composition. (The division into three parts, for example, is a transformation which is nevertheless true to the structural identity of the Psalm.) And the analysis was both formal (identification of repetitions, number of occurrences of particular words and phrases) and content-based (the semantic significance of terms like 'glory', 'strength', etc.).

2 'All brands of hermeneutical interpretations are hypothetical constructs whether they be on the expressive plane or the content plane.' We can discern two forms of this: (a) the *hypothetical–deductive*, where a model is brought to the text to aid analysis; and (b) the *hypothetical–inductive*, where a pattern is 'discovered' within the text. The basic nature of knowledge is that we discover hypotheses not by applying known rules (whether inductive or not) but by a quite serendipitous and arbitrary process. Despite the some-what forbidding terminology which Polzin employs, these are actually rather familiar processes. For example, both Christology and 'covenant renewal ceremony' as modes of interpretation of the Psalms depend upon bringing to the text a model of how to read it which is derived from sources external to the Psalter. By contrast, parallelism in all its rich variety is an internal structural system which was 'discovered' by Lowth (1839) and others, and has had a profound effect on the way that psalms are understood.

3 The one who carries out the analysis is a subject, and so the structures 'found' are in part determined by the personal structures of the analyst.[2] This point is very similar to that attributed to Barthes in which he identified the anthropological quality of the 'simulacrum' brought about by the addition of intellect to the object

of the text. Subjectivity is thus explicitly recognised to be part of the hermeneutic; but not unfettered play with the text (this is the force of Polzin's commentary (1977) regarding his first category, the object of analysis). The reader cannot but be implicated, and his or her style of reading will inevitably contribute to what is 'discovered'; but questions of agreed signification, of historical and sociological evidence, and of 'limited objectivity' retain their force. The discussion of Psalm 29 offered under aspect 5 was carried out in this spirit, and rather than attempt any further theoretical debate, I will simply ask the reader to review that section in the light of Polzin's theoretical position.

Post-structuralism, superstructuralism, deconstruction

The revolution begun by Saussure and his followers quickly developed into a much more comprehensive assault on the traditional philosophical assumption that there exists an assured body of knowledge (or truth) accessible, however imperfectly, by the power of language regarded as a tool. While Saussure, as I noted, held that *langue* was necessary to mediate between chaotic 'raw' thought and undifferentiated sound, he nevertheless preserved in doing so some kind of attachment to the priority of thought. This has now been comprehensively attacked, most famously by Derrida and the hermeneutics of deconstruction.

In order to describe this movement, I will begin with a particular manifestation of it: Richard Harland's *Superstructuralism* (1987), which as he points out can be interpreted either as '*super*-Structuralism' or '*superstructure*-alism'. Each offers a differently interesting way of taking forward the concerns of structuralism. Superstructuralism emphasises the priority of culture over nature (the latter, indeed, was a seventeenth-century innovation), and the priority of society over the individual (the latter being a cultural construct flowing from a bourgeois ethic of individualism [SS: 9–10]). What this means is that we cannot live as human beings below the level of language categories and social meanings because it is these that make us human in the first place. Hence, for 'priority of Culture over Nature' read 'priority of Sign over Objective things'; and for 'priority of Society over the Individual' read 'priority of Sign over Subjective things' (SS: 68). This comes close to replacing the Saussurian principle of language (and its signs) as the means by which we realise meaning and social identity with a more radical claim: that the sign is the substance of both meaning and identity.

This shift in emphasis is part of a larger debate about the relationship between language and thought. While the argument is primarily philosophical, it impinges upon the hermeneutical task. If thought precedes language, the interpretation of texts has a quite different objective than if language precedes thought. It may be useful, therefore, to set out the main lines of the argument in order to provide a context for the way in which deconstruction handles the matter.[3]

We may begin by identifying three classic positions which seek in different ways to understand the nature of ideas and thought. The *empiricist* case is that we must begin with raw, natural, 'objective' data. 'For empiricists, the human mind comes properly in second place; if it comes first, it can only impose distorting presuppositions and artificial prejudices upon the outside world' (SS: 71). They advocate, in short, the priority for conceptualisation of the objectivity of things. The *metaphysical* position, as argued by Plato, Spinoza and Hegel, holds that it is only through language that we know we are experiencing sense-data. Thus metaphysicians hold that it is only retrospectively that objectivity emerges, and empiricism fails because right from the beginning it employs the mind and language, which are in no way raw 'objective' data (SS: 71). Objectivity, on this view of the matter, is to be found at the level of abstract ideas, and these 'are ideas not as mental concepts in general are ideas, but specifically as abstractions are ideas. Images and perceptual data and all such mental "solids" are excluded; the universe of objective ideas is a universe of empty categories and relational forms' (SS: 74). The third position is that of the *Cartesians*, for whom the key lies in recognising the subjectivity of ideas as against the empiricist objectivity of things. This leads in turn to the characteristic mind–body dualism which has so dominated western forms of thinking about the self. For if what really matters is the inner core of subjective identity, which is that which thinks ('the transcendental ego'), it follows that mind is of a substance different from that of matter and 'I' am not a body which belongs to the realm of objective things, but a mind which transcends the mundane realm.

A major concern of post-structuralism has been to position language as a phenomenon in relation to thought or ideas. Harland's account of superstructuralism sets language within the general metaphysical tradition, but with one very important difference. The metaphysical philosophers see systems of ideas as residing 'outside' the individual (Plato's Forms; Spinoza's Modes and Attributes of God; Hegel's Categories). Thus objective ideas are prior to both subjective ideas and objective things; moreover the metaphysicians tended to lapse into religious terminology. Thus Harland (SS: 74–5) maintains that metaphysical philosophers

> tend to interpret objective ideas in terms of a religious concept of God or Spirit. Of all philosophical traditions, the Metaphysical tradition has always been the most spiritually oriented. For the concept of God or Spirit is precisely the concept of a mind outside of any individual subjective mind. But this concept is still formed upon an analogy with the individual subjective mind; there remains always a kind of inwardness about the thinking of a Divine Mind.

Superstructuralism avoids this by understanding

> signs and language categories as communicated *between* human minds rather than lying *behind* them. With the concept of signs and language categories, it becomes much easier to think of abstractions as simple external manifestations, simply on a level with everything else in the universe. . . . Superstructuralism thus represents a kind of natural next step for Metaphysical philosophy.
>
> (ibid.: 75)

Moreover, it is a development which rejects both empiricism and Cartesianism as being, in effect, two sides of the same coin – a conceptual world in which it is natural to think of objective *things* and subjective *ideas*:

> We can give a name to this conceptual dimension: it is the dimension of 'experience'. For experience as we commonly conceive it is precisely the place where objective things make contact with subjective ideas. Superstructuralist philosophy thus proposes to outleap the dimension of experience, to start from a starting point outside of experience.
>
> (SS: 76)

And that starting-point is *langue* – an objectification of language which embodies the concept of an objective idea[4] and so opens the way to a hermeneutic which avoids the mysticism of traditional metaphysics, the subjectivity of Cartesian duality and the aridity of empiricism.

The best-known post-structuralist is undoubtedly Derrida, whose technique of *deconstruction* has achieved a level of fame and notoriety rarely matched in the academic world. I shall say more about both the technique and the notoriety shortly; I want first to examine how this particular version of the language–thought problem is situated and what its roots are.

Derrida's post-structuralist theory begins from an appraisal of Edmund Husserl's account of the phenomemology of language in 'Expression and Meaning' (1970: 269–333).[5] First published in 1900, it represents an important essay towards the definition of a phenomenological approach to language. In so far as Derrida's position derives from a not-unsympathetic critique of Husserl, it is not wholly irrational to see his own starting-point as a phenomenology of language which takes the ultimate step of privileging the system of signs and relations we call language as its own final 'reference'.

Husserl, however, has a high view of intention as meaning: 'Meaning thus understood is not just meaning in the sense that *words mean*, but in the sense that *someone means them to mean*.' The *reductio* of this is that for Husserl the purest form of expression is interior monologue, where perfect communication is possible; this has the curious consequence that language is strictly speaking unnecessary because we already understand perfectly everything we might think (SS: 126f.). Derrida describes this *reductio* in an important passage from *Speech and Phenomena* (Kamuf 1991: 8):

> [According to Husserl] in solitary discourse the subject learns nothing about himself, manifests nothing to himself. To support this demonstration, whose consequences for phenomenology will be limitless, Husserl invokes two kinds of argument.
>
> 1 In inward speech, I communicate nothing to myself, I indicate nothing to myself. I can at most imagine myself doing so; I can only represent myself as manifesting something to myself. This, however, is only *representation* and *imagination*.
> 2 In inward speech I communicate nothing to myself *because there is no need of it*; I can only pretend to do so. . . . The existence of mental acts does not have to be indicated (let us recall that in general only an existence can be indicated) because it is immediately present to the subject in the present moment.

At one level, what Husserl claims seems self-evident. It is widely believed[6] that 'ideas' are prior to language and that they appear to us, in solitude, in a kind of numinous 'soup', without benefit of words and phrases. Husserl is determined on this point: the true thought is interior and therefore communication beyond the solipsistic is bound to fall short of perfection. Thus, on the problem of communication between speaker and hearer:

> The hearer perceives the speaker as manifesting certain inner experience, and to that extent he also perceives these experiences themselves: he does not, however, himself experience them, he has not an 'inner' but an 'outer' percept of them. . . . In the former case we have to do with an experienced, in the latter case with a presumed being, to which no truth corresponds at all. Mutual understanding demands a certain correlation among the mental acts mutually unfolded in intimation and in the receipt of such intimation, but not at all their exact resemblance.
>
> (Husserl 1970: 278)

This barrier which the imperfections of language causes nonetheless leaves the original thought unaffected *in the mind of the originator*. Thus:

> It is plain, however, that each assertion, whether representing an exercise of knowledge or not – whether or not, i.e., it fulfils or can fulfil its intention in corresponding intuitions, and the formative acts involved in these – involves a thought, in which thought, as its unified specific character, its meaning is constituted.
>
> (ibid.: 286)

And, again, in the context of an expression of the impossibility of achieving the ideal of a perfect communication of meaning:

> To being-in-itself correspond truths-in-themselves, and to these last, fixed, unambiguous assertions. Of course, to be able to say all this actually would require, not merely the necessary number of *verbal signs*, but a corresponding number of *expressions* having precise meanings. . . . We are infinitely removed from this ideal.
>
>   In other words, the subjective acts which confer meaning on expressions are variable, and that not merely as

individuals, but, more particularly, in respect of the specific characters in which their meaning consists. But the meanings themselves do not alter: this is in fact an absurd manner of speech if we adhere to our view of meanings as ideal unities, whether in the case of equivocal, subjectively defective expressions, or in the case of univocal, objectively fixed ones.

(ibid.: 322)

It is this strongly idealistic position which Derrida attacks. In doing so his prime concern is not (as one form of attack on Husserl might be) to return to some kind of empiricism in which language is an epiphenomenon produced as a consequence of our material nature. Rather he goes *further* than Husserl in the sense that he pushes to the limit the implications of his concept of representation. Where Husserl saw it as a 'temporary' device which would (as we saw above) in ideal circumstances be redundant, Derrida promotes language itself as the essential (as distinct from accidental) mode of communication. Discussing the Husserlian concept of the representation-free inner monologue as distinct from representation and imagination, he asks (Kamuf 1991: 9f.):

> Can this system of distinctions be applied to language? From the start we would have to suppose that representation (in every sense of the term) is neither essential to nor constitutive of communication, the 'effective' practice of language, but is only an accident that may or may not be added to the practice of discourse. But there is every reason to believe that representation and reality are not merely added together here and there in language, for the simple reason that it is impossible in principle to rigorously distinguish them. And it doesn't help to say that this happens *in* language; language in general – and language alone – *is* this.

He goes on to argue that words, phonemes, etc. are signs. As such they are not events (that is, unrepeatable instances), but *signifiers* which remain constant and recognisable; they 'can function as [signs], and in general as language, only if a formal identity enables [them] to be issued again and to be recognized. This identity is necessarily ideal' (ibid.: 10). Thus we cannot separate expression and signification from the presumed object on the basis that one is ideal and the other not. Effectively, then, the level of the ideal is transferred from the notional 'thought' to the expression. Of course, this immediately calls in question the status of that idealised 'thought', and leads to its effacement.

This is a key to Derrida's project, since with the effacement of the idealised concept comes nothing less than an assault on the privileged claims of the whole western philosophical tradition.[7]

> In both expression and indicative communication the difference between reality and representation, between the true and the imaginary, and between simple presence and repetition has always already begun to be effaced. Does not the maintaining of this difference – in the history of metaphysics and for Husserl as well – answer to the obstinate desire to save presence and to reduce or derive the sign, and with it all powers of repetition? . . . To assert, as we have been doing, that within the sign the difference does not take place between reality and representation, etc., amounts to saying that the gesture that confirms this difference is the very effacement of the sign. . . . Signs can be effaced in the classical manner in a philosophy of intuition and presence. Such a philosophy effaces signs by making them derivative; it annuls reproduction and representation by making signs a modification that happens to a simple presence. But because it is just such a philosophy – which is, in fact, *the* philosophy and history of the West – which has so constituted and established the very concept of signs, the sign is from its origin and to the core of its sense marked by this will to derivation or effacement. Consequently, to restore the original and non-derivative character of signs, in opposition to classical metaphysics, is, by an apparent paradox, at the same time to efface a concept of signs whose whole history and meaning belong to the adventure of the metaphysics of presence.
>
> (Kamuf 1991: 11)

Norris (1987: 40–1) locates Derrida's opposition to this tradition in the context of a rejection of authority; particularly the authority claimed for the spoken *logos*:

> So it is that the ethics of speech as self-presence affects the constitution of Plato's ideal Republic. Within such a system

there would always be the ultimate reference back to an authority residing outside and beyond specific differences of age, class or political interest. These differences could then be subsumed – like the problematic instance of writing – under a *logos* that would always already be established in the place of self-present truth. And if writing ever presumed to challenge this truth, to deny the paternal law of speech, then it would have to be accounted a bastard son, or an orphan deprived of all natural, hereditary rights. For it is the passage of authority from fathers to sons – rightful, legitimate sons – that ensures the continuity of tradition and the maintenance of properly exercised power in family and state. '*Logos* is a son, then, a son that would be destroyed in his very *presence* without the present *attendance* of his father. His father who answers. His father who speaks for him and answers for him.'

The authority which is here castigated is that of the western tradition which postulates ideals and pure concepts as prior, and affirms them through a spurious attachment to the spoken word as a (more) pristine form of communication by comparison with writing. This is clearly implied in the way that Husserl (1970: 276–80, §§6–8) gives priority to speech as the mode in which expression takes place. Derrida notes that Husserl supposes the concept of phonetic writing – which implies already a privileged role for speech. As Norris (1987: 68) puts it:

[It] is a fact that writing as we know it – as practised in all Western cultures – is a form of phonetic–alphabetical transcription. That is to say, written language is naturally conceived as a second-order system of signs based on the primary material of the spoken word. . . . Derrida is far from wishing to deny the appearance of self-evident truth possessed by this feature of natural language. . . . But this fact, he goes on, 'does not correspond to any necessity of an absolute and universal essence'. That is to say, there is no justification, in the strictest logical terms, for treating this priority attached to spoken language as a ground for further claims about the nature of truth, meaning or language in general.

Yet for Husserl (according to Derrida), '[t]he ideality of the object, which is only its being-for a nonempirical consciousness, can only be expressed in an element the phenomenality of which does not have worldly form. *The name of this element is the voice. The voice is heard* (Kamuf 1991: 19). The reason for this emphasis lies in the mistaken belief that in spoken language (or in writing which gives priority to speech) there is seemingly a coincidence of meaning with the immediate intent of the speaker.

> When we speak there is a sense of some peculiarly intimate relation between the words that we utter and the meaning that animates these words. In French there is a phrase, *s'entendre–parler*, that nicely suggests the intuitive logic of this natural attitude to speech. 'Entendre' means both 'to hear' and 'to understand', with the strong implication that hearing is in some way a privileged or uniquely authentic form of understanding. *S'entendre–parler* might thus be translated: 'hearing oneself speak and immediately grasping the sense of one's own utterance'. . . . Hearing/ understanding oneself talk is a *de facto* truth in our experience of language that appears so massively self-evident as almost to brook no question.
>
> (Norris 1987: 71)

It is this dominant tradition and its claim to self-evidentiality which Derrida comprehensively criticises.

The essence of his criticism lies in the affirmation that (as Saussure pointed out) language is in all of its manifestations a system of differentiated signs in which meaning resides not in any ideal correspondence between sound and sense but in structures of relationships. Speech is language, and cannot be exempted from this account; therefore the classical downgrading of writing applies equally, and for the same reasons, to speech. We cannot escape from the consequences of the ubiquity and impermeability of signs – we may replace signs with other signs, but we cannot 'replace' them with meaning in some transcendent sense.

> To think logocentrically is to dream of a 'transcendental signified', of a meaning outside and beyond the differential play of language that would finally put a stop to this unnerving predicament. Deconstruction defines its own project by contrast as a perpetual reminder that meaning is always the 'sign of a sign'; that thought cannot escape this

logic of endless supplementarity; and that writing is in at the origin of language, since that origin cannot be conceived except by acknowledging the differential nature of signs.

(Norris 1987: 85–6)

Derrida, on the contrary, makes language central and attributes to it an important reality, and so reverses Husserl's argument. For him, language is most true to itself when it is at its most self-sufficient, and this happens in the form of 'writing' which is independent of the author and able to function entirely by itself when cut off from intention. 'Husserl insisted upon the mental meaning behind the verbal meaning in order to keep verbal meaning under control.' But, for Derrida,

> the writer only discovers the meaning of his words in the act of writing them. As Derrida, on behalf of all writers, confesses, 'before me, the signifier on its own says more than I believe that I meant to say, and in relation to it, my meaning-to-say is submissive rather than active'. The written sign is not *sent* but *received*; even the writer is just another reader.
>
> (SS: 131–2)

In an important sense this is uncontroversial for those who work with texts without (known) authors and with no serious possibility of recovering intention; but Derrida goes well beyond the mere recognition of ambiguities in 'real' signs. He

> refuses to allow any meanings in the mind at all. He conceives of meaning in a new and extraordinary way that involves no movement from marks on the page to mental concepts and images. . . . The signified, so far as Derrida is concerned, is merely an illusion that human beings have invented because they have feared the consequences of a materialist conception of language. . . . [Derrida's] signifiers are above all *signifying*, that is, pointing away from themselves, pointing away to other signifiers.
>
> (SS: 134)

The foregoing, rather extensive, preliminary discussion allows us to approach the problem of a definition of just what Derrida's project of deconstruction is about. It is rooted in language, not speech; it denies the principle of reference in any objective sense; it promotes the requirement, in the face of the inevitable deferral of meaning implicit in the Saussurean idea of meaning through difference, for a constant process of reinterpretation (*reinscription*); and it stands in determined opposition to all hierarchical oppositions such as essence–appearance, spirit–matter, speech–writing. The last of these is, as we have seen, the most important focus of deconstructive philosophy. For, prior to Derrida, it has been customary to privilege 'speech' as being in some way prior, more immediate, more authentic than writing. This *logocentrism* regards writing as 'merely' a representation of speech which is privileged because it seems to be simultaneously present in utterance to both speaker and hearer.

Out of the two terms 'deferral' and 'difference' Derrida created his famous neologism *différance* which implies that meaning, which is a function of difference, is always deferred because words are required to define meaning, and they in turn require to be interpreted. To put it another way, 'the logic of writing is . . . a double logic: writing is called upon as a necessary remedy for *différance*, but at the same time it *is* the very *différance* for which remedy must be sought' (LENT: 45). Speech is no different, for the meaning of what is said and of what we hear is deferred in just the same way. 'We can never catch up with the actual moment of our sensory contact with the outside world, we are eternal latecomers to the "now" of our own experience. "The 'perceived'," says Derrida, "may be read only in the past, beneath perception and after it"' (SS: 144). Out of this comes the *ludic* aspect of deconstruction: writing is a field of limitless play characterised by the movement of *différance*. 'Deconstructive writing takes the form of a commentary on other texts and aims to turn the language of these texts against itself, usually by playing on the contradictory or "undecidable" relationship between the literal and figurative levels of the text.' While there are some links with Hegel in this process, 'In Derrida's theory, oppositions are unbalanced "without ever constituting a third term, without ever leaving room for a solution in the form of speculative dialectics"' (ibid.: 140).

While 'definitions' of deconstruction can be attempted, and have clearly some merit, Derrida is insistent that 'deconstruction is neither "method" on the one hand nor "interpretation" on the other'. Among possible defining statements, the following are plausible:

- '[deconstruction] is the dismantling of conceptual oppositions, the taking apart of hierarchical systems of thought which can

then be *reinscribed* within a different order of textual signification'; or
* 'deconstruction is the vigilant seeking-out of those *"aporias"*,
  blindspots or moments of self-contradiction where a text
  involuntarily betrays the tension between rhetoric and logic,
  between what it manifestly *means to say* and what it is nonetheless
  constrained to mean.' It is 'in the margins of the text – the
  "margins", that is, as defined by a powerful normative consensus
  – that deconstruction discovers these same unsettling forces at
  work'.

Nevertheless, we must reject definability; for 'it is precisely this idea
– this assumption that meaning can always be grasped in the form
of some proper, self-identical concept – that Derrida is most
determinedly out to deconstruct' (Norris 1987: 18f.).

The question of definition can be tackled by focusing on the
behaviour of the signs which (together with relationships) constitute
language. Thus, post-structuralism addresses the problem that the
structuralists' semiotic analysis applies equally to their own world
and their own writing and thinking – it deconstructs structures.
There are two contrasting modes of functioning for the sign: on the
one hand, that of structuralists and semioticians for whom the sign
is rigid and predictable; and, on the other, an unconventional mode
where the sign works creatively, anarchically and irresponsibly. Post-
structuralism is concerned with the anti-social sign, which has three
essential qualities:

1 it moves – the act of signifying is indeed a 'pointing-away', for
   signifiers are signs in motion, restlessly always pointing to other
   signifiers;
2 it multiplies – 'The meaning of meaning . . . is infinite implication, the indefinite referral of signifier to signifier.' Derrida
   describes this as a state of *dissemination* – 'the state of perpetually
   unfulfilled meaning that exists in the absence of all signifieds'
   (SS: 135);
3 it is material – signs *are* meaning: there is no real signified to
   which they point, and language is materialist.

One remaining concept within deconstruction requires our
attention. It is the idea of the 'supplement' (French: *supplément*).
Whereas the English expression reflects that which is secondary, a
mere accessory, in French it can mean both addition and substitution.

This means that when philosophy privileges speech as a means of direct mediation of truth, and tries to make writing inferior, by excluding it as a mere supplement or accessory, a deconstructive approach has more to say. For

> a 'supplement' is also that which is required to *complete* or *fill up* some existing lack, some hiatus in the present order of things. And in this case writing would no longer be a strictly dispensable or ancillary technique. On the contrary, it would have to be treated as a precondition of language in general, a necessary supplement in the absence of which speech itself could scarcely be conceived. What Derrida calls the 'logic of supplementarity' is precisely this strange reversal of values whereby an apparently derivative or secondary term takes on the crucial role in determining an entire structure of assumptions.
>
> (Norris 1987: 66–7)

Let me conclude this overview with a short passage from Norris (1987: 224–5) in which he contrasts structuralist and deconstructive readings:

> In a striking image, Derrida compares the upshot of structuralist readings to 'the architecture of an uninhabited or deserted city, reduced to its skeleton by some catastrophe of nature or art' (*Writing and Difference*, p. 5). The virtue of such readings is to highlight the essentially abstract or 'lifeless' character of the landscape thus revealed. 'The relief and design of structures appears more clearly when content, which is the living energy of meaning, is neutralized' (p. 5). What structuralism necessarily leaves out of account is the *excess* of meaning over form, the fact that certain elements (of 'force' or 'significance') must always escape its otherwise lucid vigil.

It is that 'excess of meaning' that we seek – forever, of course, doomed to be disappointed; yet exhilarated in the process of pursuit.

Reading again

Applications of modern hermeneutical techniques to Psalm 29 (aspect 6)

(Readers may find it useful at this point to have another look at the discussion in Chapter 5 before embarking upon what now follows. Comments of a structural nature are contained in that discussion under aspect 4.)

There are several *aporias* in Psalm 29 – those problematic points which often serve to indicate how deconstruction may proceed. Most of these have already come to our attention under earlier aspects; but we now approach them not in the spirit of wrinkles to be smoothed out but as potential openings into new perceptions.

We begin with the 'heavenly beings' of verse 1, whose very existence is subversive in relation to the way that the religion of the Jews is normally understood. With them we should associate the irruption into verse 3 of 'the God of glory', in respect of whom the English typographic convention leads us to understand a synonym for 'the LORD' – but who might have a much more counter-revolutionary role to play. The mysterious verse 7 is also to be singled out (not least because of its singularity); and this is true also of the last line of verse 9, which does not stand in parallel to anything. How these two lines 'connect' makes a considerable difference to how the poem is read. Finally, the Psalm concludes with a prayer for peace: we might wonder how that relates to anything at all in the preceding verses, which are all sound and thunder.

Externally there are points also to consider. The Psalm is ascribed to David, yet it seems to come from a more ancient milieu; the versions have great difficulty with elements of the middle section (verses 8–9), some finding examples of premature birth where others refer only to the wind destroying the forest; and verse 1 finds opinion ranging across angelic powers, mighty ones, sons of God and gods, in addition to the NRSV's 'heavenly beings'. It is also quite unclear what the mode of worship is at the end of verse 2: the phrase occurs elsewhere in the Hebrew Bible, but not in significantly different contexts, so that we are left with a puzzle which is reflected in the variety of translations on offer.

Perhaps the most obvious deconstructive point to make is that most of the English versions actually obscure the strangeness of the Psalm. The use of 'God' in verse 3 is a case in point: in English it is a simple synonym for LORD, and as a result what we read appears to be a continuous coherent paean of praise to the one deity. It does not move or develop – it occupies a single moment in time, and describes a single scene. Yet even in English *God* and LORD are different, and *heavenly beings* are mysterious, and constitute grounds to suspect that the coherence of the Psalm is not the last word. The assumption that everyone and everything is on the same side is revealed to be a modern western spectator's perspective, born out of the cultural and philosophical urge to find unity in everything. On the contrary, *god* indicates 'them' as well as 'us', and supernatural beings constitute a threat to order at least as often as they afford comfort (both in the religious language of the pre-Renaissance world and in the superstitious discourse of the modern). Conflict, therefore, is an important key to understanding this poem – conflict between the panaceas of conventional religion and the aggressive demands of zeal; conflict also between the longing for order and the unruly reality of the cosmos; and conflict between those in power and those who long for power.

The history of this poem embodies successive struggles: between El and Baal; between Yahweh and the gods of Canaan; between the LORD, symbol of order, and the unruly forces of nature, symbols of chaos; between storm and *shalom*, violence and peace; and, finally, between the anodyne nostrums of conventional religion and the often stormy search for real understanding. Perhaps the attribution to David, that complex, paradoxical character, is fitting – a man whose equal passion for love and war, for poetry and the rhetoric of deceit, in some ways mirrors the ambiguities of the Psalm itself. We do not know whether to admire David or despise him; and the deconstructed poem contains both the praise of those who are Yahweh's enemies (the divine beings, God) and the chaotic resistance of the wild woods which Yahweh created, ending with the adoration of those who stand in the temple. But what are we to make of the promise of peace from such a god of violence? And if the poem is indicative of David's character, should Uriah the Hittite hope for a generous pension from his grateful king, in return for services rendered?

The theme of conflict between Yahweh and the old gods is found in another place in the Hebrew Bible – in 1 Kings 18 where, after Elijah has defeated the prophets of Baal in a contest of fire (compare verse 7 of the Psalm), we read (1 Kings 18:39–40):

> When all the people saw it, they fell on their faces and said, 'The LORD indeed is God; the LORD indeed is God.' Elijah

said to them, 'Seize the prophets of Baal; do not let one of them escape.' Then they seized them; and Elijah brought them down to the Wadi Kishon, and killed them there.

There is something rather sinister about this passage, which appears to condone murder in the name of Yahweh.[8] Those in the temple (those who are on Elijah's side) say 'Glory' ('The LORD indeed is God') and they find *shalom* – and we must remember that in Hebrew *shalom* is the word for success in battle as well as a general term for peace and prosperity.

There is an ironic character to the Psalm's conclusion, since it suggests that peace is unavoidably bound up with conflict. We cannot achieve the former without enduring the latter. We cannot learn to worship the (true?) God without first fighting the demons, and exorcising them (the symbolic meaning, maybe, of Elijah's outwardly brutal killings). But it is an inevitable consequence of the preservation and continuing use of Psalm 29 that the old gods, far from being silenced, live on in the text to continue endlessly the challenge and the struggle (just as the attractions of Canaanite religion remained powerful throughout the Monarchic Period in both Israel and Judah). Thus that which was displaced returns to supplement our understanding of the divine, the ghosts we exorcised through the cool logic of power stand silently (but not ineffectually) at our elbow even as we cry, together with those in the temple, 'Glory to Yahweh!'

The process of deconstruction is evident within the Psalms themselves. The curious phrase at the end of verse 2 ('Worship the LORD in holy splendour') is found in two other places: Psalm 96:7–9 and its repetition in 1 Chronicles 16:28–9 (where Psalm 96 is quoted). While the language and structure is remarkably similar to that of Psalm 29:1 –

Ascribe to the LORD, O families of the peoples,
  ascribe to the LORD glory and strength.
Ascribe to the LORD the glory due his name;
  bring an offering and come into his courts.
Worship the LORD in holy splendour;
  tremble before him, all the earth –

there is a most significant change. Where Psalm 29 has 'heavenly beings' Psalm 96 substitutes 'families of the peoples' and thus dissolves the crucial tension of the older Psalm and domesticates it

– curiously, in rather the same way as the English versions: by removing the differences between the parties. Psalm 96 goes further, for it has already (in verse 5) written off 'the gods of the peoples' as idols. In many ways, Psalm 96 is what Psalm 29 became when it was thoroughly rewritten in the mode of Deuteronomistic theology. We are forever condemned both to rewrite the texts of the past in terms of our own conventions and beliefs, and at the same time to be confronted by the ghosts we have thus tried, but failed, to lay to rest. Perhaps the most urgent substitution for our own day is that consequent upon atheism, the death not just of the old gods but of 'God'. The Psalm becomes then a kind of *danse macabre* at which through the lens of time we gaze. All that remains to us is the elemental struggle between wind and storm, water and fire on the one hand, and the life forms to which the planet has given birth on the other. We have returned to the loneliness of our distant ancestors, who looked with a mixture of fear and wonder at an incomprehensible world governed by ineluctable forces. Though not quite – for the powerful knowledge which modern humanity commands (as a result of eating that tempting fruit!) means that when it all goes wrong now, we have no one to blame but ourselves.

Personal afterword (aspect 7)

I warm very much to the sense of the deep well of the past which this Psalm conjures for me. The drama of the elements may be enormously dangerous to human life, but it is tremendously exciting as well. Many years ago, when I worked for a while in Pakistan, I used to drive from the Punjab to the Murree Hills at the weekend, and I still remember vividly one journey through an almighty thunderstorm which hurled water down upon the hills and raged around me as I drove in my tiny car (it was a Morris Minor). Strangely exhilarated, I rolled the windows down and rejoiced in the cool rain and the display of natural violence. Only later, when (no thanks either to my driving skills or to my commonsense) I had reached my destination, did I discover that fears had been expressed for my safety. Yet to this day I relish that memory: there is something in us that longs to be part of the elemental struggle, and regardless of any theological import or liturgical structure, Psalm 29 is for me that siren call to danger – not, I hasten to add, danger to any purpose; simply risk for its own sake.

Of course, much older now, and sadly much wiser, I would probably stay at home these days, and enjoy nature from the safe distance between my couch and the television set. If this ancient verse can provoke me out of that false peace into something more energetic, its metaphors will have done their work.

These remarks are couched in non-theological terms; but they are themselves, of course, metaphorical, and may be read (if the reader, or the writer, so desires) as a religious trope.

Part II

APPLICATION
Select psalms

7

PSALM 2[1]

The text

In order to clarify the discussion at various points, I have provided in Parts II and III the NRSV text of each psalm under discussion, together with any suggested amendments, and notes about its structure. Amendments are given in the body of the text in square brackets. Where they represent *additions* to the NRSV the extra text is given without other comment – as in Psalm 2:12 where '[rejoice]' is an addition to the text. Where they are *alternatives* the new text is introduced by means of *or* – as in Psalm 2:1 where '[or bluster]' represents an alternative to the NRSV's 'conspire'.

In keeping with my general principle of allowing the chosen English version to 'speak for itself' I confine myself to the minimum of comments by way of supplementary elucidation of the NRSV text; there are, however, several places where this is either helpful or necessary in Psalm 2. In verse 1 the words translated as 'conspire' and 'plot' could also be taken to mean, respectively, 'make a blustering noise' and 'mutter to oneself'. The second of these is also found in Psalm 1:2, where it has the sense of 'to meditate'. Given the evident futility of the action described in verse 1, these alternative translations have particular point in emphasising one of the central motifs of the Psalm: the unbridgeable gulf between the mutinous kings and the *anointed* king.

When the Hebrew text speaks in verse 4 of God 'sitting in the heavens', the stronger sense of 'enthroned in the heavens' is implied, and would not be an erroneous translation. However, the verb does literally mean 'to sit'; it is only its regular association with the figure of the enthroned deity which suggests the more particular interpretation.

PSALM 2

VERSE		TEXTUAL NOTES AND STRUCTURE

Introduction

1 Why do the nations conspire [or bluster],
   and the peoples plot [or grumble] in vain?

The theme: the fate of those who rebel

Part i

2 The kings of the earth set themselves,
   and the rulers take counsel together,
   against the LORD and *his anointed*,
   saying,

3 "Let us burst their bonds asunder,
   and cast their cords from us."

A Structurally, 2a,b form a parallel repeated as a chiasmus in verse 10

B Rebels assert their claim to independence

Part ii

4 He who sits [or is enthroned] in the heavens
   laughs;
   the LORD has them in derision.

P-3 YHWH's mockery

5 Then he will speak to them in his wrath,
   and terrify them in his fury, saying,

P-2 YHWH's wrath

6 "I have set *my king* on Zion, my holy hill."

P-1 Content of the decree

Pivot

7 I will tell of the decree of the LORD:

P

Part iii

He said to me, "You are *my son*;
   today I have begotten you.

P+1 Content of the decree

8 Ask of me, and I will make the nations your
   heritage,
and the ends of the earth your possession.

P+2 Messiah's rule

9 You shall break them with a rod of iron,
   and dash them in pieces like a potter's
   vessel."

P+3 Messiah's vengeance

Part iv

10 Now therefore, O kings, be wise;
   be warned, O rulers of the earth.

A1 See verse 2a,b

11 Serve the LORD with fear,

12a   [rejoice] with trembling* kiss his feet
   [or kiss the son],

B1 Rebels are compelled to submit in humility

12b or he will be angry, and you will perish in
   the way;
   for his wrath is quickly kindled.

* Verse 12 begins with the word 'kiss'

Conclusion

12c Happy are all who take refuge in him.

Outcome: blessing of those who trust

A different category of explanation is required at two points in verses 11–12, where there are explicit problems with the text (a fact registered in the NRSV footnote). In verse 11b, while the Hebrew actually reads 'rejoice with trembling', most translations omit the word 'rejoice', though without any clear explanation for so doing. In verse 12a the phrase translated 'kiss his feet' is in Hebrew 'kiss the son', where (unusually) the Aramaic word for 'son' is used. This is admittedly odd, since the normal Hebrew word for 'son' appears in verse 7 (but see my detailed discussion of this point in Chapter 5, pages 64f.). 'Kiss his feet' is essentially a guess, based on the kind of ritual of subservience that the rulers of vassal states might be expected to undergo at the court of the great king. It is worthy of note that the KJV renders the Hebrew faithfully in both cases.

Comparative material from the ancient Near East

Given the fragile nature of power in the ancient world, dependent as it was on the ability of a powerful ruler to demonstrate power regularly and visibly, and on the effectiveness or otherwise of lines of communication, it is not surprising that when the ruler of an extensive and extended empire like that of Assyria died there was often a long interregnum before a successor emerged. During these times of internecine struggle for the throne, satellite states often seized their chance to claim independence and to forge local alliances – one such (between Israel and Damascus) lies behind the exchange in Isaiah 7 between the prophet and king Ahaz, and the force of Isaiah's warning to the warring rivals is that, sooner rather than later, the Assyrians will reassert their military power and crush those who so foolishly rebelled.

Such coronation texts as have survived from the wider ancient Near East are related only loosely to Psalm 2 and the biblical ceremonies. The hymn to Aten (*NERTOT*: 19) speaks of 'Your son who came forth from your body' (i.e. the king who was born of the god), and may be paralleled with the affirmation in verse 7. There are some relevant details in a Sumerian hymn to the king (*NERTOT*: 107), which records that the god

> has exalted you as shepherd over the land of Sumer,
> [and] has put your enemies under your feet

and goes on to describe the king's reign:

Under your rule men will increase and extend,
hostile lands will rest in peace,
men will enjoy days of abundance.

The language of verse 8 may be in imitation of the declaration of
world sovereignty associated with Egyptian and Mesopotamian
kings. Thus the Pharaoh is 'king of the two countries', the extent of
whose rule is dramatically presented in one Egyptian text (quoted
from Frankfort 1948: 109):

Let him grasp the Heavens
And receive the Horizons;
Let him dominate the Nine Bows
and equip (with offerings) the Ennead.
Give the Crook into his hand
so that the head of Lower and Upper Egypt shall be bowed.

Babylonian and Assyrian kings use with divine sanction the
titles 'King of the Universe' and 'King of the Four Quarters of the
World'; in a similar fashion the psalmists use language betraying a
Babylonian standpoint when, for example, they exclaim (Psalm 72:8)
'May he have dominion from sea to sea, and from the River to the
ends of the earth' or (Psalm 89:25) 'I will set his hand on the sea and
his right hand on the rivers.'

History, liturgy, social context

The most obvious historical and cultural context for this Psalm is
that of the coronation of a king, a feature it shares with, for example,
Psalms 72, 101 and 110. Certain details might well reflect elements
of a coronation ceremony – the proclamation of the decree in verses
6–7 is one obvious candidate, and some have suggested that the
metaphor of the king using his iron sceptre to smash his enemies like
a clay pot (verse 9) might have been literally enacted during the
coronation liturgy. The naming of the king as 'messiah' (literally 'the
anointed') in verse 2 further suggests a ceremonial action.[2]

We cannot, of course, associate this Psalm with a named king or
an explicit date; and (as the subsequent discussion will show) it may
be a form of pastiche, developed to express a certain hope regarding
the ideal king of messianic traditions. There is some evidence
in other parts of the Old Testament for the ceremonial appropriate
to coronation: thus 1 Kings 1:34, 39 describes the anointing of

Solomon by Zadok the priest and Nathan the prophet, and 2 Kings 11:12 records a similar ceremony for Joash. Both accounts make reference to scenes of great rejoicing (1 Kings 1:40; 2 Kings 11:14) – another reason, perhaps, for retaining that word in verse 11 of the Psalm – and both take place in the sanctuary (compare the reference to 'Zion, my holy hill' in verse 6). Interestingly, at one stage in the coronation of Joash he is presented with a 'testimony' or 'decree', which might correspond to the similar reference in Psalm 2:7.

The declaration 'You are my son; today I have begotten you' in verse 7 has prompted much speculation. There is one clear example of this style of address in the historical books, in Nathan's oracle in 2 Samuel 7:14, repeated in 1 Chronicles 17:13 – 'I will be his father and he shall be my son'.[3] Again, Psalm 89:26f. puts the following address to God on David's lips:

> You are my Father,
>   my God and the Rock of my salvation.

God is made to comment immediately after:

> I will make him the firstborn,
>   the highest of the kings of the earth.

Do such expressions imply a Hebrew concept of divine kingship? It is hard to be sure; but while formal characterisations of the king as divine, or as a representative of the gods, are found in Egypt and to some extent in Mesopotamia, there is some doubt as to their presence in Syria or Canaan, and the lack of this element in the two coronations which have been recorded suggests that the declaration in Psalm 2 should not be made to carry the burden of proof of the existence of divine kingship in either Israel or Judah.

Structure

There are a number of striking structural features in Psalm 2 (a summary is provided alongside the text on p. 104). Whether intended or not, they offer quite significant possibilities for analysis, and I develop these in the next section. The immediate task is to identify them and describe their nature.

The final part of verse 12 clearly forms a doxology, which can be related to Psalm 2 (in which case the question of an appropriate 'introit' needs to be addressed) and to Psalm 1 (which begins 'Happy are those who do not follow the advice of the wicked' – a negative formula which is structurally similar to verse 12c, and which delivers a similar semantic message). There is no need to pose these as exclusive alternatives, particularly in view of the proposal which has often been put that Psalms 1 and 2 together form a general introduction to the Psalter as a whole, or to some part of it. Indeed, there is a pattern of inclusions which works both internally to either Psalm and across the two as a unit (Table 7.1) and which allows us to examine this structural aspect as it relates to Psalm 2 alone. Thus the 'blessedness' statements at the beginning of Psalm 1 and the end of Psalm 2 on the one hand, and the bridging references to the wicked in 1:6 and 2:1 on the other, span the pair conceived as a unit; while the contrasts between the two states form a distinct inclusion in each Psalm.

These are not, however, mindless patterns, for the inclusion in Psalm 2 has been split to provide, on the one hand, an element of tension and, on the other, a further structural device. The closing phrase is of the form subject–verb–object ('all who–take refuge in –him'), but verse 1 does not provide any object of the nations' conspiracy. However, the seemingly awkward third stich of verse 2 completes the sentiment: 'against the LORD and his anointed'. The combined power of this pairing (for a Jewish reader), and its delayed appearance, serves to emphasise what has already been made plain – the vanity of rebellion. The presumed parallel with verse 12c introduces a further interesting idea; for it is by no means obvious

Table 7.1 Bridges and contrasts between Psalms 1 and 2

Verse	'Happy' parallels – linking the Psalms	The way of the wicked – bridging the Psalms	
1.1ab	Happy are those who do not follow the advice of the wicked		*Contrast between the happy and the wicked*
1.6b		the way of the wicked will perish	
2.1		Why do the nations conspire, and the peoples plot in vain?	*Contrast between the vain hopes of the wicked and*
2.12c	Happy are all who take refuge in him.		*the trust shown by the happy*

who is intended by the 'him' at the end of the Psalm. Could it be that the ambiguity is precisely that we are being prompted to a closer identification of Yahweh and Messiah? I will return to this point.

A second structural device of interest depends upon the alternative reading, in which the Aramaic word 'son' is taken to be the correct interpretation in verse 12a. The key words are indicated in italic type in the text of the Psalm; what we have is a set of four distinct ways of referring to the monarch, one in each of the four parts of the Psalm (his anointed, my king, my son [Hebrew], the son [Aramaic]). These are rather strategically placed, two being immediately on either side of the pivotal statement in verse 6b, and the other two, respectively, in the first verse of *part i* and the last verse of *part iv*. Taken with the ambiguous 'him' already noted in the conclusion, this surely constitutes an interesting formal device.

The third major feature relates to the Psalm as a whole. It is clear that verse 7a acts as a pivot for the Psalm as a whole, prompting the expectation (in conjunction with the opening and closing statements) of an overall palinstrophic character to be elucidated. The fact that verse 6 and verse 7b give alternative expression to the *content* of the decree – the former a public announcement, the latter a personal promise – strengthens this structural dimension. The column to the right of the text of Psalm 2 spells this out in more detail, though the relationship between verse 2a,b and verse 10 merits a little clarification. Even in English translation the parallel between these two verses is plain, and the underlying Hebrew has a remarkably strongly developed pattern which operates at both the formal and the semantic level, creating a dramatic chiasmus. While this is modified in the NRSV, the links between these verses remain evident (see Table 7.2). These verses change structurally in a way that echoes the change of mood from *part i* to *part iv*.

Just as the rebellious kings, arrogant in their pretensions, are reduced to abject, trembling fear (verse 11), so the paralleled verbs of conspiracy in verse 2 are replaced by the chiastically arranged verbs

Table 7.2 Links between verses 2 and 10 of Psalm 2

Verse 2a,b		Verse 10	
d,f	The kings of the earth	d1	Now therefore, O kings
e	set themselves	E1	be wise
D	and the rulers	e1	be warned
E	take counsel together	D1,f	O rulers of the earth

of warning in verse 10. One particularly nice touch is to move the descriptive phrase 'of the earth' from its place at the start of verse 2 (where it suggests a certain grandeur and power) to the end of verse 10, where it becomes sharply ironic. What kind of 'rulers of the earth' are these, who are about to 'Serve the LORD with fear, and rejoice with trembling'?

Contextual interpretations

The wealth of information gathered under the first four aspects enables us to develop a wide range of interpretations without departing significantly from the (presumed) context or contexts of the Psalm's early life. The density of structure further encourages us to believe that careful composition and deliberate poetic device have informed what we now read. And the suggestion of a closer link with Psalm 1 as part of an introduction to the wider Psalter makes it possible that, in the absence of any specific historical *Sitz-im-Leben*, we would do well not to focus on 'coronation ceremony' as the primary mode of interpretation.

The first and most obvious point to make is that the design of Psalm 2 indicates in many ways a messianic reading. It centres on the decree of Yahweh which quite obviously authenticates a king of extraordinary qualities; it matches the actions of Yahweh in *part ii* with those of the king in *part iii*; the rebellion is against Yahweh and his anointed (literally, his *messiah*); and the profound ambiguity of the conclusion in verse 12, in which every personal pronoun could be applied either to Yahweh or to the king, almost demands that we understand this king to be of unnatural quality. This reading is important both in terms of known Jewish messianic speculation and in terms of the Psalter as a complete collection. There was undoubtedly a growing interest in the figure of the ideal king from late post-exilic times onwards – even within the Hebrew Bible elements of 1 and 2 Chronicles, the romanticised oracles of Davidic paradises in several of the Prophets, and the failed movement to enthrone Zerubbabel all point in this direction. Thus, taking Psalm 2 in its context – I am referring here not to any putative but unascertainable pre-exilic use but to its redactional function – there is good reason to set it, as we now have it, within this same period of messianic speculation. It is, in short, a messianic Psalm; and from this another interesting consequence flows: namely, that at least some circles in Jerusalem regarded the figure of the king in the Psalter as essentially a messianic one, not a literal description of the long-vanished

Davidic dynasty. Whether hopes were raised of this ideal becoming a reality we cannot now say, beyond noting the evidence for a number of messianic pretenders in the first two centuries of Roman rule over Palestine.

The messiah indicated by Psalm 2 is clearly a powerful military figure, merciless towards his enemies, but a source of succour to his friends. Vengeful and despotic, he is as careless of his defeated victims as a potter is of damaged vessels: they are fit only for scrap. All this is an all-too-familiar example of the rhetoric of the underdog, which, were it to be realised, would achieve nothing more than the exchange of roles between oppressor and oppressed. It is an uncomfortable thesis to find at the beginning of a collection which, for many readers, is a source of consolation and comfort; but we do the psalmist and the Psalm no favours by masking its motifs in the saccharine language of an alien Christian messianism. There is no suffering messiah here, no gentle victim blessing his enemies and praying for his persecutors. What there *is*, surprisingly, is the hint of a divine connection for the messiah: 'You are my son'. I do not believe that this has any literal force; but it does imply (as I have already argued) a very close connection – almost surrogacy – between God and this idealised king which prepares the ground for the sort of reception received by some, at least, of the 'messiahs' we know of: Jesus, Bar Kochba and Shabbati Zvi,[4] to name but three.

A second observation arises from the style of the psalmist's language, which is at several points ironic or sardonic in tone. We cannot hope to ascertain at this distance whether the grandiose claims made for the messiah-figure in Psalm 2 are serious in intent; but it does seem clear that those of the rebellious 'kings of the earth' are the subject of mockery. I have already pointed out how the structure of the Psalm reinforces the vanity of the rebellion which sets the scene in verses 1–2. This is further endorsed by the pairing of 'why' at the beginning with 'in vain' at the end of verse 1. 'Why' has often, in the context of psalms of lament, a rhetorical meaning, and this is reinforced by the final 'in vain' which undermines the conspiracy almost before it is properly under way.

This ironic knowledge of failure to which the reader is party is strengthened by a series of figures within the Psalm. In verse 4 the laughter of God is at once sinister and demeaning: the enemies of the LORD merit mere mockery; but the mocking laughter of the deity is in some ways more awesome than God's wrath. It has some associations with Greek conceptions of the gods who, using people as playthings, first drive to madness (*até*) those whom they intend to destroy, but is rather rare in Hebrew. There is an echo in Proverbs 1:26 where Wisdom in the persona of a prophetess warns those who have rejected her:

> I also will laugh at your calamity;
> I will mock when panic strikes you.

The only other instances in the Hebrew Bible of God's mocking laughter are in Psalm 37:12f. ('The wicked plot against the righteous, / and gnash their teeth at them; / but the LORD laughs at the wicked; / for he sees that their day is coming') and Psalm 59:8 ('But you laugh at them, O LORD; / you hold all the nations in derision.'). But there is an interesting passage in Habakkuk 1:5–11 where the Chaldeans are described as an irresistible force sweeping through the land, destroying all opposition while (verse 10)

> At kings they scoff,
> and of rulers they make sport.
> They laugh at every fortress,
> and heap up earth to take it.

Reminiscent of other prophetic passages in which Mesopotamian empires are seen as the tool of God to purify Israel, the use of the theme of mocking laughter here inevitably reminds us of the portrait of God in Psalm 2 – and of the ultimate power which is believed to reside in God's hands. Even Assyrians and Babylonians, for all their impressive might, are at the end of the day only ciphers for the irresistible power of God.

We should associate with the mocking laughter of verse 4 the equally sinister demand to 'rejoice with trembling' in verse 11. While most translators and commentators (Delitzsch 1887 is an honourable exception) prefer to elide the apparently awkward 'rejoice', it provides a nice counterpoint to verse 4, conjuring the all-too-accurate picture of the terrified and trembling prince seeking both to flatter the great king and to conceal his abject fear. To display fear is to insult the tyrant – to appear calm and unconcerned is to tempt arbitrary fate. Hence the knife-edged requirement to balance pleasure (however simulated) with terror, so aptly caught in the phrase 'rejoice with trembling'.

More conventionally, the aspirations of the rebels are countered by their being absorbed into the empire of the messiah (verse 8), their power smashed (verse 9), and they themselves forced into a choice between abject humiliation (verse 11) or annihilation (verse 12). That these punishments are to be imposed (in a wholly inappropriate analogy with Assyria or Babylon) by the petty ruler of a small Judaean city is itself either a further irony – the power of the weak over the mighty, which might have a quasi-historical locus in the period of the Maccabees[5] – or a theological reminder that *all* human power is in the end subject to the desires of the Almighty.

We cannot help wondering, finally, whether (and to what extent) the kind of hopes and claims this Psalm gives voice to matched any reality in the world of post-exilic Jerusalem and Judah. The existence of a wide range of apocalyptic and eschatological material from the period, and the fact of three major wars of independence (the Maccabean Wars, the First Roman Revolt in 73 CE, and the Bar Kochba Revolt of 134) is at least some evidence of the existence of certain groups predisposed to precisely the kind of military adventure indicated in Psalm 2. Some of the sectarianism familiar from Josephus and the New Testament (Zealots, Essenes, Pharisaic opposition to Herod, Sicarii, possible messianic pretenders such as Judas the Galilean and Theudas, Simon from the household of Herod, Athronges, and Jesus son of Ananus[6]) further supports this reading. But at the same time there is a strong tradition of suspicion of messianism in Judaism, which may well have its roots in a rather more pragmatic view of the dangers of taking such idealism seriously. The probability that Psalm 2 should be linked with Psalm 1 as a preface to the Psalter, with the consequence that meditation upon and observance of the Torah is at least equally as important as is the messianic theme, encourages this latter interpretation.

Deconstructive readings

It is of the essence of deconstruction that no formal process can be specified, nor can any logically testable outcome be predicted. Nevertheless it is not arbitrary, nor is it merely destructive (the *con* is important!), as I have tried to point out in Chapter 6. Accordingly I will use (with extreme reservations) a rough paradigm as I seek to deconstruct the psalms under discussion in this part of the study. The rhetorical term *aporia* (literally, 'puzzle' or 'problem') will be used to head a list of selected questions which are not directly answered in the text (see Table 7.3); associated with that will be another selection – of absences which could provide significant meaning in the extended discussion (though not everything listed under these headings will necessarily be taken up in the immediate

Table 7.3 *Aporia*s and absence in Psalm 2

Aporia	Absence
Who are the nations whose conspiracy is described?	David
What kind of god stoops to mockery?	Jerusalem
Who is the king?	The words of the decree
Where is Zion?	'Rejoice'
Is the son of a god also a god?	The 'feet' that are kissed
'Rejoice with trembling'?	
'Kiss the son'?	

dialogue – the reader is seriously invited to continue what is, after all, incomplete in principle). This discussion will take place under the paired heading *différance* and *supplément*, which words provide probably the closest we might wish to approach to anything like a technical term for the process of deconstruction.

Différance and supplément

Any coherent reading of Psalm 2 must take account of the cluster of uncertainties and ambiguities surrounding the person of the 'king' and the location of 'Zion'. It requires only a moment's reflection to enter preliminary lists of obviously associated terms. I suggest, for example: 'tyrant – dictator – messiah – Christ – Christian' for the former, and 'Zion – Jerusalem – Israel – Palestine – Zionism – Hamas' for the latter. There is material enough in these two progressions to support a book or two: I shall confine myself to a few suggestions.

There is a profound and disturbing irony in the deferral of the meaning of *messiah* which creates the space for the difference between what a Jew and a Christian might understand when that term is used. For it is in that *différance* that the shift from Jewish sect within pagan Rome to the affirmation of secular power which is Christendom takes place, and with it the forging of an alliance of nations whose hatred for the Jews (in the name of the Christ–Messiah) culminated in the Holocaust. (The failure of the Psalm to name David is pertinent at this juncture, creating as it does an absence which will rapidly be filled with the names of pretenders.) Thus did the king in Zion, whose alliance with Yahweh enabled him to conquer and humiliate the strongest of enemies, become the Jesus who epitomised European anti-Semitism and its murderous allies in the Third Reich. We might say, I suppose, that 'all who take the sword will perish by the sword',[7] were it not for the further dark irony that these words are also attributed to Jesus. The Psalm, which both loudly proclaims the military supremacy of a certain kind of Jewish messianism and constitutes a classic Christian source for the divinity Jesus as Son of God,[8] thus creates by its unspoken associations a text which might have been in the mind of Yeats when he wrote, in *The Second Coming*, of that 'rough beast, its hour come round at last', slouching 'toward Bethlehem to be born'.

With these thoughts in mind, God's laughing mockery takes on a tragic hue: dare we suppose, then, that the answer to the question 'Where was God?' during those dark hours of Jewish history is to be found in Psalm 2:4? It is fine to run with the notion of divine scorn when it is your god whose scorn is withering others; it is quite another when we ourselves (whoever 'we' are) express that nervous or hysterical laughter which accompanies the experience of uncertainty as to whether the joke is against us. Could the reluctance on the part of translators and commentators to come to terms with 'rejoice' in verse 11 be a psychological symptom, an unconscious recognition of the fact that the gods, resentful of our mass apostasy from proper respect/fear/awe, have begun to drive us mad in preparation for our destruction? These, of course, serve also as metaphors: the death of 'god' is the coming to birth of absence, the deification of humankind, the insidious spread of the crazy belief that we – who are *of* creation – are *over and above* it. We are all messiahs now, making 'the ends of the earth [our] possession', breaking and smashing with the iron rod which represents our power; rather like small and ill-disciplined children with a large hammer and no adult supervision.

Looking at the world even in its articulation as the sphere of religious activity, the aptness of the latter metaphor is depressingly plain. Those who kiss the wrong feet (of idols, false gods and demagogues) or who call the son 'god' without knowing the parents are prone to cover their mistakes by dubbing them 'truth' and demanding (often at gunpoint) general allegiance to their cause. 'We know', they tell us, 'what is written in the decree. It is a secret, revealed to us, which tells us that the whole world must be made to agree with us.' It does not matter how the 'holy hill' is defined – be it the Zion of Zionism and a reborn Israel,[9] or the Holy City (Al Quds) of Muslim tradition, or the political Jerusalem, capital of the Palestinian State imagined in the rhetoric of Hamas, or the visionary

New Jerusalem of Christian apocalyptic. The problem is that of the Psalm itself: the exclusivity of the claims made ensures, with utter inevitability, that conflict will continue. There will always be rebellious 'kings' to challenge the status quo, just as there will always be a status quo to be defended. Perhaps, some day, the futility which this deconstructed Psalm so poignantly reveals will persuade its readers of the central absence: that there is nothing in the decree which justifies any of our claims, and that everything about it supports all our hopes. Possibly then the hope offered at the end – 'Happy are all who take refuge in him' – will be realised; though even this is open, since we do not know who is intended by 'him', nor even that it is a person. The Hebrew, after all, could indicate a thing – 'Happy are all who take refuge in it'; that is, the silence which reminds us of the equal vanity of all religious claims.

Personal afterword

While the Psalms are (in a formal sense) poetry, they belong also to the liturgy of Israel's worship after the exile, and this imposes certain limitations to their free expression of the poetic muse. We are dealing, perhaps, with Polyhymnia rather than Euterpe.[10] Thus we may expect to find both the familiar features of religious verse (repetitions, refrains, congregational responses and stock phrases) and a degree of stereotyping in the way that standard subjects are approached. If, further, the subject matter itself seems alienated from our regular discourse, the problems of reading become at a personal level rather daunting. This is, of course, not different in principle from the task of appropriating to our own use the literature of England or Scotland of past centuries. Translation is needed (if only at the level of a glossary of unfamiliar terms), subject matter may strike us as quaint, and structural devices often appear forced and overly formal. End-rhymes and strict metre impose on the modern ear a somewhat repetitive triteness; the ubiquity of alliteration in Anglo-Saxon verse may strike us (despite the best efforts of Gerard Manley Hopkins to reintroduce to English poetry its use of alliteration and 'sprung rhythm') as contrived and devoid of natural interest. Only by an effort of imagination and an act of will can we absorb something of what these texts once meant.

Notwithstanding the deconstructive readings of the preceding section, the 'natural' sense of Psalm 2 as a composition dealing with the affairs of kings takes it far from modern perceptions of what is important. We do not, in the age of the tabloid, take kings and

116

queens, princes and princesses, with the kind of seriousness implied in the Psalm. This in turn identifies a problem with the widespread assumption of the biblical world that the figure 'God is king' or 'Yahweh rules' has meaning. I suspect that the deadness of this metaphor, combined with the Psalm's concern to demonstrate the merit of its perspective in terms of military prowess, must leave most of us worse than cold. Surely we can take it that such language is no longer appropriate to the task of communicating either what 'god' means or what God's followers ought to be about.

I can suggest three tentative paths out of this impasse. One is aesthetic – to take pleasure in the elaborate and subtle structures of the Psalm, and the way that these structures are interwoven with the semantics of the text. Something of this has been attempted under the heading 'Structure' earlier in the chapter. A second is deconstructive – to refuse the overt 'meaning' of the text and engage with it dialogically. As we have seen, this produces intriguing, if negative, readings together with a sense of the openness of the material to further exploration. And the third is individual – to do what readers of the Psalms have done for generations, and to seek to take them as a direct address to the soul, spirit, mind, or will of the reader. The scholarly proposal that Psalms 1 and 2 together form an introduction to a work designed (at least in part) for personal meditation grants to this path a certain intellectual status which may, for those who may be suspicious of the introduction into a scholarly work of such solipsistic subjectivity, justify its inclusion. My arguments for a 'broad church' in the realm of interpretation make such pseudo-academic support unnecessary.

What, in conclusion, might such an individual reading deliver? In principle, and by definition, I cannot answer that question. However, for this individual it might make sense to ask, for instance, 'Am I the problem, or part of the answer? Am I offered sonship, or servitude? Is the conflict to be internalised, so that wisdom lies in coming to terms with – taking refuge in – myself the son? Of whom, other than my own folly, should I be afraid?'

8

PSALM 8

VERSE	TEXTUAL NOTES AND STRUCTURE
1 O LORD, our Sovereign, [*or* O Yahweh our LORD] how majestic is your name in all the earth!	A Refrain
You have set your glory [*or* whose glory is recounted] above the heavens.	B God's glory
2 Out of the mouths of babes and infants [*or* heavenly beings]	C God's power acknowledged
you have founded a bulwark because of your foes, to silence the enemy and the avenger.	
3 When I look at your heavens, the work of your fingers,	D God's handiwork in heaven
the moon and stars that you have established;	
4 What are human beings that you are mindful of them,	E What is humankind?
mortals that you care for them?	
5 Yet you have made them a little lower than God [*or* the gods],	D1 Humankind in relation to the heavenly council
and crowned them with glory and honour.	B1 Humanity's glory
6 You have given them dominion over the works of your hands;	C1 Human power acknowledged
you have put all things under their feet,	
7 All sheep and oxen, and also the beasts of the field,	
8 the birds of the air, and the fish of the sea, whatever passes along the paths of the seas.	
9 O LORD, our Sovereign [*or* O Yahweh our LORD], how majestic is your name in all the earth!	A Refrain

The text

The text of this popular Psalm contains two notorious problems and several minor issues most of which we do not need to concern ourselves with. One of the latter is indicated in my alternative reading for the first line of the refrain. This is intended to uncover the unusual juxtaposition in the Hebrew text of the proper name of God (Yahweh), which is conventionally read as if it were the word for 'LORD', with the actual word for Lord. Strictly speaking, it should be read as 'O LORD our LORD', which is the device adopted by most older versions (KJV, RSV) and some modern (NIV). The NRSV reading, which I believe to be substantially misleading, is shared with NEB and REB – a rare conjunction of opinion between versions which are characterised by their differences.

The two major difficulties are to be found in verse 2. One concerns the question whether the Hebrew forms a direct connection between verse 1 and verse 2 (as suggested in my alternative reading) or is a separate statement. The problem lies in an obscure verbal form which can be interpreted in different ways. The other concerns the identity and function of the 'babes and infants'. Are we to think of even the youngest praising God, or are these beings in some sense bound up with God's quarrel with the enemy? Some have proposed to see in this phrase a reference to supernatural beings, and I have included that notion in my amended version. No standard translation, however, and few commentators have endorsed it. I will take the matter up under the next heading.

Finally, the famous wording of verse 5 conceals a couple of debatable points, as the NRSV footnote makes clear. The usual word for God is found here, and though in the past it was sometimes rendered as 'angels' (thus removing a certain theological difficulty) the issue now lies between a singular and a plural word in English ('God' or 'the gods'). The other issue is whether 'a little lower' is to be understood as a reference to quality or time, since the Hebrew word can refer to both. Are human beings qualitatively close to but not identical with God, or are we temporarily of reduced status? Perhaps the ambiguity is deliberate.

Comparative material from the ancient Near East

For all that it has a somewhat exotic air, it is not easy to find parallels to this Psalm in the surrounding cultures. This arises partly from the anthropology of verse 5, which seems to be rather specific to Hebrew thought. Apart from the legend of Utnapishtim, the 'Sumerian

Noah' who achieved immortality, Mesopotamian literature is more likely to emphasise the difference between humankind and the gods. Both Egyptian and Mesopotamian myths preserve the tale, like that in Genesis, of the gods' determination to wipe out the human race. No doubt there are also traditions concerning the divine character of the king, but these can scarcely be compared with the belief expressed in this Psalm (echoing perhaps Genesis 1:27) that the entire human race is in some essential sense 'like' God. A passage from *The Teaching of Merikare* (*NERTOT*: 46) contains material which resonates with these ideas, but also appears to refer to the myth of the destruction of humankind (noted in italics in this excerpt):

> Well directed are men, the cattle of the god.
> He has made heaven and earth for their sake.
> He has driven away the water monster.
> He made the air for their nostrils to live.
> They are his images, who have come forth from his body.
> He arises in heaven for their sake,
> he has made plants for them,
> beasts, fish and plants to nourish them.
> *He has killed his adversary,*
> *diminished his own children,*
> *because they planned to rebel against him.*
> He creates the light for their sake
> and goes in the heaven to see them.

The curious connection between babes and infants and 'the enemy and the avenger' in verse 2 might bear some resemblance to the lines in italics; but it is remote in the extreme. Perhaps the most we can say is that Psalm 8, like Genesis 1–3, belongs to a pattern of creation myths from Egypt and Mesopotamia which cannot help but suggest connections. These may be little more than the accidents of a common cultural inheritance; indeed, attempts to make precise literary links between Psalm 8 and Genesis have failed to reach anything much firmer than just such an assertion of the shared *Umwelt*.[1]

The other speculation (it is little more than that) which might merit some comment is the putative interpretation of the babes and infants of verse 2 as 'heavenly beings', referred to in the textual comments as an alternative reading. It must be said that the reading is not very plausible, not least because every other occurrence of this pair of words in the Hebrew Bible[2] quite plainly refers to human

PSALM 8

children. There is one instance in the Ugaritic myth of *Shachar and Shalim and the Gracious Gods* (reproduced in Gibson 1977: 123ff.; the specific reference is to 23:23–4) in which one of the Hebrew terms seems to refer to 'the gracious gods . . . who *suck* the teats of the breasts of Athirat'. The lack of the other term, and the general obscurity of the passage, render this speculation unsustainable as an argument from shared mythic conventions. Nevertheless I retain a lingering suspicion that some kind of supernatural business is to be inferred from the language of verse 2, particularly in view of the account given of God's creation of the heavenly bodies in verse 3.

While rejecting the explanation of infants as divine beings, Dahood does draw other cosmic parallels. A parallel is drawn between 'heavens' and 'power' in Psalm 78:26 which may allow us to read 'bulwark' in verse 2 as a metaphor for 'heavens', thus giving a supernatural dimension to both the 'bulwark' and the various enemies (Dahood 1965:50; 1968: 242). We might further note that there is a myth from Ugarit of Baal's defeat (silencing) of his enemies by the building of his house – a theme which may also be present in David's urge to build a temple for Yahweh.

History, liturgy, social context

There is little to be said under this heading in regard to Psalm 8. The date of the Psalm can only be guessed at, though those who see it as derivative from Genesis 1–2 perhaps would opt for a post-exilic context. The odd double naming of God (Yahweh–LORD) in verses 1 and 9 might have arisen from similar sensibilities as those which produced Yahweh–'*Elohim* in Genesis 2–3, that is, reflecting an early stage in the process of substituting for the spoken form *Yahweh*. That, however, does not really help, since there is no unambiguous evidence as to when that development might have occurred.

There is nothing of particular significance which might be described as relevant to any social context. The potentially interesting reference to small children is so obscure as to convey little beyond the observation that the psalmist uses the weakest and most vulnerable of the human race either to announce God's glory or as a symbol of the enemy's defeat. That they are conventionally the most vulnerable is clear from the other biblical instances of 'babes and infants' listed in note 2; and their presence here in the context of power and glory prepares us in a way for the unexpectedly exalted status of humankind as a whole to be announced in verse 5. Other than that, we may record the implied sense of a unity of creation, whether heavenly bodies or earthly creatures, all same work of the same God.

The likelihood of an expressly liturgical context for Psalm 8 seems rather high. The parallel account of creation in Genesis 1 is widely held to have a primarily cultic purpose, climaxing in the theology and celebration of the Sabbath as a principal goal of creation in the Jewish understanding. The refrain in the Psalm, and the central question around which it circles – 'What are human beings?' – sets up a reflective structure which suggests a use of the creation myth in an analogous, though not identical, fashion to its use in Genesis. For the point here is not the theological *raison d'être* of a festival but the daring affirmation of a truth about ourselves. That central question is found in other places, though not the same answer. Psalm 144:3 provides a perhaps more predictable account of human nature in comparison with God:

> O LORD, what are human beings that you regard them,
>   or mortals that you think of them?
> They are like a breath;
>   their days are like a passing shadow.

The image of human life as a fleeting thing, like grass which quickly withers or a breath soon past, is a common perspective in the Hebrew Bible;[3] we may speculate that such a rhetorical question as 'What is humankind?' figured in many religious pieces. The interesting feature of its appearance in Psalm 8 is that it is not rhetorical, or rather, that its rhetoric is undermined. There is one other instance of the question in which a 'surprise' answer is given, though of a quite different kind; namely, Job 7:16b–19:

> Let me alone, for my days are a breath.
> What are human beings, that you make so much of them?,
>   that you set your mind on them,
> visit them every morning,
>   test them every moment?
> Will you not look away from me for a while,
>   let me alone until I swallow my spittle?

This graphic passage should perhaps be recited along with Psalm 8, lest we run away with the idea that being close to God is an unalloyed blessing!

Structure

The balance of themes in this brief composition is controlled by the question which is placed at the centre of things. On either side of that key enquiry the poet has balanced motifs relating to God with similar motifs relating to humankind. Thus B and C, celebrating God's glory and power, find their partners in B1 and C1 where humankind's glory is described, and its power symbolised by the declaration of dominion over the living world. In the middle section, on either side of the central question, there are statements which pertain principally to the realms above – God's handiwork in shaping the heavenly bodies (D) and the surprising positioning of men and women (*adam* is a collective term in Hebrew) in near-equality to the 'gods' (D1), the divine beings whose dwelling is in the heavens. Formally this constitutes a variety of chiasmus, bracketed by means of a common refrain.

Terms which indicate honour, glory, majesty are confined to the lines A and B, while C and D deal in one way or another with power relationships tied into the drama and order of creation in its familiar Hebrew forms. This juxtaposing of themes is strikingly absent from the Genesis material which, while it clearly indicates the dominion over the creatures of the earth which God bestows upon humanity, nowhere suggests that this is a matter of pride, merit or honour for men and women. In Genesis it is strictly a function or duty; hence in Psalm 8 the combination of the motifs in A–B with those of C–D is particularly noteworthy.

The list of creatures in verses 7–8 seems rather random and possibly repetitive; but there is more logic to it than first appears. The point is that 7a and 8a describe creatures either domesticated or within the broadly domestic realm. Cattle and sheep are farmed; birds of the air and fish from the sea may be trapped or caught, and certainly do not pose any threat. The phrase 'the beasts of the field', in 7b and 8b, on the other hand, regularly refers to *wild* animals, and 'whatever passes along the paths of the sea' should probably be understood as the large, possibly mythological, creatures with which fisherman ought not to tangle. That humankind is given dominion over *all* of these is significant; see, by way of contrast, Yahweh's bombastic language in Job 38–41.

Contextual interpretations

Although this Psalm appears at first sight to be a straightforward declaration, its structure in fact reveals it to have the character of a drama. Beginning with a refrain which establishes the proper place of the worshipper before Yahweh, it progresses through a mysterious struggle against unspecified enemies (a possible echo of the old *chaoskampf*, the fight to the death between Yahweh and the destructive gods of chaos) to a celebration of God as creator. But then, right at the climax, when we might (by analogy with Genesis) have expected to find an account of the creation of man and woman, there is a question about the status of humanity, on the presumption that they have already been brought into being. This first break with the expected flow is immediately trumped in the form of a startling answer. We have already seen that the question may have been rhetorical in its normal context, expecting the traditional response: 'Humanity is but a fleeting breath, or grass which withers within a day.' However, here the reply is astonishing: human beings are, in effect, god-like, crowned with glory (the familiar term *kabod* which is pre-eminently associated with God) and honour (a less common expression, but again one which would be more usually used of God, and occasionally the king/messiah).

The effect is to establish the human race as a partner with God; not merely (as in Genesis) a vice-regent, placed in control of the rest of creation, but now a near-equal, with god-like qualities. This is a truly astonishing claim which, on any regular understanding of Jewish theology, comes perilously close to being blasphemous. Yet it seems to have been received in the various religious traditions with remarkable equanimity. Its stark character prompts the question: how was this, as part of an ancient liturgy, understood? What would the participants in the temple (if indeed Psalm 8 served as part of the worship of Israel) have made of it? Did it, as so much liturgy does, flow unheard over the heads of the congregation, as familiar words do? Or was another possible interpretation followed – one with an emphasis on the 'lower' of verse 5a setting up a contrast with 5b: despite being lower, humankind has none the less been honoured by God? The strong reading, which I myself hear as the more probable, leads us into a final dramatic moment. For the second occurrence of the refrain is not a mere repetition, but a restatement under new conditions. Those who speak are now revealed to be God's near companions. Where verse 1 has the air of being uttered from the vast distance which separates God from creation, verse 9 is intimate, spoken by those who have a right to stand in the presence of God.

Some of these issues return in the psalms which follow this one, with a possible climax in Psalm 24 (see Chapter 9). Both Psalm 15 and Psalm 24 enquire as to the identity of those who may stand in God's presence, while 14 expresses pessimism about the folly of humankind as a whole, with Israel and Jacob as possible exceptions. In short, what seems to take place is a systematic denial of the heresy of Psalm 8, as though someone recognised rather quickly that such a bold claim could not be sustained. What might have constituted a radically optimistic view of human nature is departed from, to be replaced by the more traditional theology of the special nature of Israel, chosen, redeemed and vindicated by Yahweh (Psalms 14:7, 24: 5–6).

There is an analogy to this interpretation in the broader sweep of the mythic first eleven chapters of Genesis,[4] where we find a similar highly optimistic introduction (the anthropology of 1:1–2:3) followed by a narrative of decline (2:4–3:24) and a sequence of myths embodying various problematics of the human condition *vis-à-vis* God. The outcome of this, of course, is the selection, in 12:1–3, of Abram to be the founder of the nation which God has chosen. Thus, if Psalm 8 is indeed a liturgy based on Genesis 1,[5] then the conflicts and failures and restorations described in the psalms which follow, climaxing in Psalm 24, might well be understood as a liturgical reinterpretation of the Genesis myths.[6] This is not the place to expand upon this, but I imagine that a detailed study would reveal interesting information with which to assess the value of this hypothesis.

I propose, in conclusion, that there are grounds for surmising a context in the liturgy of the temple for something not unlike the *Enuma Elish*, the Babylonian creation epic, in which both the power of the gods and the role of humankind (both positive and negative) were celebrated. It is well known that the Genesis materials match the Babylonian sequence in a number of ways, and I have suggested that (as a working hypothesis) Psalms 8–24 represent a poetic version of the same themes. In the light of this, one further comment is in order. Many exegetes believe that Genesis 1 is in part the result of a determined essay in demythologising. The details of the language of that opening creation account reveal many etymological links with both Mesopotamian and Egyptian creation myths,[7] most of which have been redefined by the biblical writer's determined use of a matter-of-fact epistemology. A similar process could perhaps explain the hints of cosmic drama which survive in Psalm 8, in particular verses 2–3 (supernatural beings and heavenly bodies) and verse 5 (the council of the gods, *'elohim*).

Deconstructive readings

This Psalm, structurally speaking, effects closure – an effect which any good postmodernist must immediately doubt. Whenever a text seems to have been sewn up, we need to ask why, by whom, for what reason. Spin doctors *avant la lettre* may have been at work, trying to prevent us from asking the wrong questions from or arriving at the wrong conclusions (wrong, that is, from the point of view of *some* authority). The authority in the Psalms may be God, or the king, or the priestly establishment, or some dominant faction within the community which had access to the means of literary production. There is no need to establish the identity of these people in a deconstructive reading, for what concerns us is the text through which they have tried to exercise control, but which will itself prove their undoing.

This text seems to conclude with an (unholy?) alliance between humankind and God, a sort of mutual back-scratching. The people lavish praise upon God, who in turn accords to them a highly honourable status coupled with real power. At the end of the day, (divine) monarch and assembled nobility exclaim (as well they might) how entirely satisfactory the whole system is, rather like the line in Psalm 29, 'all in his temple say, "Glory!"'. But elite groups are rarely democratic, typically excluding those who do not belong. The hermeneutic of suspicion teaches us that something is less than satisfactory about this happy arrangement, and that we should subject it to closer scrutiny.

There is one blatant *aporia* in the Psalm, one which is at the same time a glaring absence. What are the identities of 'the enemy and the avenger' in verse 2 – and where do they figure in verses 3–5? If they are supernatural, are they to be counted amongst the *'elohim* of verse 5 who, it should be remembered, regularly figure as 'false' and 'other' gods in the Hebrew Bible, and as Yahweh's rivals in, for instance, Psalm 29 (see Chapter 5) or Psalm 82 (see Chapter 11)? If that were the reading, verse 5 is not quite so bold. Human beings are like inferior demons, given some kind of special status by Yahweh to keep them sweet! If, on the other hand, 'the enemy and the avenger' is code for human adversaries (a common enough signification in the Psalter) then something highly dubious has been perpetrated in verse 5. It turns out that 'human beings' is not to be taken as the human race *in toto*, but as *those of the human race who are not in opposition* – a very different matter. The silent exclusion of a swathe of humanity turns this into a highly select coterie, an arrangement between Yahweh and 'those and such as those', from which we can infer a not unreasonable analogy with the British class structure and its system, its honours regularly doled out to 'the great and the good' (ironic quotes intended!). We may, mischievously, picture the participants in this Psalm as being not unlike a parade of belted earls and ermined peers on their stately way to the Opening of Parliament, embodying in their superficial finery both the corruption of power and the exclusivity of class.

There is another strange silence in most readings of this Psalm, and it consists in a silence about the nature and character of the God with whom we consort and to whom we are compared. This is the God, remember, who ordered the genocide of the Amalekites at the hands of the Israelites. Indeed, the use of the phrase 'babes and infants' in 1 Samuel 15:3 refers to Samuel's instructions to Saul, in the name of the LORD, to 'attack Amalek, and utterly destroy all that they have; do not spare them, but kill both man and woman, child and infant, ox and sheep, camel and donkey'. A savage irony, indeed, that the same 'babes and infants' who praise Yahweh to the heavens in Psalm 8 were the victims of the LORD's inexorable rage at the hands of Samuel and Saul. And lest we should imagine that this is just an 'Old Testament' problem, let us not forget that the (presumably) same God took his own son's life to satisfy his need for justice (in one commonly phrased form of the Christian myth). Such instances could be added in profusion; but the point is the same: the pleasing image of God and humankind hand in hand, which is so often assumed of Psalm 8, has an unacceptable face – hand in glove, rather than hand in hand.

It would be a shame to leave the matter here, so let me offer one other absence which proffers a further deconstruction: the absence of God. Psalm 14 opens with the stark opinion: 'Fools say in their hearts, "There is no God." They are corrupt, they do abominable deeds; there is no one who does any good.' A common religious perspective, which arrogates all ethical behaviour to the accident of faith. But suppose the hypothesis were to be accepted, for the sake of argument. If there is no God, then the theme of Psalm 8 is of how humankind aspires (successfully) to greatness beyond its merely earthly origins: the Psalm becomes, in other words, a great humanistic hymn. It may be said that to remove God is ultimately illegitimate, an affront to the deepest principles of biblical religion. Yet is that not what developing religious traditions have in fact done? What does the loving, caring, non-judgemental, universally saving deity of vast numbers of good Christians today have in common with the God either of the Old Testament or of the New? To replace a bad god with a good one is still an act of deletion, no less a deconstruction than I have proposed for this Psalm.

Personal afterword

Regardless of the problems raised by both contextual and deconstructive readings of this Psalm, it remains curiously attractive at the personal level. This is no doubt in part a consequence of egotism and self-absorption. There is something quite irresistible about the Psalm's offer of significance to otherwise unprepossessing lives. 'What kind of people are we? Oh, *that* kind of people!' And the positive nature of the proposition could, under the right circumstances, bring about a life-affirming response.

I would set this piece in contrast with those many texts, sermons and prayers which denounce the human situation as one of inveterate and endemic evil. That Psalm 8 belongs with Genesis 1 is part of this positive reinforcement. For just as we lay too much stress upon (for example) Psalm 51 ('I know my transgressions, and my sin is ever before me'), so we have transmitted the negative myth of Genesis 3 to the detriment of the positive theology of Genesis 1. It may be accurate to represent the human condition as one in which we repeatedly fail – but both Psalm 8 and Genesis 1 encourage us to believe that this is not a necessary state of affairs. We were not (*pace* Augustine) created evil; our birth is not inevitably contaminated by the genetic inheritance of a mythic fall from grace. It has always puzzled me that intelligent people, who are well aware of the nature of genetic processes and evolutionary biology, can still propound the inexpressible nonsense that, because some legendary forefather and mother committed wrongdoing, bad blood has somehow entered the human race. The theology of creation is much better rooted in the resounding and repeated affirmation of the first chapter of Genesis, 'God saw that it was good', culminating in what ought surely, to be the last word on the subject, 'God saw everything that he had made, and indeed, it was very good.' I like that 'everything', and I believe that this Psalm encourages us to accept it as a spiritual and moral as well as a mythological truth.

9

PSALM 24

The text

The verb system in classical Hebrew is unusual in that it displays only two forms which seem to count as what in Indo-European languages we call 'tenses'. While these are generally held to describe completed and incomplete actions, respectively, there can in some circumstances be doubts as to the accuracy of this correlation. As a result, particularly in poetic texts, translators tend to treat these 'tenses' with considerable freedom, frequently rendering them not as might seem to be indicated by their form, but to suit (one suspects) the translator's convenience. I hold the somewhat unusual view that in the great majority of cases both in narrative prose and in poetry we should respect the forms of the verbs and render them accordingly.[1] The second verb in verse 2 has the form of continuing action, and my amended text takes note of this.

With regard to 'structure', one important feature of Psalm 24 is a series of emphatic forms. Not all of these are explicitly represented in the NRSV translation; accordingly I have added them in the amended text, at the beginning respectively of verses 8 and 10. A similarly minor change which has relevance to the structural character of the Psalm concerns the second verb in verse 3, which is actually 'shall arise'. This, too, is indicated in the amended text.

The phrase in verse 4, 'clean hands and pure hearts' makes use of a familiar metaphor in Hebrew – that of the heart – which appears to translate directly into English.[2] Hebrew uses it as a substitute for 'mind' or 'will', and locates the emotions in the bowels, kidneys or stomach. English readers, on the other hand, assume that 'heart' is a signifier for the emotions, an assumption which actually falsifies the literal equation of the Hebrew word *leb* with 'heart'. I have not changed this in the amended text, since it is a ubiquitous convention.

PSALM 24

VERSE	*Part i*	*"The earth is the LORD's"*
1	The earth is the LORD's and all that is in it,	Choir 1 (Pilgrims)
	the world, and those who live in it;	
2	for he has FOUNDED it on the seas,	
	and ESTABLISHED [*or* establishes] it on	
	the rivers.	

	Part ii	*"The hill of the LORD"*
3	Who shall ASCEND the hill of the LORD?	Single voice at gate
	And who shall stand [*or* ARISE] in his	
	holy place?	
4	Those who have clean hands and pure hearts,	Choir 2 (within the
	who do not LIFT UP their souls to what is	gate)
	false,	
	and do not swear deceitfully.	
5	They will RECEIVE blessing from the LORD,	
	and vindication from the God of their	
	salvation.	
6	Such is the company of those who SEEK him,	Choir 1
	who SEEK the face of the God of Jacob	
	[*or* who SEEK your face, Jacob]	
	Selah	

	Part iii	*The temple of the LORD*
7	LIFT UP your heads, O gates!	Choir 2
	and BE LIFTED UP, O ancient doors!	
	that the King of glory may COME IN.	
8	Who is [this] the King of Glory?	Choir 1
	The LORD, strong and mighty,	Choir 2
	the LORD, mighty in battle.	
9	LIFT UP your heads, O gates!	Choir 2
	and BE LIFTED UP, O ancient doors!	
	that the King of glory may COME IN.	
10	Who is [he] this King of Glory?	Choir 1
	The LORD of hosts,	All
	he is the King of glory. *Selah*	

Readers of English translations, however, should be aware of the persistent error which this rendering implies, and should make allowances for it in their interpretations.

The final amendment relates to a genuinely puzzling text at the end of verse 6. There is no dispute about the translation – the correct version is that given in the amendment. The problem lies in finding an appropriate parallel to the first line, 'Such is the company of those who seek him'. It seems strange for the second line to have a second person form of address, and moreover to pair 'him' (i.e. God) with 'Jacob'. This difficulty was recognised by those who produced the Greek version; the NRSV text is essentially that of the Greek. It should be stressed, however, that the problem is one secondary to that of actual translation; we would do well, I believe, to follow the example of the KJV ('who seek thy face, O Jacob') and let the subsequent processes of interpretation deal with the problem, if indeed it is a problem. I will return to this point in due course.

The mysterious word *selah*, which occurs in several psalms, has never been satisfactorily explained. Most likely it is some kind of musical instruction, just possibly having some etymological connection with the Greek *psallô* which means 'to play a stringed instrument with the fingers', and is the derivation of the word *psalm*.[3]

Comparative material from the ancient Near East

The closest parallel to the understanding of creation which lies behind verses 1–2 is to be found in the Akkadian creation epic. In tablets IV and V an account is given of Marduk's defeat of Tiamat and the division of her carcass to form the 'firmament' of the heavens, which holds the upper waters in place, and the dry land, which provides boundaries for the waters below.[4] This vividly expresses the utter dependence of the created order on the will and power of the god – a theme which is of central importance to Psalm 24. Apart from this mythic text, there is an interesting graffito from a chamber tomb five miles east of Lachish, possibly dating to about 500 BCE, which reads (*NERTOT*: 251):

Yahweh is the God of the whole earth.
The mountains of Judah belong to him, the God of Jerusalem.

No direct connection is implied here; I simply note evidence for the existence in Judah of the belief underlying verses 1–2.

An Akkadian invocation to an anonymous God (*NERTOT*: 128) offers a curious parallel to verses 3ff. It is of some interest because it begins with a question, and seems to be a negative version of the entrance liturgy of Psalm 24 (cf. also Psalm 15):

> Who is there who has not sinned against his god,
> who has constantly obeyed the commandments?
> Every man who lives is sinful.
> I, your servant, have committed every kind of sin.

The piece goes on to list in detail the sins of the writer, whereas both Psalm 24 and Psalm 15 assume the worshipper's probity, at least tacitly.

Finally, Gibson (1977: 41) points out a turn of phrase in Baal and Yam (tablet II, column 1, lines 27–9) which echoes verses 7 and 9:

> Lift up, gods, your heads
> from on your knees. . . .
> The gods lifted up their heads
> from on their knees.

Again, though no direct link is implied, the parallel is indicative of the poetic style involved.

History, liturgy, social context

This is a Psalm which is sublimely uninterested in matters historical, though that has not prevented speculation about the implications of the phrase 'ancient doors' in verses 7 and 9[5] and suggestions about a connection with David's transfer of the Ark to Jerusalem. On the other hand, the form of verses 3–6 (commonly described as an 'entrance liturgy') seems to indicate a well-established temple cult involving priests and pilgrims typical of the later post-exilic period, rather than the (probably) private shrine of the Jerusalem royal family. This would seem to be incompatible with either an ancient Jebusite structure or a historical connection with the Ark. It is certainly best to conclude that there is nothing internal to the Psalm which provides uncontentious historical information.

By contrast, even on a superficial reading we can scarcely doubt the liturgical nature of Psalm 24. It clearly presupposes a festival procession; it falls naturally into three strophes which appear to represent the three different stages in its progress and relate to three distinct 'places of God' (the world, 'the hill of the LORD' and the city or temple); and the question-and-answer pattern of the language powerfully suggests an antiphonal or contrapuntal mode of recital. As to the specific nature of the procession or festival, we must remain agnostic, though there are good indications of a symbolic (as distinct from historical) presence of something like the Ark. I do not propose the kind of festival reconstruction which has so dominated Psalms study in the twentieth century; but this does not rule out appropriate readings based on the strong indications of the Psalm itself.

The social context (apart from the recognition that a pilgrim procession is itself a collective cultural event) is indicated only very generally. Common world-views about the nature of creation are expressed in verses 1–2, and are presumably those of the author's community. We do not know who might have embarked upon the kind of procession indicated. Perhaps only representatives of surrounding villages (if Psalm 122:8f. is a relevant parallel); perhaps it was a purely priestly function, with music provided by the Levitical singers (if the temple arrangements attributed to David in 1 Chronicles 6 are pertinent); on the other hand the famous legend of Luke 2:41–51 might imply a tradition in which everyone – men, women and children – visited the temple for major festivals.

Structure

The three strophes or stanzas indicated by the typography of the NRSV reflect accurately enough the movement of the Hebrew text, with the three parts constituting, respectively, a hymn to the God of creation, an entrance liturgy and an account of the triumphant arrival of the LORD. *Parts ii* and *iii* can be conveniently subdivided after verses 3, 5 and 8 to reflect, on the one hand, the three stages of the entrance liturgy (question, answer, affirmation) and the two verses of Yahweh's triumphant arrival. As noted in relation to its liturgical nature, the Psalm begs to be set out in antiphonal form; the proposal in the right-hand column of the Psalm's text is one possible way in which such an arrangement can be envisaged. Naturally there is no evidence for this particular proposal – though the general principle seems strongly indicated by the text itself – and it should be regarded simply as an interesting speculation.

There are three features which form a connection between the three parts. The first, deriving from one of the core concerns of each stanza, deals with the intimate involvement of God with every sphere of human activity: the world as a whole, which belongs to and is kept secure by Yahweh; the hill country of Judah – and in particular the hill on which Jerusalem is set – which is the locus of the pilgrimage; and the temple in Jerusalem, the specially chosen dwelling place of Yahweh. In effect, we have a progression from the widest to the narrowest sphere of God's activity.

The second linking structure is the remarkable sequence of verbs of action and movement which permeates the Psalm. These are indicated by the use of upper-cases. It turns out that virtually all of the verbs in the Psalm are of this kind (the English verb 'receive' in verse 5 is in fact the same verb – 'to lift up' – as is found in verses 4, 7 and 9). Thus the fact that the Psalm is processional is mirrored by the verbal movement within each of its parts, culminating in the repeated 'that the King of Glory may COME IN' (verses 7 and 9).

The third of these links requires some explanation. Hebrew is a language in which the verb forms include a specific indication of the personal subject. Thus, in normal use, where English requires the personal pronoun '*he* does X' Hebrew simply uses a verb form without the independent personal pronoun. Where the pronoun is employed a certain emphasis is indicated. Psalm 24 contains a sequence of forms which variously provide emphasis or 'point to' aspects of the text (the reader should follow the alterative text on p. 130 for this discussion). These are: the personal pronoun *he*, the interrogative *who* and the demonstrative adjective *this*. While any one of these by itself might be unremarkable, their distribution throughout the text (shown in Figure 9.1), building to a climax, suggests a positive structural device.

The cumulative effect is to bring the reader back forcefully at the end of verse 10 to the simple personal pronoun 'he' of verse 2. The 'King of Glory' who is now established in Jerusalem is precisely 'he' who founded and maintains the whole world, and the Psalm completes a semantic as well as a structural circle.

he (verse 2)	who (verse 3, twice)	this (verse 6)
	who is this (verse 8)	
	who is he, this (verse 10a)	
	he (verse 10c)	

Figure 9.1 Distribution of verb forms in Psalm 24

Contextual interpretations

The cosmogony implied by the opening stanza of this Psalm is familiar from the Near East and the Mediterranean, and is part of the mythic language characteristic of a number of psalms. These two verses give a very vivid expression of the delicate suspension of dry land between the primeval waters which creates the space within which human and other life may flourish. Not only was Yahweh the creator of this poised system in the first place: it is through God's constant vigilance alone that this equilibrium is maintained. Thus a primary thrust of the hymn is to remind the worshippers (or pilgrims) that they are wholly dependent upon Yahweh for the preservation both of that stability and of their well-being and very lives within it. The balance is, of course, delicate only from a human perspective, for as long as God is in control there is no real danger – except from God's own strength.

It is entirely fitting, then, that those whose existence depends upon being on good terms with the deity (the technical term righteousness – ṣedaqah – which defines this relationship in Hebrew is the word which our version translates in verse 5 as 'vindication') should pay homage and make pilgrimage to the place where Yahweh's presence is most dramatically made known in Judah: the temple on 'the hill of the LORD'. For it is in the end the military prowess of God the LORD of Hosts[6] (verses 8b,c and 10b) which secures both the city of Jerusalem and the stability of the world.

Unfortunately, there is a conundrum at the heart of the Psalm which forms a kind of vicious circle: those who would (in order to keep on good terms with God) pay their respects at the temple, must first subject themselves to a trial. This trial, ironically, demands of the pilgrims that they effectively meet the conditions for being described as 'righteous' in advance of fulfilling their mission – a seeming impossibility which is resolved by the affirmation (verse 6) 'Such *is* the company of those who seek him'. The question 'who' in verse 3 is answered by the demonstrative 'this' in verse 6, just as the emphatic 'he' of verse 2 matches that of verse 10. Just as the Psalm as a whole achieves closure by circling back to its beginnings, so does the middle section turn back on itself in an action simultaneously mimicking the vicious circle at its heart and closing off its potential threat. We see, therefore, how the emphatic forms provide both a movement towards climax and a double closure within the interpretative structure of the Psalm.

The so-called entrance liturgy in *part ii* has similarities to Psalm 15, which confines itself to just this theme, providing more detail of the conditions required for admission to the sacred precinct. In detail, Psalm 15:1 matches verse 3; 15:2–5b matches verse 4; and 15:5c matches verse 5. It is of note that the pilgrims' declaration in verse 6 is not represented in Psalm 15. Some have seen in the latter Psalm a tenfold list which echoes the Decalogue, and have suggested both that the Decalogue itself might have been used as a formal test of worthiness for admission to the sanctuary and that materials of this kind should be given the genre description 'priestly Torah liturgy'. Whether Psalms 15 or 24 were actually used in such a manner is an open question; undoubtedly there were restrictions on admission to the sanctuary, whose various precincts were open only to strictly defined groups. Anderson (1972: 202) refers to an inscription on Herod's temple in Jerusalem: 'No alien may enter within the barrier and wall around the Temple. Whoever is caught [violating this] is alone responsible for the death[-penalty] which follows.'

We have more than once affirmed that Psalm 24 is a processional or pilgrimage Psalm. While the general tone of the text makes this fairly clear, it might be worth pointing to three specific indications. The first, and most obvious, is of course the language of the dramatic arrival of the deity in *part iii* (the lifting up of the gates and the doors, and the coming in of the King). I argue below that this may well have involved the symbolic presence of the Ark. The second indication is in verse 3, where the verb 'ascend' has the technical meaning of 'to go up on pilgrimage' – a usage found also in Psalm 122:4, 1 Samuel 2:3, 22 and Isaiah 2:4. This verse displays a highly detailed parallelism which binds together a series of significant terms relating to the pilgrimage and its projected destination. Since I wish to link this with the final verse of *part ii*, which has already been identified as problematic, I will set out the parallels of verse 3 in detail:

Who	shall ascend	the hill	of the LORD
and who	shall arise	in the place	of his holiness[7]

The third indication is the sequence of verbs of action and motion identified by the structural analysis: in an important sense, the whole thrust of the Psalm is a movement, both internally (the arrival of God) and externally (the presumed pilgrim procession to the temple), towards a climax.

Verse 6 requires some elucidation. I have already commented on the problems of the text, which have encouraged many translations to follow early Greek and Syriac emendations by introducing the word 'god'. I wish, however, to propose a reading of the verse which takes account of the unamended Hebrew and makes explicit the role of the pilgrims in the Psalm. Let me first set out a parallelism for verse 6:

Such is the company   of those who seek   him
                        of those who seek   your face
Jacob

The parallelism is of the form a / b / c // B / C / A. Two features of this proposed analysis merit comment – the switch from third-person ('him') to second-person ('your face'), and the status of the proper name 'Jacob'. I hope to show that a comparison with verse 3 provides a suitable explanatory context.

The verbs in verse 6 are congruent with the theme of pilgrimage, since 'seeking' God is presumably the purpose of 'ascending' and 'arising' in verse 3; moreover the object of the verbs in the proposed parallel is God in each case. Thus the motion towards the place of God in verse 3 is answered by the search for God in verse 6. Verse 3 begins with the question 'Who?'; consequently the phrase 'Such is the company' provides the answer. Who may ascend? Response: This company of pilgrims. The remaining parallel – 'Jacob' – stands therefore as an explication of 'Such is the company'. It is essentially an exclamation, an affirmation by the pilgrims of their identity as a group entitled to attend the sanctuary, and as such should be read as a collective eponymous title: the people of Jacob. This use of Jacob, which in other places parallels 'Israel', is not uncommon in the Psalms (see for example 14:7, and 22:23 in the vicinity of Psalm 24), and its presence here provides another resolution of the problem of the closed circle mentioned above: the affirmation 'we meet the conditions' is sustainable precisely because 'we are Jacob – the chosen people of God'. This, finally, explains the direct address to God in the phrase 'your face'. No longer is this a hypothetical exercise, some kind of abstract 'entrance liturgy'. It is at this moment in the Psalm an actuality. 'We are here, we are Jacob, we seek *you*, O God.' It is, consequently, only with the ringing cry of 'Jacob' that the call goes up for the gates to open and the doors to swing wide. The legitimate pilgrims are here, and the drama can now reach its conclusion.

Turning to the final movement of the Psalm, I return to an issue referred to more than once already: the role (if any) of the Ark. There is, certainly, no explicit use of that term (indeed, it only occurs once in the Psalter, at 132:8), but a number of characteristics of the processional make the association plausible. First, the word 'strong' used in verse 8b is in a number of places a characteristic of God as warrior. Psalm 68 is a striking example, where the specific occurrences of this word in 68:28 and 34 are in the context of a procession (68:24–7) which is reminiscent of 24:7–10. More directly,

Psalm 132:8 refers to 'the ark of your might', and the use of the term in Psalm 99:4 is followed by a reference to God's footstool (99:5) which in 132:7 is linked with the Ark.

Second, Numbers 10:35f. records the use of the Ark as a battle icon which is closely identified with the presence of Yahweh:

> Whenever the ark set out, Moses would say,
> "Arise, O LORD, let your enemies be scattered,
>   and your foes flee before you."
> And whenever it came to rest, he would say,
> "Return, O LORD of the ten thousand thousands of Israel."

The record of the battle with the Philistines and its aftermath in 1 Samuel 4–6 provides a narrative instance – albeit a disastrous one for the Israelites – of this tradition, in which it is clear that the loss of the Ark in battle meant the loss of Yahweh's presence in Israel. Thus when we find Psalm 24 describing Yahweh as 'the LORD, mighty in battle' and 'the LORD of hosts', we are perhaps justified in making a link with the rhetoric of the Ark.

Third, the element of procession is common to Psalms 24, 68 and 132, and Psalm 99 reads like the encomium delivered upon the arrival and subsequent enthronement of Yahweh at the temple. There is, I believe, a strong circumstantial case for seeing Psalm 24 in the context of a procession involving a symbolic object (the Ark?) which embodies the presence of Yahweh the great warrior God and King of Jerusalem.

Deconstructive readings[8]

This text is marked by questions (see Table 9.1), and one characteristic of questions is uncertainty. The fact that answers seem to be provided does not elide the uncertainty; rather it introduces a confidence which may be something of a sham. The mysteriously powerful deity whose identity is queried is a military figure without enemies. How can such a figure survive? Without enemies to conquer, his credentials are in question. Alone he sits in his awesome, isolated splendour, surrounded by the ruins of the gates of the temple, devoid of company. The world with all its inhabitants has been left behind, the pilgrims were last seen protesting their fitness at the foot of the hill.

This is the silence of fear, of victory without peace. Who dare ascend the hill of the LORD? Anyone who is willing to risk being

Table 9.1 Aporias and absence in Psalm 24

Aporia	Absence
Who shall ascend and who shall stand?	Peace
What is purity?	The enemy
Who is Jacob?	Humankind in verses 7–10
How can gates lift up their heads?	
Who is the king of glory?	
Selah	

found out in failure – for is there a human being who can claim without hubris to have fulfilled the conditions of verse 4? What kind of God will such a person meet? The God they deserve, of course, whose aspect is war, whose attribute is power, whose presence is glory, whose need is for enemies to humiliate and destroy. Take pause, pilgrims. Hear that warning 'Selah', and stand off; for there is in truth no human who can ascend the hill of the LORD, or arise in his holy place – and that is why the Holy of Holies in the temple was by definition empty.

There is an enemy, as there always was. It is God – who made us – and ourselves, who fear the God whom we made; and the peace which is the absence implied by the presence of war will never be ours (as it is significantly absent from this Psalm) until we admit that the questions we began with are unanswerable except in the form 'No one' and 'The enemy'. But Jacob, bless him (poor Esau), was ever the bold-faced, tricky, younger son, the one who knew the answer without knowing the question, the one who had the key which would unlock the door to the castle treasury. And so, of all the people of earth (keeping safely distant) Jacob will dare to ascend the hill and take up the struggle (at Jabbok and everywhere) with God. And peace will never be, has never been, his. The rest of us wait, and watch, and sometimes allow ourselves to be suborned by one side or the other (always living to regret it), for this is a private feud, a family feud, which we should respect as such.

On the other hand, there is a nice physical act of deconstruction in this text which may serve as a warning to those of us who would rather not get involved. The man-made solid structures of the city or the temple gates are forced to unbuild themselves to let the LORD through – the same LORD whose power underpins the complex dance of atoms and sub-atoms which constitutes the fragile universe. It is ironic that the earth, which seems so unstable, remains while the work of man, which appears permanent, crumbles. And the lesson for modern man, who has successfully disposed of God, is that the whole fragile universe is now his building, his designer raw material. Out of it we may build wonders, may harness unlimited power, may visit distant galaxies, may erect Ozymandian monuments – but who will gaze upon their ruins is the question we should fear.

Purity may save us – a catharsis – a purging both of the ambition to ascend to God (did we never learn from Babel?) and the desire to constrain deity. If we lock God up in an ark in a temple, an explosion will inevitably follow; if we worship what is false, we will fall predictably into deceit. If there is such a thing as a god, we can neither aspire to it nor control it. But catharsis is itself dangerous if it leaves simply a clean slate, a blank page upon which to scribble once again the old seductions. Something akin to the restoration of a gloomy old painting might be closer to the mark, a recovery of pristine awareness, of an innocence which poets dream of as the child's condition, and which anthropologists hypothesise as the early condition of humankind. Yet these too are false idols, to which we lift up our souls at our peril. We cannot escape, but we can strive to escape; we cannot return, though we can strive to return; we cannot achieve purity, though we can reject its opposite. Perhaps, in the end, this is why we need the symbol of a warrior deity without external enemies – as a sign of the condition in which we thrive, of the struggle with the only important enemy: ourselves.

The common, but almost wholly unexplained, term *selah* is of course an *aporia*. In Psalm 24 it stands next to the mysterious *Jacob*, which is a crux of the Psalm. The silence of *selah* prompts us to think of the silent partner of Jacob, his brother Esau. The biblical traditions are ambivalent in the extreme about Esau, who appears at times as Jacob's sworn rival, but at others as his close and beloved brother. Esau is the eponymous ancestor of Edom, in respect of whom the traditions are similarly ambivalent. The irony of this silence is of course that the great Herod who built the temple which is, in an important sense, the focus of Psalm 24 was an Idumean (the Latin form of the word *Edomite*). It was as a result of the aggressive empire-building of the Hasmonean rulers of the second century BCE that Idumea became part of the Judean world. Thus the former enemies of Israel become the founders of the temple which is the defining characteristic of Israel. But (the last irony) the man whose project it was is the last man who could have sworn on oath to fit the description of righteousness in Psalm 24!

Personal afterword

For anyone rooted in a continuing liturgical tradition Psalm 24 has obvious resonance. Mishnah *Tamid* 7.4 records, as does the title given to it in the Septuagint that this Psalm was sung on the first day of the week. It survives in the liturgy of Communion in Christian traditions, where verses 7–10 provide a natural processional for the bringing in of the elements which, in that religion, symbolise the presence of God in the person of Jesus. This distinguishes it from the majority of psalms, in that there remains a close similarity of use between that presumed in a procession of the Ark and that assumed in the Eucharist.

However, on a more directly personal note, what also impresses is the sheer grandeur of the risk we take when we invite the total otherness of 'god' to invade our personal space. Here is no docile, simpering Jesus of pious wishful thinking, but the unutterable given form. If, for a moment, I entertain the Hindu understanding of creation as an expression of the ultimate which partakes of the ultimate, then this magnificent processional envisages creation itself entwined with the individual in a dizzying spiral of encounter upon encounter which brings home (however faintly) the truth of the oneness which is our only hope.

Thus, strangely, when I as a Christian of a particular kind sing the words of the metrical Psalm based on our text, to a tune composed in Edinburgh, I find myself drawn out of that particularity into an all-embracing sense that (in truth) there is but one mystery, whose impenetrability we can joyfully share.

10

PSALM 74

The text

The Hebrew text of verses 5–6 is (as the NRSV footnote puts it) 'uncertain'. While the detail is undoubtedly obscure, its general import is clear enough, describing as it does a vicious and violent attack on the structures of the temple. I do not, therefore, need to present an alternative text in this case, and we will content ourselves with the interpretation offered by NRSV.

There is also some difficulty in verse 11, though here also the overall implication allows us to pass over the particular problem. Since the term 'hand', particularly applied to God, is a figure for power, the complaint of this verse is clearly that God, who by definition has the power to do whatever God wills, has deliberately withheld that power.

The only other textual point which may be of interest is that the word for 'winter' (*ḥorep*), which comes close to the end of the section headed *Review of the Past*, is almost identical in form to the word (*ḥerep*) in the next verse (also found in verses 10 and 22). Since the mockery of God's enemies is a significant motif in this Psalm, it may be that this is a deliberate play on words providing a contrived but suggestive link between verses 12–17 and verses 18–23. Accordingly in the indication of seven themes which is given in my display of the Psalm's text, the theme of 'winter' is included with that of the scoffing of the enemy. The themes are discussed more fully under 'structure'.

Comparative material from the ancient Near East

Undoubtedly the popular background to verses 12–17 includes familiar legends about the victory of the gods over the sea-monsters

Leviathan (Lotan) and Tanin in Canaan, and possibly Tiamat in Babylonia. Ugaritic legends of the conflict between Baal and Mot and other monstrous figures speak of both Lotan and Tanin (literally 'dragons') as slippery seven-headed serpents associated with the sea. Thus

> Did I not destroy Yam the darling of El,
> did I not make an end of Nahar the great god?
> Was not the dragon [*tanin*] captured and vanquished?
> I did destroy the wriggling serpent,
> the tyrant with seven heads.
>
> (Gibson 1977: 50)

And

> Have you forgotten, Baal, that I can surely transfix you,
> for all that you smote Leviathan the slippery serpent
> and made an end of the wriggling serpent,
> the tyrant with seven heads.
>
> (ibid.: 68)

There may also be a hint, in verses 14–17, of the Tiamat legend of the creation which we discussed in Chapter 9; but the primary association is surely with the Canaanite material.

In terms of the more general lament genre, a number of examples of this form have survived from the ancient Near East. Beyerlin (*NERTOT*: 170) gives an example of the kind of questioning of the gods which is found in verses 1 and 10f. of the Psalm; and in a Lamentation to Ishtar we read:

> How long, O my Lady, shall my adversaries be looking upon
>   me,
> In lying and untruth shall they plan evil against me,
> Shall my pursuers and those who exult over me rage against
>   me?
> How long, O my Lady, shall the crippled and weak seek me
>   out? . . .
> I – what have I done, O my god and my goddess?
> Like one who does not fear my god and my goddess I am
>   treated . . .
>
> (*ANET*: 384b–5a)

(The Lament form)

VERSE   *Introduction*

1 O God, why do you cast us off *forever?*[e]
    Why does your anger smoke against
        the sheep of your pasture?[b]

2 *Remember*[a] *your congregation,*[b] which
    you *acquired*[d] *long ago,*[e]
    Which you *redeemed*[d] to *be the tribe
        of your heritage.*[b]
    Remember[a] Mount Zion, where you
        came to dwell.

3 Direct your steps to the *perpetual*[e] ruins:
    the *enemy*[f] has destroyed everything
        in the sanctuary.

Lament Proper

4 *Your foes*[b],[f] have roared within *your holy
        place;*[b]
    they set up their emblems there.

5 At the upper entrance they hacked the
        wooden trellis with axes.

6 And then, with hatchets and hammers,
    they smashed all its carved work.

7 They set *your sanctuary*[b] on fire;
    they desecrated *the dwelling place of
        your name,*[b]
    bringing it to the ground.

8 They said to themselves, 'We will
        utterly subdue them';
    they burned all the meeting places of
        God in the land.

9 We do not see our emblems;
    there is no longer any prophet,
    and there is no one among us who
        knows *how long.*[e]

10 *How long,*[e] O God, is the *foe*[f] to *scoff?*[g]
    Is the *enemy*[f] to *revile*[g] *your name*[b]
        forever?[e]

11 Why do you hold back *your hand;*[b]
    why do you keep *your hand*[b] in *your
        bosom?*[b]

Review of the Past

12 Yet God my King is *from of old*,[e]
     working *salvation*[d] in the earth.
13 *You*[c] *divided the sea*[d] by your might;
     and broke the heads of the dragons
          in the waters.
14 *You*[c] crushed the heads of Leviathan;
     and gave him as food for the
          creatures of the wilderness.
15 *You*[c] cut openings for springs and
          torrents;
     you[c] dried up ever-flowing streams.
16 Yours is the day, yours also the night;
     you[c] established the luminaries and
          the sun.
17 *You*[c] have fixed all the bounds of the
          earth;
     you[c] made summer and *winter*.[g]

Petition

18 *Remember*[a] this, O LORD, how the
     enemy[f] *scoffs*,[g]
     and an *impious people*[f] *reviles*[g] your
          name.[b]
19 Do not deliver the soul of *your dove*[b] to
          the wild animals;
     do not forget[a] the life of *your poor*[b]
          forever.[e]
20 *Have regard for*[a] your *covenant*,[b,d]
     for the dark places of the land are
          full of the haunts of violence.
21 Do not let the downtrodden be put to
          shame;
     let the poor and needy praise *your*
          name.[b]
22 Rise up, O God, plead *your cause*;[b]
     remember[a] how *the impious*[f] *scoff*[g] at
          you *all day long*.[e]
23 *Do not forget*[a] the clamour of *your*
          foes,[b,f]
     the uproar of *your adversaries*[b,f] that
          goes up *continually*.[e]

Note: Themes are indicated by superscript letters to the italicised text.

Since the bulk of the poetic material which has survived is public in character, we do not have many parallels to what seems to be the more intimate character of Hebrew laments. Perhaps the Hebrew material also depends ultimately on the public domain of the royal temple of the pre-exilic period, and is a later reworking of what was originally more like the Mesopotamian examples. On the other hand, there is also the intriguing possibility that some post-exilic Hebrew psalms of lament are based on the experiences and knowledge of what we might describe as 'the Babylonian tendency' in the priestly circles of the Second Temple Period.

One of the striking stylistic features of Psalm 74 is the sequence of second-person addresses to God in verses 12–17. There is a remarkably similar device in the Hymn to the Moon God found at Nineveh and dated to the reign of Ashurbanipal (668–633 BCE):

> In heaven who is exalted? Thou! Thou alone art exalted.
> On earth who is exalted? Thou! Thou alone art exalted.
> Thou! When thy word is pronounced in heaven the Igigi
>   prostrate themselves.
> Thou! When thy word is pronounced on earth the Anunnaki
>   kiss the ground.
> Thou! When thy word drifts along in heaven like the wind it
>   makes rich the feeding and drinking of the land.
> Thou! When thy word settles down on the earth green
>   vegetation is produced.
> Thou! Thy word makes fat the sheepfold and the stall; it makes
>   living creatures widespread.
> Thou! Thy word causes truth and justice to be, so that the
>   people speak the truth.
> Thou! Thy word which is far away in heaven, which is hidden
>   in the earth is something no one sees.
> Thou! Who can comprehend thy word, who can equal it?
> O LORD, in heaven as to dominion, on earth as to valor, among
>   the gods thy brothers, thou hast not a rival.
>
> (*ANET*: 386a)

History, liturgy, social context

Unlike the majority of psalms, this is one which offers some hope of a positive dating. It is written from the context of a military defeat, when the temple was apparently subject to extensive damage, and possibly complete destruction. The two specific incidents most

146

commonly proposed are the fall of Jerusalem to the Babylonians in 587 BCE and the desecration of the sanctuary by Antiochus IV Epiphanes in 167 BCE.

The plausibility of the first alternative is heightened by the general view that Book III of the Psalter (Psalms 73–89) has a particular *raison d'être* in the context of the immediate post-exilic period. If not actually composed as a response to the events which put an end to the Judaean royal dynasty, it does seem to have been informed by that crucial episode. This interpretation is further supported by the resonances which echo between the Book of Lamentations and this section of the Psalter. It is not necessary to postulate composition in the immediate traumatic aftermath of 587; even if Book III and Lamentations form a more distanced literary and liturgical response to conquest and depopulation, the connection remains. Part of the argument lies in the assumption that Psalms 73–89 (dedicated largely to Asaph and Korah) may be taken as a unity in some significant sense.[1] Thus it is of relevance that Psalm 79 bears a particularly close resemblance to Psalm 74.[2] The fact that Jeremiah 10:25 'quotes' Psalm 79:6f. may therefore be noteworthy, as is the occurrence in verse 1 of a rare turn of phrase – 'the sheep of your pasture' – in both Psalm 79:13 and Jeremiah 23:1.[3] Jeremiah 10.16 uses a phrase almost identical to 'the tribe of your inheritance' (in verse 2). With reference to Lamentations, there are resemblances between verse 4 and Lamentations 2:7, verses 7–8 and Lamentations 1:10, verse 9 and Lamentations 2:9, and verse 11 and Lamentations 2:3. These various signs of intertextuality suggest that the descriptive style used in Psalm 74 to depict the disaster is similar to other accounts in texts from the late sixth or early fifth centuries BCE. The likelihood, then, is that Psalm 74 is also from that broad period, and refers (as those texts may be presumed to do) to the Babylonian invasion of 587.

Turning to the other historical incident, at the beginning of the Maccabean revolt, the evidence here is less persuasive. The Greek version of Psalm 79:2f. is quoted in 1 Maccabees 7:16f.; but this tells us little more than that a later writer found the material applicable to a similar situation. The statement 'there is no longer any prophet' (verse 9) might be thought to refer to the conditions presupposed by 1 Maccabees 9:27: 'Thus there was great distress in Israel, such as had not been seen since the time that prophets ceased to appear among them.' (See also 1 Maccabees 4:46 and 14:41.) The account given of the act of destruction in 74:3–8 is similar to that in 1 Maccabees 4:38:

And they saw the sanctuary desolate, the altar profaned, and the gates burned. In the courts they saw bushes sprung up as in a thicket, or as on one of the mountains. They saw also the chambers of the priests in ruins.

(See also 1 Maccabees 1 *passim*, and 2 Maccabees 1:8, 8:33). Apart from the general improbability that this section of the Psalter is as late as the time of the Maccabees,[4] and the strength of the positive case for 587, we should note that, far from the people being bereft of hope and powerless, the Maccabean Period is one in which active revolution produced within a very few years a restoration of the sanctuary and quasi-independence for the people of Jerusalem. This is wholly at odds with the sense of long-standing loss which pervades Psalm 74 (see in particular theme *e* in the Psalm's text). We must, I think, conclude that this is not a Psalm produced as a result of the events of 167; though there are indications that it was found by the writer of Maccabees to be appropriate as a way of referring to what had happened at the hands of Antiochus.

This brings me to a further important point. The apparent basis in events of Psalm 74 should not tempt us into thinking that, having made this connection, there is nothing more to be said. On the contrary, there is everything still to play for in seeking meaning, not least because a lament thus restricted to a past event (however momentous) is little more than a museum object. Two observations take us into the wider discussion: first, that the Psalm appears also to have been applied to the Maccabean Period suggests that within its early development it was seen to have more than localised relevance; and, second, that the central section of the Psalm (verses 12–17) is mythic in nature indicates that from its inception this composition was intended to have universal resonance.

The best way to bring this out is to highlight the liturgical dimension. Under the schema devised by Gunkel (1930) and others, this is a *community lament*, a religious piece which would have functioned at a relevant point in some festival liturgy. While I have indicated that it is not my purpose to retrace the paths taken by those who have sought to uncover the festivals to which psalms may have applied, it is none the less useful to set out the details of how Psalm 74 fits into the formulaic type to which it is usually allocated. The broad outline is given in the Psalm's text (pp. 144f.); in detail it is as follows in Table 10.1.

The Psalm ends at this point, although in the standard *gattung* we might expect a response in the form of a confession (Psalm

Table 10.1 Psalm 74: formulaic indications

Introduction	Invocation of God's name (verse 1a – 'O God') Plaintive questions (remainder of verse 1) Cry for help (verses 2–3)
Lament proper	Against the enemies of Israel and God (verses 4–8) Inward, regarding the community itself (verse 9) Against God (verses 10–11)
Hymnic review of the past	While this usually refers to historical events, here we have a mythic hymn to God the LORD of creation
Petition	Plea for attention (verse 18a – 'Remember this, O LORD') Reasons for God to act (verses 18, 20, 22, 23) Plea for God's intervention (verses 19, 21)

38:17–22), or a vow (Psalm 80:18), or a hymn of thanksgiving (Psalms 12:6–8, 60:12, 79:13). It is further proposed that between the petition and the response there would have been, in the actual performance of the liturgy, a break during which someone – a temple prophet, for example – might pronounce a suitable oracle. Not surprisingly, few such laments have survived, though among other community laments examples might be Psalms 12:5 and 85:8–9. Having already argued for the connectedness of the Psalms in Book III, it is interesting that Psalm 75 begins on a note of thanksgiving, and goes on to celebrate a God who, far from being the object of derision, takes dramatic vengeance on his enemies. There is something to be said for seeing 74 and 75 as a linked pair, at least within the movement of the presumed liturgy.

Transferring the Psalm thus out of the context of an eyewitness response to a particular disaster gives it depth and resonance. This is surely the function of the inclusion in liturgical form of material which at first glance looks like history – and would apply with greater force to more strikingly historical Psalms like 78. History becomes meta-history, transformed by the seeming straightjacket of liturgical structure into something which, paradoxically, offers far greater freedom both to the worshipper (who needs to be able to apply it to his or her situation) and to the reader (for whom the mere historical accidents of the poem may be rather drab and uninteresting).

Not only does this liturgical transformation grant the Psalm a longer life; it serves to deconstruct the specifically historical investigation with which I began this section. This is not, I think, to say that it was a fruitless exercise (the 'history' still gives the liturgy its point); rather it reminds us that 'merely factual history' is but raw material, which can only live and confer meaning when it is reconstructed as story, or legend, or myth or tradition: in short, when it is taken possession of by those for whom it can, somehow, be understood as immediate.[5]

Structure

Apart from the structure associated with the lament form, which I discussed in the second section, this Psalm is characterised by a series of verbal links which bring to the fore its numerous themes and motifs. I have picked out seven of these (the number is structurally significant, as we shall see!) and indicated them by italic type and superscripted letters in the text displayed at the start of this chapter.

(a) The plea to God to remember is a characteristic motif of laments. In various forms it is found seven times in Psalm 74 (twice in verse 2, and once in each of verses 18, 19, 20, 22 and 23). Not surprisingly, it is confined to those sections of the lament which concern the cry for help – the *introduction*, and the *petition* proper.

(b) The description of various things and people as *belonging to* God is a striking feature, occurring in all four sections of the Psalm. In association with the personal address 'you' in verses 12–17 (see below), this is a dominant theme constituting one of the most powerful arguments at the psalmist's disposal. I have identified nineteen examples.[6]

(c) Seven occurrences of 'you' as an address to God in verses 12–17.[7] In Chapter 9 I drew attention to the importance of pronouns when used for emphasis in conjunction with verbs in classical Hebrew. The possible significance of this sequence will be addressed in the next section.

(d) Motifs associated with the exodus. There are five terms which belong firmly within the theological complex of the exodus, and two others (not typographically indicated) which could be included. The two verbs ('acquire', 'redeem') in verse 2 are associated with the forging of Israel as a nation out of the Egypt experience; the verbs 'working salvation' and 'dividing the sea' relate specifically to the crossing of the Red Sea (verses 12f.); and the covenant (verse 20) marks the consummation of these events at Sinai/Horeb. In addition, we might include Mount Zion (verse 2), which is in many ways a symbol of the mountain at which the Decalogue was given and whose location had been long forgotten, and the theme of God's 'dwelling', which is in Hebrew a technical term (used, for example, in Exodus 24.16, when 'the glory of the LORD *settled* on Mount Sinai'). If we take the wider definition of the motif, the number of items in the set is again seven – a possibly significant point.

(e) Persistently throughout this Psalm the writer bewails the length of the time during which the people have had to endure oppression. Thus 'forever' with its various synonyms constitutes a fifth thematic group. There are nine instances, in verses 1, 2, 3, 9, 10, 12, 19, 22, 23.

(f) Being a lament, it is not surprising that enemies figure largely. There are nine references to 'enemies', 'foes', 'adversaries' and the 'impious', confined to the first, second and fourth sections of the Psalm. Maybe Leviathan and the dragons in verses 13f. should be included in this list; but they are of a quite different kind, and should be interpreted within the mythic material in verses 12–17.

(g) Mockery is the last of my thematic sets. Just as we observed that God's mockery (discussed in Chapter 7 in relation to Psalm 2) is a particularly sinister phenomenon, so the mockery of the enemy serves to add salt to the wound. The relevant terms are found four times (verses 10, 18 [twice], 22); we might add the use of 'winter' at the end of verse 17, where it may be a deliberate word-play.

Themes a, c and d each have seven items, and the total number of themes is seven. While the last point is no doubt the consequence of a subjective decision about what constitutes a theme, the significance of the number seven has a particular relevance to verses 12–17, where it may indeed be an intended device.

Table 10.2 Distribution of themes in Psalm 74

Verses	Theme a	Theme b	Theme c	Theme d	Theme e	Theme f	Theme g	
1–3	•	•		•	•	•		5
4–8		•				•		2
9–11		•			•	•	•	4
12–17			•	•	•		? •	3?4
18–23	•	•		•	•	•	•	6

151

The themes are distributed unevenly, as Table 10.2 shows. Excluding theme (c), which is confined to verses 12–17, and is in many ways a special case, the common themes are rarer in the two sections which directly describe the conflict – verses 4–8, where the enemy destroys the sanctuary, and verses 12–17 where God destroys the cosmic enemy. This indicates a broad A–B–C–B–A pattern for the Psalm as a whole, where the A passages are in essence the petition to God, C is the case against God, and the B passages describe the two opposed forms of conflict.

Contextual interpretations

The appeal to God to remember which pervades this Psalm is a potent one; for when God remembers, God also acts. This is no anodyne request that Yahweh keep the people in mind – that is a modern use of the term which would not be understood in the context of the Psalm. To think about someone without acting upon the thought is to do nothing of substance. When in Exodus 20:8 we read 'Remember the Sabbath day, and keep it holy', we are not commanded to carry out two different kinds of action: the Hebrew in fact says 'Remember the Sabbath in order to keep it holy', which implies that 'remember' is equivalent to 'observe' – a point made explicit in Deuteronomy 5:12. And in the story of Hannah in 1 Samuel 1:17–20, the answer to her prayer provides an equally active meaning of 'remember':

> Then Eli answered, 'Go in peace; the God of Israel grant the petition you have made to him.' And she said, 'Let your servant find favour in your sight.' . . . Elkanah knew his wife Hannah, and the LORD remembered her. In due time Hannah conceived and bore a son. She named him Samuel, for she said, 'I have asked him of the LORD.'

Thus the prayer has a twofold significance – pointing back to God's past deeds and the relationship with Israel, and looking forward to God's effective intervention to deal with the present situation.

The basis of this appeal is to be found in the exodus theme. Israel was once *acquired* and then *redeemed* by God. The first of these words can mean both 'to purchase' and 'to beget', and the second is a legal term which is also used explicitly in respect of the traditions of the Red Sea. The predominant metaphor is monetary – as though the psalmist is encouraging God not to waste a valuable investment.

This is also the thrust of the repeated insistence on God's possessions in the Psalm: what is at stake is *God's* congregation, *God's* heritage, *God's* name, *God's* sanctuary, *God's* hand, *God's* covenant, etc. They are even *God's* foes and adversaries. Why, the poet laments, does God not do something to protect this expensive family silver, instead of sitting back, doing nothing, and letting a crowd of violent barbarians run amuck in the holy places, leaving a trail of devastation and the sound of their mocking laughter in the air?

However, the arguably more profound creation theme is by no means absent. The language of the mythic section, which begins with a very clear reference to the exodus motif of the dividing of the sea, goes on to describe the great battle between God and the sea monsters who must be defeated in order for the act of creation to take place. While undoubtedly informed, as we have seen, by Ugaritic and Canaanite traditions, there is also more than a hint of the Babylonian Tiamat legend in the language of verses 15–17. Salvation and redemption thus find their locus in the great drama of creation, in which God prepares the heavens and the earth (verses 16–17 – compare Genesis 1:6–10, 14–19) to receive humanity in the very image of God. The plea, therefore, is to God as creator, God as ultimate progenitor, to protect the progeny which faces the threat of annihilation. Hosea's moving account of the matter (Hosea 11:1, 8–9) might well be in the reader's mind here, if not the psalmist's. God is speaking:

> When Israel was a child I loved him
>   and out of Egypt I called my son. . . .
>
> How can I give you up, Ephraim?
> How can I hand you over, O Israel? . . .
>
> My heart recoils within me;
>   my compassion grows warm and tender.
> I will not execute my fierce anger;
>   I will not again destroy Ephraim;
> for I am God and no mortal,
>   the Holy One in your midst,
>   and I will not come in wrath.

Would that *this* God might be heard again!

The use of a mythic piece where a historical reprise might have been expected (compare, for example, Psalms 77:11–20 and 83:9–12) is a reminder of the fluidity of genres in the cultures of the ancient world. We are prone to draw a sharp dividing line between what counts as history and what belongs to the sphere of legend and myth. Not so the ancient writers, who present the events of the supernatural world in as matter-of-fact a manner as those of narrative history – and vice versa! The God of creation and the cosmos, who battles with legendary monsters, is also and equally the God of Israel and its history. This being so, the 'events' which constitute that history segue readily into the 'events' of the cosmic realm. Dividing the Red Sea and splitting the carcass of Tiamat, or the heads of Leviathan, are but different ways of expressing the one truth. The broken body of Leviathan, scattered as food for the creatures of the wilderness, is one and the same as the broken power of the Pharaoh and the shattered bodies of the Egyptians, left to rot in the desert.

If the details of myths are important, and were known to our poet, then the sequence of the seven emphatic personal pronouns 'You' might be taken as a representation of the victory of God over the seven-headed Leviathan; each declamation of the divine 'You' delivering by a kind of poetic mimesis a fatal blow to one of the seven heads. Hebrew texts are ambivalent in their attitude to this fabled monster. Some, like the present text and Job 3:8, emphasise its terrible, dark power. In others, like Isaiah 27:1 and Job 41:1ff., Leviathan, while still being beyond human imagination, is clearly one of God's creatures – and thus something natural rather than supernatural. But in Psalm 104:25f. we find this once terrifying nightmare reduced to the bathetic dimensions of a porpoise or a dolphin following a ship:

> Yonder is the sea, great and wide,
>> creeping things innumerable are there,
>> living things both small and great.
> There go the ships,
>> and Leviathan that you formed to sport in it.

How, then, are the mighty fallen! But even though nightmares may fade by day, in the context of this dramatic lament they are still very real, still unresolved, still dependent on the whim of what appears to be a most capricious God.

The remaining three themes – the long wait, the enemy at the door, and the unbearable mockery of those who desecrate the sanctuary, come together dramatically in verse 10, which is the very centre of the Psalm in the A–B–C–B–A structure deduced from the distribution of themes (Table 10.2). The complaining questions –

'Why?' 'How long?' – are of course quite characteristic of the lament as a genre, and are no different from the same question put by those who suffer in any age or place. It seems to the psalmist that things have been this way forever: no one can remember a time when life was good, and our enemies have complete freedom to deride our traditional beliefs and practices with impunity. This has an obvious personal resonance, though here its most immediate context is probably to be found in the institutions of Israel. The terrible thought expressed in verse 11, that God has somehow quite deliberately and pointedly withdrawn, is matched in verse 9 by a powerful evocation of the loss of every familiar resource. The loss of prophecy is explicit; that no one 'knows' how long points to the demise of the guild of sages and wise men; and if, as a number of scholars have proposed, the 'emblems' (which were replaced by enemy emblems in verse 4) are those of the priestly rituals of the temple, then the absence is complete: Priest, Prophet and (to reach for an alliteration) Professor have all gone. And in the gap they leave there is nothing but mockery. With this analysis a more detailed palinstrophic structure for the Psalm is given in Table 10.3:

We thus see that, although the Psalm is technically unresolved, in that it concludes with the noise and clamour of God's adversaries in uproar, the structure allows us some hope, based on the reversal of fortunes in the hymn in verses 12–17.

Table 10.3 Psalm 74's palinstrophic structure

Verse	Theme	
1a	Invocation: 'O God'	A1
1	Plaintive questions	A2
2–3	Cry for help	A3
4–8	Human enemies triumph	B
9	Failure of human institutions	C1
10	The enemy's mockery of God	C2
11	Failure of divine power	C1
12–17	God defeats cosmic enemies	B
18a	Plea for attention: 'Remember this, O LORD'	A1
18, 20, 22, 23	Reasons for God to act (answers to questions)	A2
19, 21	Plea for God's intervention	A3

Deconstructive readings

I offer only three suggestive readings in the face of a text as extensive and as complex as this one: the number seven; the winter/scoffing pun; and the uproar which formally concludes the text.

Seven is such a mystical number that even the suggestion of its presence (as in the hymnic section) tends to multiply meanings. In Hebrew, it provides the root which means 'to swear', 'to make an oath' – as though to say that sevenfold repetition is a magical and powerful thing. On the seventh day of the week the Israelites marched seven times around the walls of Jericho before they fell to the ground. Is there then an oath implied by the seven cries of 'You' – an oath which gives the reader hope that God will in due course take on and destroy the invincible enemy? Curiously, in verse 12 of Psalm 79 (a Psalm which is almost the twin of 74) we read:

> Return sevenfold into the bosom of our neighbours
>   the taunts with which they taunted you, O LORD!

These taunts are from the same root as that which provides the verb 'to scoff' in Psalm 74, and prompt a depressing and cynical interpretation of the latter: that not only do we face the violence of the invading enemy, but we have to put up with the cynical mockery of our neighbours. In that case, the cosmic enemy is none other than the man or woman next door – a truth we do well to attend to; for if we cannot live with each other, we have no chance of living with Leviathan.

The sense of continual mockery, of permanent warfare and dispute which imbues this Psalm makes it particularly difficult to reach for the inverse terms – peace and harmony. There is, however, one dramatic set of connections which leads in a surprising direction. Out of the death by sevenfold command of the seven-headed Leviathan comes the miracle of heaven and earth, sun and moon and stars, and the regular round of the seasons, culminating in 'summer and winter'. This combination is found only in one other place in the Hebrew Bible – in Genesis 8:22, God's promise to Noah after the flood:

> As long as the earth endures
>   seedtime and harvest, cold and heat,
> summer and winter, day and night,
>   shall not cease.

Creation out of the conflict with the primeval waters, and re-creation out of the conflict with the flood, issue in the same scenario. But where, in the flood story, is Leviathan? One of the oddities of that tale is the ambiguity about the number of each animal taken on board; for in Genesis 7:2 Noah is instructed to take 'clean' animals in by sevens, 'unclean' in pairs. Whatever is intended by 'clean' and 'unclean' this raises the fascinating possibility that Leviathan, inherently seven, is the very symbol of 'cleanness' – the hope of survival after the flood. But of course, creation is 'very good' (Genesis 1 *passim*) and is judged to be so by none other than God, the very God who defeated Leviathan, who created Leviathan, and who permits Leviathan to swim happily alongside the ships! Seven, on this reading, becomes the mystical key which converts our foes to friends, our nightmares to dreams, and the mockery of the wintry cynic to the kindliness of summer. Thus we discover the meaning in the pun: 'to scoff' may be an icy, unforgiving thing; but in the rich economy of God winter/scoffing is always mediated by summer. 'Now,' to quote another bard, 'is the winter of our discontent made glorious summer'.

The text ends with a scene of total confusion – the 'uproar' which 'goes up' continually, despite a fervent plea to God to 'rise up'. An upbeat ending, we might conclude, though not in the popular sense of that term. The 'continually', which is the last word, promises more, and loops back to the 'forever' of the opening line, thus condemning us to an endless cycle (as is the way with palinstrophic compositions). But not merely a cycle, for as we approach it again we read it differently. This is not a vicious circle, but a natural one – summer and winter, heat and cold, the benign and destructive forces of nature constantly taking our tacky sanctuaries apart, breaking them down in order to permit the new growth without which there would be nothing but stagnation. Without that clamour, that uproar, that continual rush of the universal spirit, we could not live; nor, indeed, could we die.

Personal afterword

I treasure particularly one little phrase in this Psalm: 'Do not deliver the soul of your *dove* to the wild animals'. Only here in the Hebrew Bible is this particular word used of Israel – its other occurrences are almost all in the context of sacrifice. This was a helpless creature more familiar with the priest's knife than the love of God. The commoner word for dove (*yonah*) has a wider range of meanings, including that dove which was sent out from the Ark by Noah, and the proper name of the strange prophet who got entangled with a big fish (Leviathan again?!).

The connection through the Latin word *Columba* with a whole swathe of Scottish religious tradition, and the happy accident that Iona would transliterate directly as *yonah*, makes the serendipity particularly pleasurable. The parallel of 'your dove' with 'your poor' in verse 19, and the fact that 'wild animals' and 'life' in that verse are the same in Hebrew, opens up a rich seam of suggestive interpretation which I will refrain from embarking upon, and leave it to readers to pursue (or not) as they will.

11

PSALM 82

	Choir	Genre	*Judgement motif*
		TEXTUAL NOTES	
1 God has taken his place in the divine council [*or* council of El]; in the midst of the gods he holds judgement:	Chorus	The Divine Council	The court convenes
2 'How long will you judge unjustly and show partiality to the wicked? *Selah*	Single voice	Lament	The charge is laid
3 Give justice to the weak and the orphan; maintain the right of the lowly and the destitute.		Prophetic oracle	Precedents are quoted
4 Rescue the weak and the needy; deliver them from the hand of the wicked.'			
5 They have neither knowledge nor understanding, they walk about in darkness; all the foundations of the earth are shaken.	Chorus	Wisdom Creation myth	Proof of guilt is adduced
6 I say [*or* It was I who said], 'You are gods, children of the Most High, all of you;	Single voice	Judgement oracle	Judgement is passed
7 nevertheless you shall die like mortals, and fall like any prince.'			
8 Rise up, O God, judge the earth; for all the nations belong to you! [*or* that you may take up your inheritance in every nation]	Chorus	Petition	The court rises

159

The text

The opening line of this Psalm is somewhat peculiar in Hebrew, since precisely the same term is used for 'God' and 'the gods'. Literally it reads:

> 'elohim has taken his place in the council of 'el;
> in the midst of 'elohim he holds judgement.

Granted that Hebrew regularly uses the grammatically plural form 'elohim to refer both to the God of Israel in general terms and to any collectivity of deities, it is still odd to find both uses in the same sentence. A possible explanation may lie in the fact that Psalm 82 belongs to what has been called the 'Elohistic Psalter' (Psalms 42–89) – that part of the collection where the divine name Yahweh is used comparatively rarely. That being so, perhaps the first 'elohim is a substitute for Yahweh; this would fit well with the divine name 'el, familiar as the head of the Canaanite pantheon, but also used as a generic title in Hebrew. We might then postulate a dramatic encounter between Yahweh and the rest of the gods, held under the aegis of El, and translate verse 1 as follows:

> Yahweh has taken his place in the council of El;
> in the midst of the gods he holds judgement.

In the amended text of Psalm 82 I have restricted myself to replacing 'divine council' with the more literal 'council of El'; the further proposal regarding Yahweh is too speculative to merit formal recognition, interesting though it may be on other grounds.

In verse 6 the NRSV misses both the past tense of the verb and the presence of the emphatic personal pronoun 'I'; the amended form takes account of these linguistic points, and defines (I believe) a stronger contrast between the past tense of verse 6 and the future threat in verse 7.

The proposed amendment in verse 8b appears more drastic. It follows principally from an anomaly in the Hebrew text. The verb concerned – 'to inherit, to take possession of' – normally takes a direct object. There are just five instances in the Hebrew Bible where it is followed by the preposition 'in', and in each of the others the translation given reflects this. Thus, for example, Numbers 18:20: 'Then the LORD said to Aaron: You shall have no allotment in their land.' It seems therefore logical to retain this linguistic feature in verse 8. The other aspect of the amendment concerns the relationship between the imperative 'Rise up', the conjunction 'for' (which in Hebrew also means 'that') and the future form of the verb 'to inherit'. This combination is rather rare in the Psalms. Apart from the present example, it is found in 5:2; in 42:5, 42:11 and 43:5 (three instances of exactly the same refrain); and in 86:3, 4. In each of these a translation of the form 'that X may Y' is both grammatically and semantically possible; I propose it in Psalm 82 because it offers an outcome of the process of judgement – something happens as a result of God's judging the earth which has real force for the psalmist's implied complaint. I return to this in due course when discussing the contextual interpretation of the Psalm.

Comparative material from the ancient Near East

The scenario of the divine council with the gods present in force, overseen by El, has already been discussed in Chapter 5 in relation to Psalm 29. Other comparable texts of some interest may be identified in a prayer to the Moon God and in two passages in the Ugaritic legend of Keret. The first of these sets a scene strikingly similar to that in verse 1:

O Anu of heaven whose designs no one can conceive,
Surpassing is thy light like Shamash thy first-born.
Bowed down in thy presence are the great gods; the decisions of
    the land are laid before thee;
When the great gods inquire of thee thou dost give counsel.
They sit in their assembly and debate under thee.

(*ANET*: 386b)

The interest of the first Keret reference (see Gibson 1977: 91) lies in the occurrence there of a phrase, 'the company of the gods', which uses a close cognate of the Hebrew word for 'council' in verse 1. The coincidence is the more curious because the phrase 'council of El' is unique in the Hebrew Bible to Psalm 82.

Finally, the second Keret passage contains a piece of 'prophetic' rhetoric remarkably similar to that of verses 2–4 of the Psalm. King Keret is being addressed:

You have been brought down by your failing power.
You do not judge the cause of the widow,
    you do not try the case of the importunate.

161

You do not banish the extortioners of the poor,
you do not feed the orphan before your face
nor the widow behind your back.
(Gibson 1977: 102)

History, liturgy, social context

This is certainly not in any sense a historical Psalm, nor one which readily conveys any sense of social conventions or norms. The setting of the law court is a stereotype of prophetic literature; that it matches any cultural reality is doubtful, given that under this literary convention God acts as judge, prosecuting counsel and jury: there seems to be no defence! Equally, the demand for proper care for the weak, for orphans and so on, is a stock-in-trade of prophetic oracles, a substitute for any deeper social analysis. That there were in ancient Judah orphans, widows, poor people and those who suffered injustice can scarcely be doubted; this hardly constitutes, however, a useful social insight.

There remains the question of a liturgical context. This is problematic: the Psalm does not at first sight strike the reader as particularly suited to any ritual setting, having more of the character of a speculative theological piece on the problem of evil. Yet there are hints. There are two passages of direct speech, and the Psalm concludes with a prayer or petition, raising the possibility of contrapuntal performance: chorus (verse 1), single voice (verses 2–4), chorus (verse 5), single voice (verses 6–7), chorus (verse 8). Moreover, the setting of the 'assembly of the holy ones' recurs in Psalm 89:5–7, the royal hymn of celebration which concludes Book III. Thus in the wider context of the collection as a whole we may be justified in proposing a liturgical interpretation.

Discussions about the date of the Psalm (leaving aside the presumption made in Chapter 11 that Book III belongs to the exilic or early post-exilic period) have tended to focus on the drama of the divine council and the demotion of the gods. On grounds of content, this theme has encouraged some to take the view that we have here an archaic, primarily Canaanite, composition. This, however, is a very weak argument, given that 1 Kings is certainly at the earliest a sixth-century composition, and that we have a very similar narrative of the demotion of a divine figure in Ezekiel 28:2. It is much more likely that we have here the lively survival of mythic language, which may or may not have had continuing force as a world-view in post-exilic Jerusalem, similar indeed to the world-view lying behind the curious story in Genesis 6:1–4 of the sons of the gods bedding the daughters of humankind.[1] Thus we cannot derive any dating information from this aspect of the Psalm. Indeed, its eclectic literary type (see under Structure) might point precisely in the opposite chronological direction.

Structure[2]

In the text of the Psalm (diplayed on p. 159) I have attempted to set out three structural features which provide organisational frameworks for Psalm 82. Since they are quite different in substance it is not clear whether they cohere or simply offer three alternative perspectives from which to view the piece. Each has its own dramatic force: the contrapuntal choral performance relating to the style of the composition; the range of genres testifying to the literary skill – even agility – of the poet; and the judgement motif providing the narrative drive. Further analysis of these will be provided in the next section.

In addition to these internal structures, it is useful to highlight two verbal threads which are closely related to the theme of the Psalm – the naming of God and the gods (three times in verse 1 and three times in verses 6–8) and the use of words to do with justice and judgement (verses 1, 2, 3 and 8). Each of these serves to 'bracket' the Psalm, providing a secure context within which the writer employs his or her freedom to explore a range of literary genres. Without this stable framework the diverse genres might seem merely arbitrary, a display of dilettante rather than sagacious virtuosity; but with them we are drawn at the end to the realisation of a deeply satisfying conclusion (perhaps even a deceptively satisfying conclusion – but I shall return to that point).

Contextual interpretations

The theme of the divine council is employed to dramatic effect in a number of places in the Hebrew Bible. Perhaps the two most familiar are 1 Kings 22, where the prophet Micaiah reports a vision of God consulting with his council to plan ways of misleading the kings of Israel and Judah, and the prologue to the Book of Job, where again God is found invoking the aid of another supernatural being to cause trouble for humanity. It is therefore interesting that in Psalm 82 the purpose of calling the council is to pass judgement on these same deities for their failure to deal justly with the human beings for whom they are responsible. This represents a development of the old Canaanite idea of the pantheon in the direction of ethical and moral questions. Of course there are profoundly ethical issues bound up in Job and 1 Kings 22, but they do not relate to the dissolution of the divine council itself. A parallel to this feature of Psalm 82 may be found in Ezekiel 28:1–10, where the king of Tyre is denounced in words bearing a remarkable similarity to verses 6–7 (Ezekiel 28:2, 6–9):

> Mortal, say to the prince of Tyre, Thus says the LORD God:
>   'Because your heart is proud
>   and you have said, "I am a god;
> I sit in the seat of the gods,
>   in the heart of the seas,"
> yet you are but a mortal, and no god,
>   though you compare your mind with the mind of a god. . . . '
> Therefore thus says the LORD God:
> 'Because you compare your mind with the mind of a god,
> therefore, I will bring strangers against you,
>   the most terrible of the nations. . . .
> They shall thrust you down to the Pit,
>   and you shall die a violent death
>   in the heart of the seas.
> Will you still say, "I am a god,"
>   in the presence of those who kill you,
> though you are but a mortal and no god,
>   in the hands of those who wound you?'

The reference to the seas, in verses 2 and 8 of the above passage, together with the occurrence of the name *Danel*,[3] familiar from one of the Ugaritic epics, suggests that we have here, in a relatively late composition, the survival of a number of Canaanite themes. In both Psalm 82 and Ezekiel 28 the likely interpretation seems to lie in the context of a theology of the God of the nations (Yahweh) in conclusive conflict with the old 'gods of the nations', a line of inquiry which I now develop in relation to the third structural frame – the judgement motif.

This clearly constitutes, at first sight, the predominant theme of the Psalm, running through the whole piece. But here is no normal judiciary process, for the appellants are not human, nor is the judge, and the crime, ultimately, is that of stupidity! For, although the statement of the charge against the accused (verse 2) and the precedents quoted (verses 3–4) fall within a rather predictable range of social misdemeanours, when we come to the statement of guilt in verse 5 it amounts to a charge of blundering incompetence rather than malign criminality. The opening declaration, 'They have neither knowledge nor understanding', is a classic Wisdom formulation – the words 'to know' and 'to understand' are prevalent in Wisdom literature both as a pair and independently. Likewise the following phrase, 'they walk around in darkness', finds its closest parallels in Proverbs 2:13 and in Ecclesiastes 2:14 and 6:4. There is surely satirical force here. The reader would naturally think of the gods as beings with supernatural powers and knowledge; but the psalmist portrays them as ignorant fools, blundering about in their ignorance, threatening to undermine the fabric of the universe which (as we will recall from Psalm 24) is held together by the power of Yahweh.

We may draw two broad conclusions from this piece of burlesque. The first is that God is in effect charging 'the gods' (whoever they are – and that is a point to which I must return) of deliberate abdication of their responsibilities. If gods are ignorant, that ignorance is wilful, and results in both natural and moral disasters: the stability of the earth is threatened and the inhabitants of the earth suffer injustice. It is not out of place to point to the contrast in both these respects to the themes of Psalm 24, where a powerful, aware deity holds the earth under control, and confers righteousness upon those who are morally upright. This, if you like, constitutes a moral warning to the congregation: abandon morality and knowledge of God and the consequences will be apocalyptic. The second conclusion turns in quite different direction: it is that the psalmist is here affirming the absolute superiority of Yahweh over any other gods whatever, be they the older gods of Canaan or the rival deities of other nations and peoples. We are reminded now of the rhetoric of Deutero-Isaiah, where on the one hand Yahweh is affirmed as the one God of all nations (thus, for example, Isaiah 40:10–26) and on the other the 'gods' are mocked as mere idols, vain constructs of human skill and ingenuity. Isaiah 45:20 is a good example:

Assemble yourselves and come together,
    draw near, you survivors of the nations!
They have no knowledge –
    those who carry about their wooden idols,
and keep on praying to a god
    that cannot save.

So too is the famous satire of the carpenter who cuts down a tree, and uses part of it to carve an idol and part to build a fire to cook his food and to keep himself warm (Isaiah 44:13–20). If the general context of Psalm 82 is that of a response to the exile and the loss of Jerusalem, this is a bold claim: to argue for the supremacy of Yahweh at a point in time when Yahweh's temple and city were in ruins indicates a brave new world indeed.

The punishment to be meted out to the gods (verses 6–7) is thus both poetic and politic. Poetic, in that it is fitting that those who are ignorant and morally blind forfeit any claim to immortality or divine power. Politic in that it prepares the way for the triumphalist note of verse 8: the God of Judah has now become the God of *all* people, claiming an inheritance in every nation (and here my preference for a petitional form in verse 8b has point: 'that you may take up your inheritance in every nation'). The alternative reading of verse 6 – 'It was I who said . . . ' – gives the punishment still sharper force. Lest it should be argued that these rival or older gods can scarcely be dismissed by Yahweh's fiat, the poet insists that even in the past they held divine status only with Yahweh's consent, on God's say-so. The one who once said 'you are gods' can certainly now say 'but no longer!'

Returning to the question of the identity of these 'gods' in the mind of the psalmist or of his or her likely audience, there are a number of possibilities. I have already suggested that there could have been a continuing lively belief in the older Canaanite pantheon, which would naturally link up with knowledge of the gods of Egypt, Babylon, etc. In other words, whatever the status of monotheism in Judah at the time (and this is by no means a straightforward matter), people were probably familiar with the notion of pluralities of gods. For readers of this kind Psalm 82 must have had an immediate mythic effect as a proclamation of the defeat of those gods by the God of Judah. Others, as the rhetoric of Deutero-Isaiah implies, must have treated the 'gods' as vain or meaningless idols, the residue of a superstitious past which (because of its effects on the naive and the weak-minded) still required to be denounced. For them, this is a Psalm which uses dramatic language to make a rational point: there are no other gods; to believe otherwise is to indulge ignorance.

I wish to propose two other interpretations which seem also to be plausible within the exilic or post-exilic context. The first is hinted at by Deuteronomy 32:8–9, in the reading now favoured by most modern versions:

When the Most High apportioned the nations,
  when he divided humankind,
he fixed the boundaries of the peoples
  according to the number of the gods;[4]
the LORD's own portion was his people,
  Jacob his allotted share.

This seems to imply the notion of a semi-divine tutelary being (the Septuagint has 'angels') responsible for each nation, with Yahweh having overall charge. Somewhat similar ideas are indicated in Isaiah 24:21–2 (which also speaks of the punishment of these beings):

On that day the LORD will punish
  the host of heaven in heaven,
  and on earth the kings of the earth.
They will be gathered together
  like prisoners in a pit;
they will be shut up in a prison,
  and after many days they will be punished.

Again, in Ezekiel 28:14 we read (with reference to Tyre): 'With an anointed cherub as guardian I placed you.' It is worth noting that both Psalm 82 and the Deuteronomic passage link the reference to the gods with the title 'Most High', while Isaiah associates earthly kings and punishment with the fall of the gods, just as in the Psalm. While the precise dating of these various passages is unclear, there does seem to be a broadly post-exilic setting for them. It might follow, then, that a contextual reading of this Psalm would see it as a response to the ill-treatment of Judah by other nations, with the hope or prayer that in due course God would exercise judgement over them (a theme not unlike that of Psalm 137, though expressed in rather less bloodthirsty tones). The fall of the gods, in this reading, is a metaphor for the defeat of the nations – or, more precisely (and benignly), the defeat of their failed rulers, the coming of Yahweh's universal rule and the establishment of the eschatological kingdom of God. Here the alternative reading of verse 8 comes into its own, and brings the theme of the Psalm at its end into the same vision as that of Isaiah 2:2–4.

The second interpretation has a more contemporary character in that it would see the gods as symbols of the powers of evil in the world. The Psalm in that case would constitute a study in theodicy, the problem of reconciling the justice and goodness of God with the undoubted existence of evil[5] and suffering in the world. The solution offered is perhaps primitive, in that it seems to suppose the existence of demonic (or supernatural) powers which exercise a certain freedom to do mischief under the aegis of God. We may take this as either a limited scope for wickedness or a limited term upon their freedom of action; whichever we adopt, the device clearly does not solve the problem of evil, but does serve to defer it by attributing suffering neither to arbitrary forces of nature nor directly to God, but instead to the malign activities of more or less uncontrollable evil spirits.

In the Hellenistic and Roman period this sort of mythology had considerable popularity. The world was infested by a complex array of angels and demons, and both Judaism and Christianity were of their age in accepting this world-view unquestioningly. Whatever the explanation for this development, whether it be an indigenous extension of the role of the mysterious forces of the underworld, a debasement of the idea of the gods (thus Genesis 6:1–4), an importation of the dualism of Persian religion, or the effect of an uneducated understanding of the daimonic intermediaries of middle-Platonism, it is clearly represented in popular religion of the time and is arguably built into Christianity's dualistic understanding of the struggle between God and Satan. There is much here for further thought, but not within the compass of the present study. However, it does bear on the conclusion of the Psalm, which I described above as being 'deceptively satisfying'. If the Psalm encourages us to believe that Yahweh has defeated the gods, the forces of evil, who is responsible for the evil which continues? This is equally the problem of Christian theodicy. Christ's supposed annihilation of evil on the cross presents Christianity with the same dilemma: what is the status of a victory which leaves the enemy in control of the territory? Once again, the alternative reading of verse 8 provides something of an exclusion clause: since it forms a prayer rather than a statement, we may suppose that the psalmist anticipates a future settlement and not a present achievement.

Finally, what can we conclude about the use of this Psalm from the structures illustrated in the text (p. 159)? Interestingly, although there is a certain narrative drive to the drama of the judgement motif, there is also a palinstrophic pattern both to the choral structure and to the way that the words of the conclusion actually predicate a renewed situation of judgement. Thus, though God in the beginning takes God's place in the council (i.e. stands up in judgement), at the end the deity is once more called upon to rise up in judgement. Looking at the text from the perspective of the seemingly random use of genres, a similar structuring can be discerned, though this time verse 1 constitutes the introduction. The centre of the Psalm is the Wisdom-like passage on the ignorance of the gods, on either side of which there is oracle, flanked in turn by two elements from the language of the lament. These lend themselves to the thought of a public and dramatic liturgy, which in turn accords with earlier proposals by Mowinckel (1962) and Weiser (1962) to include this Psalm in their Enthronement or Covenant Festivals.

Deconstructive readings

Any text which presumes to deal with the issues of divine power and human suffering in conjunction with notions of justice is pretty well bound to deconstruct itself without further help from the reader! The *aporia* of the opening scene, where the same word is used in Hebrew for 'God' and 'the gods', while we are supposed to see them as opposing sides in an encounter, undermines with precision the whole thesis which is so often taken to be the Psalm's point. We cannot, in truth, distinguish between deities who mean us harm and those who love us, for the results are the same. Evil powers often tempt us with attractive propositions, while moral gods inflict upon us the most horrendous tortures for our own good. It follows that we should desire, not the death of false gods, but the death of all gods – and once again this is what the deconstructed Psalm delivers. For the 'God' who speaks the words of verse 6 is lexically indistinguishable from the 'gods' who are condemned. This is not a punishment – it is a suicide note. Nietzsche was right, then: God is dead, by god's own decree.

But what do we make then of verse 8, in which God rises from the dead to judge the earth? It speaks, of course, to the persistence of the belief in God, which survives and transcends every rational and humanistic argument for its demise. It may also testify to the ultimate inadequacy of rational argument when we come face to face with the imponderables of the universe. If our language systems and our logic cannot contend with love, good, evil, suffering and justice without discarding the hypothesis of god, might it not be that it is our systems which are lacking? Deconstruction is at pains to remind us of the hopelessness of language to deal with ultimate reality; this Psalm's deconstruction of its own deconstruction of god is, surely, a nice example of that 'truth'.

Of course this Psalm is couched in mythic language, which apparently does not need not to answer to the demands of rationality.

Nevertheless, 'myth' is in origin 'what is spoken' (the Greek *muthos* and its related verb mean respectively 'that which is spoken' and 'to speak'), and so even myth cannot avoid the problematic of words. We do not absorb the truth of myths by some mysterious non-verbal process. However, since myths work by encouraging us to suspend our capacity for reason, we may conclude that this is the special function of the genre. But this is a deconstructive function, and therefore when myths communicate paradox they do so knowingly.

There is a neat example of this situation in verse 5, where the anonymous voice proclaims that the 'gods' are ignorant and blind, blundering about in the cellars of the universe, endangering the whole delicate balance of things. A myth, to be sure, and a myth about knowledge. Therefore we might expect it to be irrational – and certainly it is, as the very next verse reveals. For what do we find there but the omnipotent God who used to think these ignoramuses were gods! What kind of 'God' is this who cannot tell the difference between fools and deities? Is this a God who learns from his/her mistakes? But can we tolerate belief in a God about whom we cannot even be sure that he/she has reached full maturity? It gets worse, for verse 6 proceeds to inform us that these same blundering demiurges were 'children of the *Most High*', who is usually identified with God in the Hebrew Bible. Human parents can perhaps be excused some of their children's misbehaviour, but it is somewhat disconcerting to learn that God Most High has the same domestic problems, and deals with them as callously as the most heartless of human parents: 'you shall die like mortals, and fall like any prince'.

Some of these tentative explorations of the inner recesses of this text may seem far-fetched, and some may be disturbing. Before the reader rejects them out of hand, however, may I recall him or her to the orthodox premise of this Psalm? It is that a great God passes judgement upon the incompetence of lesser gods, who are held to be to blame for the world's ills and the sufferings of the weak and the orphans, and in so doing affirms that God's supremacy over the whole world. We are, presumably, expected to rejoice over these cosmic deeds, and sleep easier at night as a result. Is that, in the end, any more plausible than the deconstruction?

Personal afterword

I like this Psalm. It has chutzpah. It dares to use the polytheist language of Canaan to undermine polytheism. It risks the reputation of Yahweh in a bold attempt to solve the problem of evil. It paints

170

a marvellously comic picture of the gods lost in the basement of the universe, like incompetent DIY enthusiasts unable to find a spare lightbulb to dispel the gloom of their ignorance (and too embarrassed to call in the real expert). Perhaps, after all, its power lies in the unlikely conjunction of humour and grandeur which by a neat sleight of hand has us mocking the gods and honouring God in almost the same breath, without noticing the paradox.

Part III

YAHWEH COMES HOME TO ZION

The Psalms of Ascents (120–34)

12

THE PSALMS OF ASCENTS AS
A UNIT

Rationale

So far this study of the Psalms has been concentrated on the reading of individual poems, though we have not entirely ignored the existence of groupings which (sharing the same heading, linguistic style or themes) clearly in some substantial sense belong together. If the study is to provide an approach to reading which deals with the collection as we find it, the existence of groups of psalms is a matter which requires its own treatment. It was observed in Chapter 5 that, while in recent years some work has been done on these groups, by far the dominant approach has been to analyse individual psalms using a broadly form-critical paradigm, often accompanied by the assumption that one of the 'recovered festivals' can serve as an explanatory device.

The collection – Book V of the Psalter – known as the 'Psalms of Ascents' presents a particularly interesting case for the kind of approach I have tried to elucidate in Parts I and II. Traditionally these Psalms have posed something of a problem, not least because of the highly distinctive Psalm 132 which departs from the overall style of the group and seems to belong to a different – archaic – age. Perhaps as a consequence the attempt to apply genre analysis to these Psalms leads to a quite fragmented reading, and fails to offer any explanation of the Psalter's positioning of Psalm 132 at this point. It is explained simply as an ancient dramatic ritual piece, to be associated with the Ark narratives in 1 and 2 Samuel, without an understanding of how it came to wander so far from its presumed origins. At least Psalm 29 (held to be similarly archaic) is found at a more appropriate point in the Psalter.

Some work has been done on the group as a whole: for example, the book-length study by Keet (1969), the article by Liebreich (1955) which suggests a connection with the Aaronic blessing in Numbers, and the work by Auffret (1982: 439–531) which proposes a detailed and elaborate structuralist account of the linguistic patterns in the collection, as part of a wider study of the Psalter and, indeed, of the Old Testament itself. None of these has really had much effect on the standard exegetical work, which (if the commentaries are a reliable guide) remains very traditional. Two sources discuss the literary coherence of the collection: Beaucamp (1979), and an important recent study by Crow (1996). My own work, carried out independently of Crow, uses similar tools but reaches different conclusions. Crow, for all his application of substantial literary analysis, has in the end opted for a redactional explanation which retains older hypotheses. What I hope to do is to free these Psalms to speak for themselves – to read them, in short, within their own frame. The broad pattern of my approach will be first to look at the evidence for their coherence as a group, then to give (Chapter 13) a brief discussion of each psalm under aspects 1, 2 and 4 of the traditional elements set out in Chapter 5. Next I look at the collection as a whole (Chapter 14), tying together the evidence thus far and proposing a context and an interpretation of the Psalms of Ascents which use both historical and structural indicators (aspects 3 and 5). The final chapter addresses the matter of deconstructive readings, both of the Psalms of Ascents and of the Psalter in its entirety, and serves as a conclusion to the book as a whole.

Introductory remarks

The titular coherence of the collection commonly known as the Psalms of Ascents (120–34) is impressive. The word *ma'alot* used to describe them, whatever it means, is in the Psalter unique to these fifteen Psalms. The most likely meanings of the term have been thoroughly canvassed by the standard commentaries, and there is an excellent summary in Crow (1996: 1–27). Mowinckel (1962, I: 3) claims that 'the special "festival Psalms", 120–134, were sung at the water-pouring rite on "the great day of the festival" [Tabernacles], i.e. the eighth day of celebration'. Elsewhere he reports a mishnaic tradition 'that at the feast of tabernacles . . . the singers used to stand on the fifteen steps leading from the court of the people to that of the women, and sing the fifteen "festal songs" . . . while two priests blew on horns from the gate behind them' (1962, II: 82f.; see *Mishnah Middoth* 2:5). Dahood (1970: 195), noting the frequent occurrence of step-parallelism, speculated that the title constituted a technical literary term. Many have understood *ma'alot* to denote some element of pilgrimage, either of the exiles back to Judah, or of worshippers going up to a festival in Jerusalem. The former of these, based on the KJV reading of 126:1, is less favoured today. Finally, in a text from Qumran, which reads[1] 'Your praise is pleasing, O Zion; it rises up in all the world' (*Apostrophe to Zion*), the word *ma'alah* indicates the ascents of praise to Zion. Possibly, then, the ascription of the term to this group of Psalms simply indicates that they were composed in praise of Zion. Undoubtedly Zion is a major focus; but it is not the only theme, nor do the individual Psalms fall unequivocally into the genre of hymn, so that this must be deemed to be an unlikely explanation.

The broad consensus is that this group of Psalms must have had some locus in a festival, possibly with an element of pilgrimage. And in that context it is necessary to remark upon the unique character of Psalm 132. Strikingly distinctive within the collection as a whole, it appears to be connected with a ceremonial of the Ark and readily yields the kind of dramatic liturgy which seems also to be implied by 2 Samuel 6:1–19. It is difficult to avoid the conclusion that the central meaning of the festival in question relates to the claims of the 'Davidic'[2] dynasty to have a special relationship with both Jerusalem and Yahweh, symbolised by the residence of the Ark in the temple.[3] It is not my intention to deny these natural implications; what I seek to do is to demonstrate the internal coherence of these Psalms (lexicographically, syntactically and thematically) and identify an appropriate context for such a festival.

The first of these objects is necessary because too often scholars, while admitting the factors which connect the Psalms of Ascents, have continued to cling to what is arguably an inappropriate quest for the individual *Sitz-im-Leben* of each psalm – a quest rooted in several fundamental (but by no means obvious or trivial) assumptions. These are, first, that the majority of the psalms are pre-exilic in origin; second, that some sort of oral tradition lies behind them (whether as memorised liturgies or popular hymns); and, third, that they have a liturgical function in the setting of the supposed royal cultus of the house of David in Jerusalem. Because the priority of orality over conscious literary device is scarcely questioned, it is assumed that form-critical methods will produce a reliable account of each Psalm in its liturgical context. Hence questions of literary device, of conscious pastiche, and of primary composition for reading rather than performance are rarely discussed; still less the possibility of 'through-composition' of groups of psalms. In part the dominance of this approach is a tribute to the innovative work of Gunkel and Mowinckel; but its continuation is less easy to explain. Historians for some time now have been undecided about the character of the Davidic and Solomonic 'empire' and its associated religious rituals. Whether it is in the extreme scepticism which questions the very existence of David and Solomon, as in the moderate doubt expressed about the extent of their rule and the probable Canaanite character of early Israel, we encounter serious reservations about the kind of religious cultus presupposed by work on the 'lost festivals'. And, perhaps more seriously, there is a problematic failure to explain how such a mass of liturgical material could have survived the destruction of the temple and its services in 587 BCE. Written records would most certainly have been destroyed in the conflagration; certainly none have survived. And if they were oral traditions who would have remembered them, and why? Indeed, Psalm 137 appears to express the contrary! On the other hand, with the appearance of the exilic and post-exilic voices of Lamentations, the Deuteronomists and the Chronicler, we find a context in which a written tradition can be comfortably placed and explained.[4]

There is no intention to deny any pre-exilic content, or to rule out oral traditions, although it must be said that little has been produced by way of evidence in favour of orality. Culley's 1967 study of the subject, based on the theories of Parry as described in Lord (1960), was rather inconclusive[5] – perhaps not surprising given that their work was carried out on major epic compositions (the *Iliad* and *Odyssey*, and the Yugoslavian oral tradition of the early twentieth century). No alternative theory which has been tested on other literature has, as far as I am aware, been proposed in respect of the Psalms. There remains therefore reasonable doubt about the propriety of oral composition theories in respect of the Psalms. At the very least, orality ought not to be assumed without further argument.

My counter-proposal is that at various times (probably not earlier than the so-called Second Temple period[6]) skilful work was carried out with the overt intention of producing a liturgical collection appropriate to the claims of the leading groups in Jerusalem. This is not incompatible with the theory that interested individuals collected surviving fragments of religious poetry from the cult of monarchic Jerusalem with the intention of providing a book for meditative purposes:[7] if Christian hymnography is an appropriate analogy, the two functions can cohere. The stylised first-person address characteristic of many of the psalms is well-suited to this double use, and agrees with many other examples in the Hebrew Bible of individuals giving vent to joy, sorrow, fear and passion in first-person terms.

It is often said that the individual consciousness in ancient Israel was subordinate to 'the collective identity'. Whatever the utility of that commonplace of Old Testament scholarship, we can surely agree that for first-person language to be effective there must be a real sense of individuality; this is as true of the ancient world as it is of our own. Conversely, modern readers are surely just as capable of perceiving the collective implication of seemingly personal statements as any Judean. The implication of these comments is that, in ancient Israel just as much as in modern literature, writers are aware (at some level) of writing within broad and well-established genres. The wider evidence of the ancient Near East makes it abundantly clear that from considerable antiquity 'psalms', together with most of the poetic conventions they display, were an established part of the literary world. It is hardly to be doubted, then, that where Jewish poets work within this wider context (as post-exilic poets surely did) they will contrive apparent circumstances for their compositions which reflect reality but which are not intended to be historically precise or biographically accurate.

It follows that the search for a *Sitz-im-Leben* is often in reality a quest for a literary invention or convention which, while reflecting a social reality, is not produced by it. It further means that the *appearance* of antiquity cannot be taken as a conclusive argument for dating without further discussion,[8] since there exist examples of archaising texts both in the Hebrew Bible and elsewhere.[9] Thus when we make our objective the recovery of a realistic *Sitz-im-Leben*, we run the risk of ignoring information which does not fit that approach. In the case under investigation, the widespread conviction that Psalm 132 is an early poetic liturgy closely related to the Ark narrative (1 Samuel 4–6; 2 Samuel 6) is difficult to reconcile with indications of lateness in the collection of Psalms of Ascents as a whole. This in turn prompts the 'discovery' of historical references in others of the collection. Psalm 126 may be claimed for the Ezra–Nehemiah period, for instance; 122 could be pre-exilic; and so on – all of which subtly pre-empts the discussion by assuming that the collection was brought together eclectically rather than composed as a whole. Even those, like Beaucamp, who see the force of maintaining unitary composition, are forced by these historical conventions to place the collection (improbably) in the pre-exilic monarchic period.

A major part of this chapter will be devoted to a survey of the evidence supporting the proposal that the Psalms of Ascents, far from having been fifteen originally disparate pieces put together as a collection for a later purpose, have considerable internal coherence in terms of the vocabulary used, the style of writing and the themes taken up. Moreover, these features mark them out as distinctive within the Psalter, thus increasing the likelihood that we have here a specific group in terms of composition as well as designation. It is interesting that Goulder has made similar claims in his studies for (1982, 1990, 1996) the Psalms of Korah, David and Asaph.[10]

It seems increasingly likely that the form-critical approach initiated by Gunkel, and followed (dare one say, slavishly?) in commentary after commentary, stands in need of radical modification. For its essence lies in an identification of each psalm individually in accordance with speculative types (laments, praise, thanksgiving, etc.), the criteria for which may well be secondary rather than primary defining characteristics of the Psalm in question. If the Psalms of Korah truly represent a special composition, then the primary *Sitz-im-Leben* is surely to be found in whatever they have in common, whatever moved the writer(s) to produce the collection. That they may have used here a lament form (e.g. 42–3), there one of praise (e.g. 46, 47, 48), does not address the spirit of Gunkel's enterprise,[11] in which the identification of genre was only part of a much more comprehensive project. Sadly, the assumption of cultic origins within pre-exilic Jerusalem has become the starting-point rather than the conclusion of most Psalms' study, and the specifying of cultic genre merely a confirmation of that presupposition. Thus even Michael Goulder, one of the pioneers of the study of groups of psalms, retains his belief in historically identifiable pre-exilic contexts for the four collections he has analysed.

Following linguistic analysis and some discussion of the individual members of the group, I approach the problem of the coherence of the group (Chapter 14), and attempt to offer a possible account of its unified function. It is not my purpose to reject cultic or festival explanations; simply to set them in proper context and to apply a different set of priorities. By this I mean, for example, that if I can demonstrate the unity of the collection, and if I can show that it is probably later, then the question of Psalm 132 will be addressed in the light of that evidence, and not from an *a priori* acceptance of historical context in the pre-exilic Davidic traditions.

Pre- or post-exilic? Preliminary notes on the dating of the Psalms of Ascents

While we cannot resolve the question of dating at this stage in the discussion, if at all, there are some points worth making in relation to the general editorial character of these Psalms. Much the most stimulating study in this field is attributable to Wilson (1985). What emerges clearly from his work is a radical distinction between the formation of Books I–III and Books IV and V, in part supported by the much more volatile state of the latter two, and especially Book V, in the Psalms' scrolls from the Dead Sea. Wilson wrote (1985: 121) regarding the latter:

> While evidence in support of the MT [Masoretic Text] arrangement of Psalms is fairly consistent throughout, examples of variation, practically non-existent in the first three books, increase markedly in Books Four and Five. While this evidence does not 'prove' Sanders's thesis, it is certainly suggestive, especially when combined with an analysis of the information in relation to the relative age of the Mss in which it occurs. . . . There is a direct correlation between date and support or contradiction of the MT arrangement, with contradictory Mss occupying the earliest position and totally supportive Mss only appearing much later. . . . The impression gained from this analysis is of a certain looseness in Psalms arrangement which continued until ca. AD 50 and apparently died out soon thereafter.

In an article published a year later (1986: 87) he is more confident:

> This difference in organizational technique between the earlier and later books points to the possibility of a separate redactional history for these two segments and the editorial process which lies behind them. The growing evidence for the distinct character of these two segments leaves little or no doubt of this conclusion. To sum up: 1. Organizational technique is distinctly different. 2. The use of *hhllwyh* and *hwdw* Psalms is restricted to the last two books. 3. The organizational use of author designations and genre categories is limited to Books One through Three. 4. The marked concentration of 'titled' Psalms in the first three books stands in direct contrast to the relative paucity of such Psalms (28 out of 61) in the final books.

THE PSALMS OF ASCENTS

A reiteration of this belief is given in McCann (1993: 42). While we cannot claim certainty, I believe that Wilson has established a powerful case for dating the redaction of Books IV and V to the post-exilic period. If (as seems plausible) Book III reflects the production of lament material in the exilic period – the connections with Lamentations have been often noted – we really cannot identify the beginnings of work on Books IV and V prior to 500 BCE. Finally, the evidence from the Dead Sea suggests that Book V was subject to much greater variation even than Book IV; one obvious explanation for this might be that as Book IV reached some form of closure, later materials were added in a supplement. The fact that the 'stray' Psalms in the 'Qumran' Book IV are those now numbered 146, 147 and 148 raises the possibility that by the end of the redactional process these had been removed from Book IV and adapted to form the concluding 'doxology' to the whole Psalter (thus Wilson, who regards 'Psalms 146–150 as a conclusion to the fifth book and the whole Psalter'[12]).

These observations point to an interesting hypothesis. The Psalms of Ascents, whatever their origins, were not collected until the latest stage of psalms' formation. The Dead Sea evidence suggests a contemporary fluidity rather than a fixed alternative order and content. Thus, assuming that these sources provide information relating to the third century BCE at the earliest, and more probably to the second, we come very close to an old hypothesis, discredited for much of the twentieth century,[13] which might be due for a return: a Maccabean or Hasmonean context for at least some of the compositions in Book V. I return to this speculation at the end of Chapter 14.

The language and structure of the Psalms of Ascents

Idiomatic phrases

Loren Crow provides two useful tables, one of 'unusual linguistic features in the Songs of Ascents', and the other of six 'repeated formulae in the Songs of Ascents' (1996: 148f. and 131). In line with the remit of this book to deal with the English text, I will not comment on the first of these, since it depends on the Hebrew text.[14] However, the phrases given in the second table are equally clear in English, and represent in many cases forms either unique to the Psalms of Ascents or confined to the Psalter. Table 12.1 shows the distribution of these six phrases across the collection.

Table 12.1 Distribution of six formulaic phrases across Psalms 120–34

Psalm	Who made heaven and earth	From this time on and for evermore	Let Israel now say	Peace be upon Israel	May the LORD bless you from Zion	O Israel, hope in the LORD
120						
121	verse 2	verse 8				
122						
123						
124	verse 8		verse 1			
125		verse 2		verse 5		
126						
127						
128				verse 6	verse 5	
129			verse 1			
130						verse 7
131		verse 4				verse 3
132						
133				verse 3 (in 11QPs^A)		
134	verse 3				verse 3	

The individual expressions are of interest in themselves, and deserve some comment. Three refer to Israel, and are found only in the Psalms of Ascents; this may not seem significant at first sight, but it is more than a little strange to discover, for example, that the prayer 'Peace be upon Israel' is unique to Psalms 125, 128 and (if we accept the Qumran version [11QPs^A) 133. Taken together with the phrase 'O Israel, hope in the LORD', a very important theological motif emerges as part of the characteristic thinking of the collection, and which is decidedly not drawn from any older resources of which we know. *Israel* is supremely a theological concept here, an observation which will be reinforced when I come to look at the occurrence of certain key words in the Psalms of Ascents.

The benediction which concludes Psalms 128 and 134 – 'The LORD bless you from Zion' – is also unique to these Psalms, though a variant is found in Psalm 135:21, 'Blessed be the LORD from Zion'. No other examples are to be found in the Hebrew Bible. The concluding verses of Psalm 135 (19–21) have several verbal links with the Psalms of Ascents, which may suggest a conscious literary device providing a bridge into the wider context. Just as with the formulae involving Israel, the reference to Zion is thematically significant, and is taken up in what follows.

The description 'Maker of heaven and earth', applied to Yahweh three times in these Psalms, is found also in Psalms 115:15 and 146:6, but nowhere else in the Hebrew Bible – again, a somewhat surprising fact given the ubiquity of the theme of Yahweh the creator in post-exilic literature. We might have expected to find a declaration of this kind in the opening chapter of Genesis, for example, or in Deutero-Isaiah. The closest parallel is actually in Genesis 14:19, where the same phrase is found in English, though the Hebrew verb is different. It occurs as part of the exchange between Abram and Melchizedek, which is a curious late fragment inserted into a chapter which is itself usually regarded as a supplement to Genesis. I discuss the hermeneutical significance of these features in Chapter 15.

The remaining expression, 'From this time on and for evermore', is not in essence an unusual idea in the Hebrew Bible, though its only exact equivalents are to be found in Psalms 113:2 and 115:18, Isaiah 9:7 and 59:21, and Micah 4:7. Both of the Isaiah passages have an eschatological or messianic theme, which is pertinent to the Psalms of Ascents, as we shall see; likewise Micah 4:7, which is an eschatological vision of well-being situated immediately after the oracle of the nations coming to the mountain of the LORD, which is shared with Isaiah 2. There is, in short, a close thematic coherence to most[15] of the occurrences of this particular form of the expression 'forever'.

There are also formulaic repetitions within individual psalms, but since these are for the most part covered by the analysis of step-parallelism (see pp. 188f.), they do not need to discussed here. However, two other features might reasonably be included in the analysis of formulae. First, each of Psalms 123, 124, 127 and 129 begins with a repeated introductory phrase (respectively, 'As the eyes', 'If it had not been the LORD who was on our side', 'Unless the LORD' and 'Often have they attacked me from my youth'). The repetition *within* a psalm of some feature is of course what constitutes parallelism, but the use of the same literary device in four *different* Psalms constitutes the kind of formulaic repetition which Crow has identified.

Second, though this may be only a minor curiosity, there is a relatively high occurrence of simile in the Psalms of Ascents. Taking Book V as a whole, there are thirty-seven examples. In Psalms 120–34 there are fourteen, and in Psalms 140–4 there are nine. These latter two ratios represent unusual densities (respectively,

Table 12.2   Distribution of formulaic aspects and similes across Psalms 120–34

	120	121	122	123	124	125	126	127	128	129	130	131	132	133	134
F				2	1–2			1		1–2					
S		3		2	7	1, 2	1, 4	4	3, 3	6		2		2, 3	

two-and-a-half and three times as frequent as might be expected). Table 12.2 sets out the distribution of these two additional features.

Characteristic words

While it is hazardous to claim statistical significance in literary matters, there are certain words which occur with a far higher frequency in the Psalms of Ascents than in the Psalter as a whole. It is my modest contention that these contribute towards the overall character of the collection. I will give only a few of the more readily accessible examples here, again keeping in mind the principle that these are available through the English version.

*   *Mighty One of Jacob* occurs in verses 2 and 5 of Psalm 132; it is found also in Genesis 49:24 and Isaiah 49:26 and 60:16. The title *Mighty One of Israel* occurs in Isaiah 1:24.
*   *David*. It may seem strange to single out this name in particular as a special characteristic of the Psalms of Ascents; however, for all that many superscriptions attribute psalms to David, he is rarely referred to by name in the actual text of psalms. Excluding the editorial comment in 72:20, there are just twelve uses of 'David', five of which are to be found in Psalms 122 and 132. It is also relevant that the description of the king as *the anointed* is over-represented (twice in Psalm 132 out of a total of twelve in the Psalter). Finally, in this summary of words relating to David, mention of his *throne* is also statistically more frequent here, being found twice each in Psalms 122 and 132 out of a grand total of eighteen occurrences.[16]
*   *Jerusalem*. Similar remarks apply to Jerusalem, which is mentioned five times (122:2, 3, 6; 125:2; 128:5) out of a grand total in the Psalter of seventeen references; six of the remaining twelve are in Psalms 135–46, a curious fact which is, however, consistent with the observation in note 14 about the distribution of the late Hebrew relative conjunction.

- Even the familiar name *Israel* is significantly over-represented in the Psalms of Ascents, where it turns up nine times; there are in total sixty-two uses in the Psalter as a whole. The disparity in this case is by no means as striking, but it is still pronounced, representing something like four times the expected frequency.

- *Zion.* As if to complete a set with Jerusalem and Israel, the familiar religious name for the sacred city turns out also to be a significant expression within the Psalms of Ascents, where it is found seven times out of the total of thirty-six in the Psalter.

- Perhaps surprisingly, in a book supposedly representative of the religious observances of the monarchy and the temple, the word for priest (*cohen*) is found only five times, twice in Psalm 132, and elsewhere in 78:64, 99:6 and 110:4. *Aaron* also, though found only in Psalm 133 among this collection, is rarer than might be expected overall, occurring otherwise only eight times. The reference to the *Ark* in 132:8 is, surprisingly, unique in the Psalter, though there are other places where it seems to be indicated, such as Psalm 24:7–9 and Psalm 68 *passim*.

- *To hope for/to desire* (130:5, 7; 131:3; 132.13f.). The expression of hope is significantly represented in Psalms 130 and 131, and there are only four instances of the word for 'desire' in the whole Psalter, of which the two in Psalm 132 are unique in having Yahweh or God as the subject.

- *Slumber.* The references to Yahweh and David refusing to sleep (121:3f. and 132:4) are unique in the Hebrew Bible. The word itself is rare, and only here is it used with these subjects. The closest thematic parallels are in Proverbs 6:4 and 6:10 (= 24:33), which warn against falling asleep when danger is near.

- Both *blessing/to bless* and *peace (shalom)* are more frequent than statistically expected, the latter more the emphatically. *Shalom* occurs seven times out of a Psalter total of twenty-seven, and it is over-represented to about the same extent as is Jerusalem, with which it forms an appropriate play on words in Psalm 122:6–9.[17]

There are important hermeneutical observations to be made on the basis of these words and phrases, and I take up that task later. For now, I hope that they are sufficient to give a flavour of the special linguistic character of Psalms 120–34 as a whole. Table 12.3 shows how the various expressions are distributed across the collection of the fifteen Psalms of Ascents; together with Tables 12.1 and 12.2 they constitute a graphic presentation of that special character.

Table 12.3 Distribution of characteristic words across the Psalms of Ascents

	120	121	122	123	124	125	126	127	128	129	130	131	132	133	134
Jacob													2.5		
Israel		4	4		1	5			6	1	7,8	3			
Jerusalem			2,3,6			2			5						
David			5										1,10,11,17		
Anointed													10,17		
Throne			5,5										11,12		
Zion						1	1		5	5			13	3	3
Aaron														2	
Priest													9,16		
Ark													8		
Desire/Hope											5,7	3	13,14		
Slumber		3,4											4		
Peace	6,7		6,7,8			5			6						
Blessing				6					4,5	8			15,15	3	1,2,3

'Staircase' or step-parallelism in the Psalms Of Ascents

One of the commonest claims made regarding the poetic structure of Psalms 120–34 is that the collection displays an unusually high incidence of 'step-parallelism' (the technical term is *anadiplosis*, defined in the *SOED* as 'the beginning of a sentence, line, or clause with the concluding, or any prominent, word of the preceding'). It is difficult to resolve the question conclusively for, apart from the element of subjective judgement involved in determining what counts as an example of the phenomenon, it would appear to be a daunting (if not impossible) task to ascertain relative frequencies for the occurrence of *anadiplosis* in a manner similar to the analysis carried out above.

There is also the question whether repetition at the end of a line of a prominent element from the preceding line should count as *anadiplosis*. I propose to take a generous view of what constitutes step-parallelism, while noting that some examples may also be classified under other types of parallelism. Most commentators on the Hebrew of the Psalms of Ascents have, however, reported a strong, if necessarily subjective, sense of step-parallelism as an important and characteristic aspect of the collection,[18] and the phenomenon certainly persists in translation, though some instances are lost because of the change of word-order involved. Psalm 132 appears to be the exception: the absence of step-parallelism could be a consequence of the different purpose of Psalm 132, and its far greater length. I have identified thirty examples (there are significantly more in the Hebrew text) which arguably constitute instances of step-parallelism within the Psalms of Ascents (the details are set out in Table 12.4).

Table 12.5 represents a palimpsest of each of the aspects I have examined in order to provide an overall presentation of the linguistic and structural evidence for the inner coherence of this collection. It is not complete, since it is based on a study of these Psalms in English. A review of the Hebrew text would certainly increase both the number of instances of step-parallelism and the number of significant words. In any case I would not wish to claim any precision for the figures in the final column – though they do introduce the intriguing paradox that the one Psalm in this collection which is commonly regarded as the only real pilgrimage song (Psalm 126) turns out to be one of the least well represented by the shared literary features of the collection!

A question does, however, linger concerning the status of Psalm 132, which the reader will recall as something of a bone of contention

Table 12.4 Examples indicative of step-parallelism in the Psalms of Ascents

	Detail of step-parallelism	*Total*
120:3	What shall be given . . . // what more shall be done	
6–7	those who hate peace. // I am for peace	2
121:1–2	from where will my help come? // My help comes	
3–4	he who keeps you will not slumber. // He who keeps Israel // will neither slumber nor sleep	
5	the LORD is your keeper; // the LORD is your shade	
7–8	The LORD will keep you . . . // he will keep your life. // The LORD will keep	4
122:2–3	O Jerusalem. // Jerusalem – built as a city	
4	To it the tribes go up, // the tribes of the LORD	
5	there the thrones for judgement were set up // the thrones of	3
123:2	As the eyes . . . // as the eyes . . . // so our eyes	
2–3	mercy upon us. // Have mercy upon us, O LORD, have mercy upon us.	
3–4	more than enough of contempt. . . . // the contempt of the proud	3
124:1–2	If it had not been the LORD . . . // if it had not been the LORD	
4–5	the torrent would have gone over us; // then over us would have gone	
7	the snare of the fowlers; // the snare is broken	3
125:2	surround Jerusalem, // so the LORD surrounds	
3	to the righteous, // so that the righteous	2
126:2–3	"The LORD has done great things for them." // The LORD has done great things for us	1
127:1	Unless the LORD builds. . . . // Unless the LORD guards	
1–2	in vain / . . . in vain. // It is in vain	2
128:4–5	blessed who fears the LORD. // The LORD bless you	1
129:1–2	Often they have attacked me from my youth . . . // often they have attacked me from my youth	
8	The blessing of the LORD be upon you! // We bless you	2
130:5–6	I wait for the LORD, my soul waits . . . // my soul waits	
6	more than those who watch for the morning, // more than those who watch for the morning	3
7–8	great power to redeem. // It is he who will redeem	
131:1	not lifted up, // . . . not raised too high	
2	like a weaned child . . . // my soul is like the weaned child	2
132		
133:2	running down upon the beard, // on the beard of Aaron, // running down over	1
134:2–3	bless the LORD. // May the LORD . . . bless you	1
Total		30

Table 12.5 Aggregation of evidence presented in Tables 12.1–12.4

| | Instances of features | | | | Total | No. of verses | Significance |
	12.1	12.2	12.3	12.4	(n)	(vv)	(n:vv)
120			2	2	4	7	0.57
121	2		3	4	9	8	1.13
122		1	10	3	14	9	1.56
123		2		3	5	4	1.23
124	2	2	2	3	9	8	1.13
125	2	2	4	2	10	5	2.00
126		2	1	1	4	6	0.67
127		2		2	4	5	0.80
128	2	2	6	1	11	6	1.83
129	1	3	3	2	9	8	1.13
130	1		4	3	8	8	1.00
131	2	1	2	2	7	3	2.33
132		19			19	18	1.06
133	1	2	3	1	7	3	2.33
134	2		4	1	7	3	2.33
Average							1.26

in the argument over dating and function. Although it has a significant number of features, these are concentrated on lexical items,
some of which (Ark, anointed, priest) are limited to that Psalm. To
counter that observation, there are repetitions at the beginnings of
lines (verses 3, 4; 5a and 5b; 6a and 6b; 7a and 7b; 11c; 12a and 12c
['sons']) and indications of step-parallelism in verses 13–14 which
I feel are not strong enough to be included in the listing of features
but which certainly tend towards the common pattern. The David–
throne link with Psalm 122 is also an important indication. Finally,
as we shall see in Chapter 14, Psalm 132 effectively takes up almost
all of the themes evinced throughout the sequence as a whole.

This examination may not have established the unity of the Psalms
of Ascents beyond all doubt, but I believe that there is sufficient
evidence now to defend that unity as beyond all reasonable doubt,
and to conclude that our reading of the collection must take account
of its having been composed as a deliberately coherent group. Here I
must part company with Crow, who argues for a redactional process.
That seems to me to fall to Occam's razor – it is an unnecessarily
complex hypothesis, one not required by the evidence to hand, and
largely arising from prior assumptions about both the date of individual psalms and the way that biblical materials were developed.

The models of redaction applicable to Torah and the Prophets are not obviously relevant to the Psalms, and we should use better tools first. In the next chapter I discuss the group as a whole and its individual members (necessarily briefly) under the rubric of aspects 1, 2 and 4, as set out in Chapter 5.

13

PSALMS 120–34

Preliminary exegesis

Psalm 120

	TEXTUAL NOTES AND STRUCTURE	

1 In my distress I cry [or cried] to the LORD, that he may [or might] answer me:
2 'Deliver me, O LORD,
    from lying lips,
    from a deceitful tongue.'
	Lament and plea	A

3 What shall be given to you?
    And what more shall be done to you,
    you deceitful tongue?
4 A warrior's sharp arrows,
    with glowing coals of the broom tree!
	Proposed solution	B

5 Woe is me, that I am an alien in Meshech, that I must live among the tents of Kedar.
6 Too long have I had my dwelling
    among those who hate peace.
7 I am for peace;
    but when I speak,
    they are for war.
	Repeated lament	A1

Textual points and comparative material from the ancient Near East

Since there is rather little to be said on both of these aspects in respect of the Psalms of Ascents, I have combined them under a single heading throughout this chapter.

The first verb in verse 1 is in past-tense form, which would yield not a present plea but a memory of a past prayer: 'In my distress I cried to the LORD, that he might answer me.' Verse 2 would in that case constitute the content of the prayer, which could then be taken as both past and present, since the implication of the final verse is that the experience of being surrounded by lies and conflict is a continuing one. This is reinforced by the language of verses 5 and 6 which clearly indicate a lengthy sojourn in alien territory (the verbs in verse 5, as in verse 1, are expressions of past time continuing into the present).

Verse 4 might also mean that the warrior's arrows were sharpened and hardened in a charcoal fire, rather than constituting a pair of separate weapons. This is in some ways a more attractive option, since it provides a precise metaphor for the cutting and wounding effects of deceit. It may be of passing interest that the broom bush is also that under which Elijah slept in 1 Kings 19:4f. (the only other instance of the word apart from Job 30:4).

If the places Mesech and Kedar are to be taken literally, they seem to be located, respectively, in eastern Anatolia, near the Black Sea (Genesis 10:2, 1 Chronicles 1:5, Ezekiel 38:2), and in the Syro-Arabian desert. The name Kedar is that of the second son of Ishmael (Genesis 25:13) and so presumably of an Arab tribe of herders (Isaiah 21:13–17, 42:11, 60:7; Jeremiah 49:2a).

Structure

(The discussion of Psalm 120 in Chapter 4 (see pp. 56–8) is also relevant to the present chapter.)

Various features have been picked out in the second column of the Psalm's text indicating its main structural points. Overall the poem seems to represent a complaint which remains unresolved, with the middle section representing more of a vain hope than a confident expectation. The primary metaphor is of a war of lies and deceit, and the Psalm is replete with references to both. Thus 'distress' in verse 1, the 'warrior's sharp arrows' in verse 2, 'those who hate peace' in verse 6 and those who 'are for war' in verse 7 all contribute to the sense of embattlement which is central to this composition. But that the war is not conventional is demonstrated through the second sequence of metaphors concerning conflict through speech ('lying lips' in verse 2, 'deceitful tongue' in verses 2 and 3, and the battle of words in verse 7). It may not at first be obvious that the 'distress' of verse 1 is the distress of war, but Dahood (1970) proposed the translation 'when I was besieged', recognising that the word in question is used in a number of places to describe the effects of war.

The Psalm ends by juxtaposing war and peace, thus introducing what will be a key motif – *shalom* – of the Psalms of Ascents and at the same time creating a shift of metaphor: just as war is inconsistent with peace, so does the combination of lies, deceit and verbal conflict prevent the resolution of religious strife (both individual and communal). In addition, and providing a third metaphor, we find a poignant portrayal of alienation in verse 5. Meshech and Kedar are alien places, as far away from each other as possible, and for the psalmist to be encamped in their territories suggests eloquently both the trials of war (a besieging army in a strange land) and the sense of loss associated with distance.

One last observation is due to Dahood. A number of words suggest in some way parts of the mouth. 'Lip' and 'tongue' are obvious; in Hebrew the adjective 'sharp' is derived from the word for 'tooth'. Hence we have a graphic association of the three participants in speech (mouth–lips–teeth) in the context of speech as a deadly weapon (compare 57:4, 64:3; Jeremiah 9:8; and the passage in 3 James which describes the dangerous power of the tongue).

Psalm 120 is not a lament in time of war, as is plainly shown by the primacy of idle talk as the focus of complaint in verse 2. If war is involved, it is the war of words, and the strangers and foreigners are not those of remote and mysterious regions, but those within the community of Jerusalem who oppose and contradict the psalmist's principles. Of course, just as we can rarely identify the military enemies so vividly described in many psalms, so we are likely to remain frustrated in any attempt to identify the competing religious positions hinted at here.

Psalm 121

Textual points and comparative material from the ancient Near East

There are no problems in the Hebrew text of Psalm 121 which need delay us, though it may be worth reminding readers of the question-mark at the end of verse 1, which is certainly present in the original text.

Comparative material is relevant to two points in the Psalm: the theme of the wakefulness and watchfulness of Yahweh; and the belief expressed in verse 5 that both sun and moon can have harmful effects

---

PSALM 121

	TEXTUAL NOTES AND STRUCTURE	
1 I lift up my eyes to the hills – from where will my help come?	Rhetorical question	A
2 My help comes from the LORD, who made heaven and earth.	Pilgrim's answer	B

3 He will not let your foot be moved;
     he who keeps you will not slumber.
 4 He who keeps Israel
     will neither slumber nor sleep.
	(Priestly) blessing	C

5 The LORD is your keeper;
     the LORD is your shade at your right hand.
 6 The sun shall not strike you by day,
     nor the moon by night.		

7 The LORD will keep you from all evil;
     he will keep your life.
 8 The LORD will keep
     your going out and your coming in
     from this time on and for evermore.		

---

on the unwary or unprotected. Regarding the former, apart from the notorious contest of Elijah with the prophets of Baal in 1 Kings 18[1] in which he mocks their god for perhaps having gone to sleep, there is a passage in an Egyptian hymn to Amon-Re (*ANET*: 366c) which describes him as he who 'spends the night wakeful, while all men are asleep'.

The dangers of the sun are well known, those of the moon less so. Weiser (1962) claims that in antiquity the moon was regarded as the cause of diseases; and the association of the moon with madness lingers on in the English word 'lunacy'. Some Babylonian sources indicate that the seventh, fourteenth, twenty-first and twenty-eighth days were unlucky – perhaps a connection with the phases of the moon is discernible.

Structure

Permeating this Psalm is a sense of danger – located at first in the hills (and the thought of stumbling surely belongs to the risks associated with travel around Jerusalem, whether for business or on pilgrimage), but then in the hot sun and bright moon, and lastly in the generalisation 'all evil'. This univerality of physical danger intrudes paradoxically into the phrase 'who made of heaven and earth' which is used of God, the supposed defence against danger.

The psalmist constructs a very childish, almost fearful, set of protective devices: a God who helps and who – repeatedly – watches ('keep', 'keeper') is the first requirement. Just as a small child becomes uneasy when its parent disappears from view, so in this Psalm God is expected to be everywhere, at all times. Thus the two complementary motifs of 'wakefulness' (verses 3b and 4b) and 'presence' ('will not let your foot be moved'; 'your shade at your right hand'; 'will keep your going out and your coming in').

All of this depends, finally, upon Yahweh's having the power to meet the poet's heavy demands. Hence the two 'heavyweight' lines which form an *inclusio* around the blessing: 'Who made heaven and earth' and 'from this time on and for evermore'. Both, of course, are characteristic formulae in the Psalms of Ascents; this is the only Psalm in which they are found together, though one or other recurs in 124 (where help is again associated with creation), 125 and 131. Their significance is to remind the reader that, although danger may be ubiquitous, the LORD is all-powerful and ever-present.

Overall, the Psalm appears to be some kind of dialogue, though commentators do not agree as to how it works. The problem is the continuation of the first-person form through verses 1 and 2. Weiser resolves this by amending the text to read 'help', so that verse 2 can serve as the response by a different speaker to the psalmist's query. This is unnecessary, however, if the question and its answer are treated rhetorically, and this is the option I have preferred. It fits better, in general, with the individualist, somewhat introspective, mood of Psalms 120–3.

Psalm 122

Textual points and comparative material from the ancient Near East

The first line might be better translated 'I rejoiced among those who said to me . . . ' perhaps reflecting what appears to be the context – a group of pilgrims at the entrance to the holy place. Other linguistic points (such as the rather obscure Hebrew of verse 3) are too recondite to affect our reading of the Psalm in English.

PSALM 122

	TEXTUAL NOTES AND STRUCTURE

1 I was glad when they said to me,
　　'Let us go to the house of the LORD!'
2 Our feet are standing
　　within your gates, O Jerusalem.

Part (i) The pilgrims await　A

3 Jerusalem – built as a city
　　that is bound firmly together.
4 To it the tribes go up,
　　　the tribes of the LORD,
　　as was decreed for Israel,
　　　to give thanks to the name of the LORD.
5 For there the thrones for judgement were set up,
　　the thrones of the house of David.

Part (ii) The city of Yahweh awaits　B

6 Pray for the peace of Jerusalem:
　　'May they prosper who love you.
7 Peace be within your walls,
　　and security within your towers.'
8 For the sake of my relatives and friends
　　I will say, 'Peace be within you.'
9 For the sake of the house of the LORD our God,
　　I will seek your good.

Part (iii) The pilgrims' prayer for the city　C

If, as I have suggested, this Psalm refers to a festival procession or pilgrimage, it represents a relatively rare phenomenon. For, although processions of various kinds were part of religious observance in Egypt, Canaan, Babylon and Assyria, the surviving texts do not often tell us directly of the routines involved. More often they preserve the words used on such occasions, since presumably the actual performance was familiar to those involved and did not require to be recorded.

One of the background questions which this Psalm prompts is whether the pilgrims were representative of their various villages (as the wording of verse 8 seems to suggest), or whether whole communities went up to Jerusalem together for major events (compare Luke 2:41–4, where the 'relatives and friends' are part of the party). In the story of the birth of Samuel, his father Elkanah is specifically said to go up every year to worship at Shiloh (1 Samuel 1:3), as though this were a noteworthy thing, implying that not everyone followed this practice. While belonging to a different context, this may nevertheless support the contention that pilgrimage or participation in festival processions was either specialised or representative, and not the business of the people as a whole. In view of the extensive liturgical demands that are involved, this seems a reasonable hypothesis.

Structure

There are three pairs of lines in this Psalm which use the device of a repeated introductory phrase in a rather pointed fashion: verse 4 ('the tribes / the tribes'); verse 5 ('the thrones / the thrones'); and verses 8–9 ('for the sake of . . . I will say / for the sake of . . . I will seek'). While these are no doubt aspects of step parallelism, they also create a bonding effect for the poem as a whole which nicely mirrors the key declaration that Jerusalem is 'bound firmly together'. That binding is further demonstrated in the step-wise repetition of the city's name at the end of part (i) and the beginning of part (ii). This is a composition in celebration of Jerusalem (which is named also at the beginning of part (iii)). But it is not the secular stronghold alone which is the subject. The Psalm is bound together by a very significant *inclusio*, 'the house of the LORD', in verses 1 and 9: it is Jerusalem as Yahweh's place that is important. Finally, in the pivotal verse 5 a third ingredient completes the picture: 'the house of David'. The temple of Yahweh – the throne of David – the city of Jerusalem: epitomes of the priestly, royal and civic foci of this sequence of Psalms. The civic dimension is seen also in an emphasis on the people for whom this holy place signifies – 'the tribes of the LORD' and the psalmist's 'relatives and friends'.

At the end of Psalm 120 I noted the poet's poignant plea for peace, daring to speak the sacred word *shalom* though surrounded by cries of violence. This faint call is now echoed and magnified in the repeated prayer for peace, prosperity and good which informs the petition in the third part of Psalm 122. No longer an isolated voice, but a representative of all those who adhere to the true Jerusalem, the singer now boldly demands what at the beginning of the sequence he or she was almost forcibly prevented from whispering.

The designations A, B, C for the three parts of this Psalm are intended to echo the A, B, C of Psalm 121. The first part in each Psalm describes the condition of a (the?) group of pilgrims about to set out. The second part in each Psalm provides a form of assurance (or, in the case of Psalm 121, reassurance). The third section of Psalm 121 consists of a (priestly?) blessing on the pilgrims as they embark upon their journey, while the third part of Psalm 122 contains a prayer *by* the pilgrims for a blessing upon Jerusalem, the goal of their journey.

Psalm 123

	TEXTUAL NOTES AND STRUCTURE
1 To you I lift up my eyes, O you who are enthroned in the heavens!	The faithful A look to God in trust

2 As the eyes of servants
       look to the hand of their master,
    as the eyes of a maid
       to the hand of her mistress,
    so our eyes look to the LORD our God,
	B
	
	B1
	
	A1

3 until he has mercy upon us. Have mercy upon us, O LORD, have mercy upon us,	Linking C Plea C+

for we have had more than enough of
       contempt.
 4 Our soul has had more than its fill
       of the scorn of those who are at ease,
       of the contempt of the proud
	The proud D
	look upon
	the D+
	faithful
	with contempt

Textual points and comparative material from the ancient Near East

As a parallel to the sequence 'As the eyes . . . as the eyes . . . so our eyes . . . ' Dahood suggests the following (I have taken the version from Gibson 1977: 76):

> Like the heart of a heifer yearning for her calf,
>   like the heart of a ewe yearning for her lamb,
>   so the heart of Anat yearned after Baal.

Textually, the most problematic verse is the last one, which in the Hebrew appears to contain a grammatical solecism. More interestingly, the final phrase, 'the contempt of the proud', could be read as holding a reference to or a pun on the Hebrew for 'Greeks' (*yewanim*;

compare 'Ionian'). This offers the remote but tantalising possibility that those who represent the opposition in this Psalm (and hence presumably in the Psalms of Ascents as a whole) are either Greeks, or Hellenised Jews. For the period from the fourth century onwards this is by no means an improbable scenario (though it must be stressed that the reading in question is highly speculative, depending on an interpretation of a marginal gloss).

The principal metaphor of the first half of the Psalm is that of the relationship between master or mistress and servant (male or female). Generally speaking, servants and/or slaves were a regular feature of ancient society, and the fact that both in Hebrew and in Greek the word for individuals of this status covers both of the English terms should warn us against seeing this relationship as inherently unjust. Both words, of course, are also used to describe the relationship of human beings to God, though it is not normal in that context to translate them as 'slave'. The discussion of the legal status of 'slaves' in Exodus 21:2–11 appears to recognise a certain voluntary status of servitude, and in the ancient world generally it was by no means impossible for bonded servants to achieve high status. The Mesopotamian materials, for example, discuss cases of both male and female servants marrying free women and free men.

This air of ambiguity suits the context of this Psalm very well, since presumably the reasons for servants to 'keep an eye on' their superiors are to do with both reward and punishment – to be there for the former, and to avoid, if possible, the latter.

Structure

There is a delicate formal structure evident in Psalm 123, though it is masked by the verse divisions of the NRSV. The first part, verses 1–2, excluding the last line of verse 2, presents in palinstrophic form the comparison between our attention to God and the way that servants keep an eye on their superiors. Thus there appears to be a kind of closure here, as though a simple point had been made to the poet's satisfaction.

But skilfully and almost imperceptibly the writer slips into a more disturbing theme. For the middle section, which begins with the prayer 'until he has mercy on us', rapidly shifts to the unhappy reason for the prayer: the scorn and mockery of those who think they are superior. The formal device used here is not chiastic but climactic, indicated by the notations C, C+ and D, D+. In each case the opening statement ('until he has mercy' at the end of verse 2 and 'we have had more than enough of contempt' in verse 3) is followed by a double repetition, as I think is clear from the text. The effect of this is to undermine the rather cosy air of the opening verses, so that by the time we arrive at the climax of the Psalm, in verses 3b–4, the atmosphere is tense indeed. No resolution has been reached, no closure achieved, and the metaphor of the opening part remains only a metaphor.

Lexically there are two key patterns which bind the Psalm into a poetic whole. The fourfold repetition of 'eyes' in verses 1–2 is contrasted with the words 'contempt' and 'scorn' in verses 3–4, reminding us that our 'looking' to God is the reverse of the look of scorn and contempt bestowed those who despise us (a look which we strive to avoid). We are the cynosure of the proud, who despise the God to whom we look. The other pattern shows the contrast of power which goes along with these different forms of looking. Legitimate power (of Yahweh, or of the master/mistress) is defied by spurious authority (those who are at ease – perhaps the apathetic and the proud).

Psalm 124

Textual points and comparative material from the ancient Near East

The translation 'enemies' in verse 2 is very weak. The Hebrew is *'adam* which must mean, in the context, 'the whole world', 'everybody'. This is important, because the mood of the Psalm is concerned not with a specific enemy attack but with the cosmic fear of total annihilation. The floods and the rivers as foes belong to the mythology of Canaan and Babylon. It is the sea monster Leviathan (Canaanite *Lotan*, Babylonian *Tiamat*) which swallows the living whole. Elsewhere in the Hebrew Bible *she'ol* (the world of the dead) is portrayed in exactly the same terms (Isaiah 5:14–15; Proverbs 1:12).

The Proverbs passage provides an additional link, since it goes on to describe how a bird can be snared through its ignorance of the nature of the trap (a theme revisited in 7:23). This gives the redemption described in the Psalm greater force, for it is not simply an arbitrary image but comes out of a literary precedent. Perhaps (to trespass on the aspect of interpretation) we may see flight into the air as a dramatic contrast with descent into the waters: two contrasting elements symbolising life and death.

PSALM 124

		TEXTUAL NOTES AND STRUCTURE
1	If it had not been the LORD who was on our side – let Israel now say –	What might have been A
2	If it had not been the LORD who was on our side, when our enemies [*or* everybody] attacked us,	
3	then they would have swallowed us up alive when their anger was kindled against us;	
4	then the flood would have swept us away, the torrent would have gone over us;	
5	then over us would have gone the raging waters.	
6	Blessed be the LORD, who has not given us as prey to their teeth.	What actually happened B
7	We have escaped like a bird from the snare of the fowlers: the snare is broken, and we have escaped.	
8	Our help is in the name of the LORD, who made heaven and earth.	What made A+B the difference

---

Structure

I have suggested descriptive titles to summarise the pattern of this Psalm. The opening sequence is highly formalised, both in terms of the opening phrase which is repeated, and in terms of the way that only two words are used to introduce each of the five lines – *if, if, then, then, then*. What this surely indicates is a hypothetical event. Of course, had the cosmic enemy actually triumphed there would have been nothing else to say. The form of the first part makes the substance of the second possible!

Each part begins with a reference to Yahweh; and these constitute all of the direct references to the deity: 'If it had not been Yahweh'; 'Blessed be Yahweh'; 'Our help is in the name of Yahweh'. These form three motifs which structure the movement of the Psalm: what would have happened had we not had Yahweh on our side, how things actually progress, and the climax (which is also a reprise of the opening of Psalm 121), which affirms the power of Yahweh to make a difference. This contrasts with, as well as echoing, the earlier Psalm in which (the reader will recall) the daunting dangers of the created order were imagined and defied in the form of an anxious repetition of the mantra 'the LORD protects'. Now we know why it is safe to trust in God.

Finally, there is an emphatic 'us and them' and 'us and Yahweh' theme in Psalm 124 – seven of the first eight lines refer to 'us'! For this is not a dispassionate poem imagining what might happen to others; it is a visceral account of the very real fears of those (like us) who face the worst that nameless demons can do.

Psalm 125

	TEXTUAL NOTES AND STRUCTURE
Part i	
1 Those who trust in the LORD are like Mount Zion, which cannot be moved, but abides for ever.	Two metaphors of stability A1
2 As the mountains surround Jerusalem, so the LORD surrounds his people, from this time on and for evermore.	
Part ii	
3 For the sceptre of wickedness shall not rest on the land allotted to the righteous, so that the righteous may not stretch out their hands to do wrong.	Two dramas B1 of instability
4 Do good, O LORD, to those who are good, and to those who are upright in their hearts.	
5 But those who turn aside to their own crooked ways the LORD will lead away with evildoers.	
Conclusion	
Peace be upon Israel!	Prayer A1+B1 to resolve conflict

Textual points and comparative material from the ancient Near East

There is a textual difficulty in verse 1 in the word 'abides'. The problem is that the Hebrew verb does not occur anywhere else with this meaning, or with an inanimate subject. Half-parallels occur in Psalm 9:7 ('The LORD *sits enthroned* forever') and 29:10 ('The LORD *sits enthroned* over the flood; // the LORD *sits enthroned* as king for ever'), but in each case Yahweh is the subject. There appears to be a parallel in Psalm 122:5, where the NRSV reads the same verb as 'there the thrones for judgement *were set up*'. This is strictly speaking a mistranslation, since the verb is active, and should be rendered 'there they set up thrones for judgement'.

There is, of course, no objection in principle to a grammatical usage which occurs only once. In a language like classical Hebrew, whose stock of texts is relatively small, such phenomena are to be expected; but this is a rather common verb (*yashab* occurs 1,085 times in the Hebrew Bible), so the presumption must be that one of the 'normal' usages is if possible to be preferred. In this spirit Dahood (1970) follows the Septuagint, which takes the form to be a participle: 'he who dwells; he who is enthroned'. The resulting translation is of some interest:

> Those who trust in Yahweh
>   are like the Mountain of Zion.
> Never will be upset
>   the Enthroned of Jerusalem.[2]

Another of Dahood's suggestions is of interest. The Hebrew which the NRSV translates as 'those who turn aside' (verse 5) could be taken to come from the root 'to be moved' which occurs in verse 1 (and also, incidentally, in 121:3), thus providing both an *inclusio* for Psalm 125 and a happy link with 121.

The same word which in Hebrew describes the 'crooked ways' of the wicked is found in Ugaritic descriptions of 'the twisting serpent' (see for example Gibson 1977: 50, 68). Taken together with the slightly sinister final words 'the LORD will lead [them] away with evildoers', this is reminiscent of the descent into *she'ol*, with its Mesopotamian parallels in the myth of Ishtar (*ANET*: 106–9). See also Proverbs 5:5, 7:24–7.

Structure

This is a Psalm of contrasts culminating in a prayer which offers hope of a resolution of its conflicts. The prayer is terse, almost thrown in as an afterthought; but significantly it takes the form of one of the standard phrases which characterises these Psalms (see also 128:6 and

133:3 in the Qumran version). The first part of the Psalm (verses 1–2) engages with the theme of stability, assurance, constancy, while verses 3–5 (excluding the closing phrase) contrast the fate of the righteous with that of the wicked, while at the same time making the reader aware of the uncertainty which besets even those who would do good. These opposed themes are developed through both individual words and phrases and the poetic structures in each section, as we shall now see.

Images of stability are conjured by the key terms *Yahweh* (LORD), *Mount Zion* and *Jerusalem*. Naturally these are concentrated in the first part; but it is important that God's personal name is repeated twice within the second. Thus in the midst of the disarray confronting both righteous and wicked, God stands as an emblem of constancy. A second group of phrases, all but one of which includes a verb, represents the twin themes of rest and stability on the one hand and movement and uncertainty on the other. Rest and stability are represented in the first part ('cannot be moved', 'abides for ever', 'surround(s)', 'from this time on and for evermore') while movement and uncertainty are confined to the second ('shall not rest', 'may not stretch out', 'turn aside', 'will lead away'). These metaphors and phrases are directed to a single subject, variously represented as 'those who trust', 'his people', 'the righteous', 'those who are good / upright in their hearts', 'Israel' – a series of terms to denote the faithful people to whom this Psalm, and the others in the series, are directed. In this individual Psalm, as in the collection as a whole, the focus is on those represented by the psalmist's voice.

The formal patterns which I have identified in Psalm 125 match well its theme of the balance and contrast between stability and uncertainty. Thus the first part consists of a pair of similes or metaphors (verse 1a, verse 2a and b), each followed by an expression of permanence ('which cannot be moved, but abides for ever'; 'from this time on and for evermore'[3]) – a reassuringly predictable format which reflects well its content. The second section, on the other hand, presents a number of chiasmuses and oppositions which equally well highlight the uneasy sense of menace which is present. Thus the righteous and the wicked are opposed, and verse 3 is (broadly) an a–b–b–a chiasmus, matching this contrast (semantically it has the pattern wicked–righteous–righteous–wicked). Verses 4–5 are grammatically chiastic (action–description–description–action) but this time the good–bad contrast is at odds with the chiasmus (good–to the good–to the evil–evil).

While these structural details may seem (unnecessarily!)

complicated, they help to show how the language works to achieve that unsettling of the comfortable picture in the first two verses which gives the poem its force, and makes the conclusion both pertinent and poignant. 'For God's sake, give us peace' might be a fair contemporary representation of its sentiment.

Psalm 126

	TEXTUAL NOTES AND STRUCTURE	
Part i		
1 When the LORD restored the fortunes of Zion, [*or* brought back those who returned to Zion] we were like those who dream.	'Refrain'	A
2 Then our mouth was filled with laughter, and our tongue with shouts of joy;	Summary of theme	B
then it was said among the nations, 'The LORD has done great things for them.' 3 The LORD has done great things for us, and we rejoiced.	Elaboration	C
Part ii		
4 Restore our fortunes, O LORD, like the watercourses in the Negeb.	'Refrain'	A1
5 May those who sow in tears reap with shouts of joy.	Summary of theme	B1
6 Those who go out weeping, bearing the seed for sowing, shall come home with shouts of joy, carrying their sheaves.	Elaboration	C1

Textual points and comparative material from the ancient Near East

As the footnote to verse 1 in the NRSV makes clear, the interpretation of the Hebrew of this verse is by no means clear. The form rendered 'fortunes' by the NRSV is unusual, and may be derived either from a root denoting captivity or from one meaning 'to turn back'. The whole phrase occurs in a number of places in the Hebrew Bible, and there is a growing consensus that the more probable meaning overall is 'to restore the fortunes of . . . '. In the Psalms some form of the phrase is to be found in 14:7 (= 53:6) and 85:1, as well as the two occurrences in verses 1 and 4 of the Psalm under discussion. The simple formulation 'Restore us' is found as a refrain in Psalm 80:3, 7, 19, and in 85:4. I am disinclined, therefore, to interpret Psalm 126 in the context of the exile, or of the return from Babylon, despite the Psalm's description of how the nations proclaim God's greatness (verses 2–3). This fits just as well a context in which the people celebrate their past good fortune in the land of Israel, and contrast that with urgent prayers for the present (verses 4–6). Indeed, Psalm 85, to which I have already referred, preserves in verses 1–4 a structure similar to that of Psalm 126, with a very similar transition in verses 3–4.

The motifs of the second part of this Psalm are bedded in the physical and mythological terrain of the Negeb. I have already commented on the cosmic threat symbolised by the torrential waters described in Psalm 124; here they are transformed into a positive (but still mysterious) phenomenon. The flooding of the wadis in the wet season is both a prerequisite for successful agriculture and a random event in the power of Yahweh. Only if God sends the rains will the 'watercourses in the Negeb' be full, only when they are full can a good harvest be expected.

Mythologically the language of verses 5 and 6 may be reminiscent of myths of the dying and rising fertility god which sometimes included scenes of weeping and rejoicing. Osiris in Egypt, Dumuzi or Tammuz in Mesopotamia, Baal in Canaan, and both Adonis and Dionysus in Greece are familiar examples. One literary example will suffice: in the epic of Baal and Mot (*NERTOT*: 216, 218–19), there are two interesting scenes. The first shows the goddess Anat weeping over the dead god; the second is a vision of reclaimed harmony when he is restored to life.[4]

> Shapshu the light of the gods went down to her [Anat].
> Until she had had her fill of weeping,
> she drank the tears like wine.
> She called loudly to Shapshu the light of the gods:
> 'Lift the mighty Baal onto me!'
> Shapshu the light of the gods heard her.
> She lifted up mighty Baal,
> she laid him down on the shoulders of Anat.

She brings him to the summit of Zaphon,
she bewails him and buries him,
lays him in the caves of the gods of the earth.

In a dream of kindly El, the gracious one,
in a vision of the creator of creatures,
the heavens rain oil,
the wadis bring forth honey.
The kindly El, the gracious one, rejoices.
He puts his feet firmly on his footstool;
he opens his mouth widely and laughs;
he raises his voice and shouts:
  'I will sit and take my rest,
  and my soul shall be at ease in my breast,
  for the mighty Baal is alive,
  the prince, the lord of the earth exists!'

While these are not likely to be direct literary influences, they serve as a reminder of the kind of cultural and literary context within which the poets of Israel and Judah worked, and of the fact that Hebrew poetry and religious writing was not something entirely unconnected with the wider world. A further reminder of this may be seen in another ancient text, which belongs to the royal conventions of Assyria. It is, of course, even less probable that such a text could have been known to a Jewish poet; my reason for giving it is to bring out a feature of the Psalms of Ascents which can easily be forgotten in a piece like 126: namely, the centrality of an idealised concept of *kingship*. In the ancient world the well-being of society as a whole depended crucially on the king's relationship to the deity, and that well-being was undoubtedly largely dependent upon agricultural prosperity. The favourable conditions sought in the second part of Psalm 126 are bound up with the desire for a king in good standing with Yahweh. The following inscription (Saggs 1984: 162) belongs to the reign of Sargon II of Assyria (727–705 BCE):

[H]e set his mind to . . . open up fallow land, and plant orchards; he set himself to gain a crop on steep rocky slopes which formerly had never produced vegetation; he set his heart on putting furrows into waste land which under former kings had known no plough, to have people sing for joy!

One last connection is worth noting. In Isaiah 55:10–13 there is an oracle celebrating the prosperity of the land as a metaphor for the power of Yahweh's word. Verses 10 and 12 are particularly apt – an indication, perhaps, that just as Isaiah uses agricultural imagery explicitly for a deeper religious purpose, so Psalm 126 may well suggest matters deeper than the ground dug by the plough.[5] The mystical or mythic references may indeed be an important part of the meaning of the Psalm, for ancient and modern readers alike.

Structure

There is an eloquent similarity of form between the two parts of this Psalm. Each begins with an almost identical form of words ('When the LORD restored the fortunes of Zion' and 'Restore our fortunes, O LORD'), and each opening phrase is then expanded in a simile ('like those who dream'; 'like watercourses in the Negeb'[6]). Any reservations about the integrity of the Psalm as a whole must be dispelled at once, together with the old reading of 'captivity' in verse 1. For if the two parts form a whole, then the prayer in the second part must be the reason for the reminiscence in the first, which in turn surely speaks of past prosperity in general.

This similarity of form does not end with the opening verses, for each part goes on to explore the themes of laughter and sorrow in structurally connected ways. Thus each proceeds to a summary of the theme (in the form of a declaration in the first part and a prayer in the second), followed by an elaboration of the theme. Joy and sorrow, laughter and tears are the motifs. The joy deriving from the hymn to past good fortune in verses 2–3 is modified by the sorrow which accompanies the uncertainty of the prayer in the second part. In keeping with this essential contrast between the genres, the parallelism employed is synonymous/chiastic in the first part and antithetic/chiastic in the second. The detail is set out below.

Then our mouth was filled with laughter,	a / verb / b
and our tongue with shouts of joy;	A / / B
then it was said among the nations,	a1
'The LORD has done great things for them.'	d
The LORD has done great things for us,	D
and we rejoiced.	B1

May those who sow in tears	p / q
reap with shouts of joy.	–p / –q

209

Those who go out weeping,	Q
bearing the seed for sowing,	P
shall come home with shouts of joy,	–Q
carrying their sheaves.	–P

The chiastic effect in the first part is within the elaboration; in the second it consists of a reversal between the statement and the elaboration.

Psalm 127

	TEXTUAL NOTES AND STRUCTURE	
Stanza 1		
1 Unless the LORD builds the house, those who build it labour in vain.	Building the house	A
Unless the LORD guards the city, the guard keeps watch in vain.	Guarding the city	B
Stanza 2		
2 It is in vain that you rise up early and go late to rest, eating the bread of anxious toil; for he gives sleep to his beloved.	Uselessness of solitary toil	C
Stanza 3		
3 Sons are indeed a heritage from the LORD, the fruit of the womb a reward.	Sons maintain the house	A1
4 Like arrows in the hand of a warrior are the sons of one's youth.	Sons defend the city	B1
Stanza 4		
5 Happy is the man who has his quiver full of them. He shall not be put to shame when he speaks with his enemies in the gate.	Blessedness of corporate action	C1

Textual points and comparative material from the ancient Near East

Commentators have puzzled over the seeming disparity between the two parts of this Psalm and, as Allen (1983) observes, 'a sizeable number of scholars have regarded it as an amalgamation of two separate, unrelated sayings'. Yet in the end both he and Davidson (1998) affirm the unity of its composition, while continuing in the majority tradition of allocating it to the Wisdom genre. The fact that it bears the title 'Of Solomon' to some extent supports this interpretation – at least to the extent that ancient readers may have shared the modern view. However, it has also been suggested that the reference to 'his beloved' at the end of verse 2 may have prompted the unusual attribution, a point discussed in detail in Chapter 3 (pp. 39–40). While this must remain speculative, there is an interesting coincidence of theme between 2 Samuel 7:11b–16 (even more so its parallel in 1 Chronicles 17:10b–14) and Psalm 127. Both are concerned with the house to be built by or in honour of Yahweh, and with the dynastic succession. In view of the established use by Chronicles of passages also found in Psalm 132, we may be justified in identifying a significant intertextuality to which the name of Solomon accurately directs us.

While there is in the NRSV a footnote indicating an alternative translation for the last line of verse 2, the difficulty is not at the level of the Hebrew text, but rather one of puzzling out what the text *means*! The translation 'he gives sleep to his beloved' is accurate enough. The only other point of a textual nature is to note the various meanings which can be carried by the Hebrew word rendered 'house'. Apart from that basic sense, it is used also to indicate special houses, such as the temple ('the house of Yahweh') or the king's residence (palace). Further, it denotes a household or family, including the sense of a dynasty. This multiplicity of reference helps to explain how the two seemingly separate parts of Psalm 127 are to be held together.

We would not expect to find any very particular ancient near-eastern parallels for a psalm such as this, though Weiser (1962) comments that 'there is . . . an inscription on a Babylonian building which says of the god Marduk: "There is no house whose foundation is laid without thee . . . who can do anything without thee?"' One other observation is pertinent, concerning the reference to 'the gate' at the end of the Psalm. It is perhaps a commonplace now that local justice was dispensed by 'the elders' at the town gate (De Vaux 1961: 152–3), though beyond the few instances in the Hebrew Bible which seem to fit this description there is surprisingly slight documentation available. Boecker (1980: 26) comments in respect of the wider ancient Near East:

Speaking quite generally, the justice of elders must go back to a developmental stage prior to the king's justice. But it was not fully suppressed by the latter. It is not easy to determine the relation of the administration of justice by elders to that by the king, particularly as the source material is so meager on this point. Courts of elders were particularly active in the smaller towns. *The assumption that the local elders' court was appealed to in slight affairs, the royal court in more important affairs, is so much in the nature of things that it cannot be totally false.*

(1980: 26; emphasis added)

The relevance of this comparison is that, just as the military language in Psalm 120 is surely metaphoric, so here we should read verse 5 not as dealing with the conditions of war but rather with the general conflicts of everyday life.

Structure

My proposal is to see this Psalm as a four-stanza composition, rather than the two normally set out. In the text of Psalm 127 I have suggested headings for each stanza to clarify how they link to each other. *Stanzas 1* and *3*, while each serves as an introduction to its half of the Psalm, are connected by the bond between 'house' and 'sons'. The latter provide the means of ensuring the successful outcome of the prayer in the former. The link is not merely human, however, for it is the LORD who provides in both cases.

Stanzas 2 and *4* form a contrast between the vain, isolated endeavour of the solitary provider and the blessed state of the pater-familias who is surrounded by his family[7] and who therefore does not need to face his opponents unsupported. In addition, the phrase 'shall not be put to shame' in verse 5 provides a further element of contrast with the futility of *stanza 2*. But each also includes linguistic ties with its preceding stanza. Thus *stanza 2* picks up the idea of vanity which takes the form of a warning in *stanza 1* and explores its consequences, while *stanza 4* develops the metaphor of the warrior's arrows in its depiction of the scene 'in the gate'.

The position of Psalm 127 in the Psalms of Ascents is significant in view of the language of Psalm 128, in which domestic well-being is described. This in turn echoes Psalm 126, since the 'fruits' to which the family of the blessed are compared are surely the result of the kind of successful harvest which that Psalm anticipates.

Psalm 128

	TEXTUAL NOTES AND STRUCTURE	
1 Happy is everyone who fears the LORD, who walks in his ways.	The blessed state of the	A
2 You shall eat the fruit of the labour of your hands; you shall be happy, and it shall go well with you.	individual	B C
3 Your wife will be like a fruitful vine within your house; your children will be like olive shoots around your table.		B1
4 Thus shall the man be blessed who fears the LORD.		A1
5 The LORD bless you from Zion. May you see the prosperity of Jerusalem all the days of your life.	The blessed condition of the nation	D E F
6 May you see your children's children. Peace be upon Israel.		E1 D1

Textual points and comparative material from the ancient Near East

An almost innocent Psalm, this, in the sense that there are no difficulties in the text meriting any comment and (given the intensely domestic scene which it portrays) little to be added of a comparative nature. The description of family life is quite unique in the Psalter, matched only by the metaphor of weaning employed in 131:2. The pairings of the vine and the olive on the one hand, and the house and table on the other, are rather rare. The first is only otherwise found in Hosea 14:4–7; but that is a quite significant parallel, since it uses these terms to describe Israel restored through the merciful love of God. The vine by itself is more frequently found as a metaphor for Israel – positively in Hosea 10:1 and in Psalm 80:8–18, and problematically in Jeremiah 2:21 and 8:13, and in Ezekiel's parable (17:1–10). It is of interest that only in this Psalm are these symbols used explicitly of 'women and children'; though we may note the special character of Hosea with its emphasis on the more feminine characteristics of the deity. The link with Psalm 80 is noteworthy in the light of my earlier reference to that Psalm in connection with Psalm 126:1, 4.

The second pairing finds just two parallels, in Psalm 23:5–6 and in Proverbs 9:1–2. The latter describes Wisdom (a female figure) building her house and laying her table to attract acolytes; the former speaks of God's spreading a table for the psalmist, who looks forward to an everlasting dwelling in God's house. Again, as with the pairing of vine and olive, these are very suggestive comparisons.

Structure

How should this Psalm be divided? Do the three stanzas indicated by the NRSV properly reflect the inner forms of the poem? Allen (1983) proposes two parts, the first ending with verse 3, so that the repeated 'who fears the LORD' becomes the introduction to the second stanza. The use of the adjective 'blessed' perhaps supports this approach, since that term is not found before verse 4, but recurs in verse 5. Dahood (1970), on the other hand, regards the phrase 'who fears the LORD' as an *inclusio* rounding off the first section, thus implying two stanzas of unequal length.

While there is no single 'correct' structure, the solution I have chosen (see p. 213) is based, first, on the recognition of a palinstrophic pattern in the second part of the Psalm. It then turns out that Dahood's suggestion matches a corresponding palinstrophe in the first part, which provides a satisfying completeness to the pattern of the Psalm. In addition, two verbal themes are important for the unity of the Psalm: a sequence of terms relating to fruitfulness (fruit / fruitful, wife / children / children's children), and a set of expressions describing an air of contentment (happy, blessed, prosperity, peace).

There are several features which connect Psalm 128 closely to its predecessor. The opening word, 'happy', takes up the last verse of 127, and the theme of fruitfulness reverses the negative note of 127:2 ('the bread of anxious toil'; compare 'the fruit of the labour of your hands') and continues the positive theme of 127:3 ('the fruit of the womb a reward'; compare 'Your wife will be like a fruitful vine'). We may also note that in both Psalms the public and private spheres are paired. Psalm 127 begins with the temple (the public household) and the city, and ends with a celebration of family life. Psalm 128, conversely, devotes its first part to the happiness of the fruitful family, and uses that as grounds for a prayer for blessing on the community as a whole. Notice in particular how the public structures (Zion, Jerusalem) in lines D and E are matched by the personal in E1 (children's children) and D1 (Israel).

Psalm 129

	TEXTUAL NOTES AND STRUCTURE	
1 'Often have they attacked me from my youth' – let Israel now say –	The assaults of the wicked	A
2 'often have they attacked me from my youth, yet they have not prevailed against me.		B
3 Those who plough ploughed on my back; they made their furrows long.'		C
4 The LORD is righteous; he has cut the cords of the wicked.	The intervention of the	D
5 May all who hate Zion be put to shame and turned back.	LORD	D1
6 Let them be like the grass on the housetops that withers before it grows up,	The defeat of the wicked	C1
7 with which reapers do not fill their hands or binders of sheaves their arms,		
8 while those who pass by do not say,		B1
'The blessing of the LORD be upon you! We bless you in the name of the LORD!'		A1

Textual points and comparative material from the ancient Near East

The distressing image of the enemy ploughing furrows in one's back strikes the modern reader as an unnatural cruelty. It finds a context, however, in Canaanite language associated with the death of Baal, his role in the fertility of the land, and the form of mourning which his supporters employ. Thus Anat, finding the body of the slain Baal (Gibson 1977: 74),

> [harrowed] her collar-bone,
> she ploughed (her) chest like a garden,
> she harrowed (her) waist like a valley, (saying):
> 'Baal is dead!'

Elsewhere (Gibson 1977: 78) we find a lament concerning the circumstances of Baal's absence from his proper role in the process of ploughing and planting (El is speaking):

The furrows in the field are cracked, O Shaphash,
the furrows in the fields of El are cracked.
Baal should be occupying the furrows in the plough-land.[8]

Finally in the same myth (*ibid.*: 77) there is an account of Anat's killing of Mot (Baal's enemy) which is couched in the language of agriculture:

She seized divine Mot,
with a sword she split him,
with a sieve she winnowed him,
with a fire she burnt him,
with mill-stones she ground him,
in a field she scattered him.

Given that the final curse upon the psalmist's enemies takes the form of agricultural blight and drought, there are signs here of a secularised form of these traditional mythic motifs. This seems to be the only such instance in the Hebrew Bible, though there is a troubling passage in 2 Samuel 12:31 in which David appears to be putting the people of the defeated city of Rabbah to a particularly horrible torture, involving placing them under saws, harrows and axes, and driving them through a brick kiln. The KJV is essential here, since the full unpleasantness of the Hebrew is masked in modern translations, which amend the original to give something marginally less revolting (as indeed does the parallel in 1 Chronicles 20:3). Perhaps we need occasionally to be reminded that the ancient world was often brutal and inhumane (though why the twentieth century should require any such reminder is passing strange).

There are difficulties with the Hebrew of verse 6, but they need not detain us since the interpretation provided in the NRSV is perfectly acceptable. The scene is familiar – flat, mud-roofed houses upon which a growth of grass appears in the wet weather, only to wither as soon as the sun returns. An exchange of the kind indicated in verse 8 (which is surely to be read as a blessing exchanged between two parties) is recorded in Ruth 2:4 – 'Just then Boaz came from Bethlehem. He said to the reapers, "The LORD be with you." They answered, "The LORD bless you."' Finally, the phrase 'the cords of the wicked' in verse 4 has a parallel in Isaiah 5:18 – 'Ah, you who drag iniquity along with cords of falsehood, who drag sin along as with cart-ropes.' The 'cords' are clearly drawn from the same metaphoric context as the other agricultural references in the Psalm.[9]

Structure

A clue to the structure of Psalm 129 is to be found in the formal similarity between the repeated lines in verses 1 and 2a, and those in verse 8. This is suggestive of a palinstrophic distribution, a possibility further strengthened by the paralleled ploughing and reaping motifs in verse 3 and verses 6–7. From these hints I have built up the schema indicated in the text (p. 215). Verse 2b parallels verse 8a in that both use the common negative 'not' to signal the failure, on the one hand, of the enemies' designs upon the righteous and, on the other, of blessings for those 'who hate Zion'.

The middle section (verses 4–5) could be read either as a single statement, or (as I have done) as an antithetic pair. Thus 'The LORD is righteous' finds its opposite in 'May all who hate Zion', while God's positive action ('he has cut the cords of the wicked') is paralleled in the passive fate of the enemy ('put to shame and turned back').

Psalm 130[10]

	TEXTUAL NOTES
1 Out of the depths I cry to you, O LORD	Invocation
2 LORD, hear my voice! Let your ears be attentive to the voice of my supplications!	Repeated pair (1)
3 If you, O LORD, should mark iniquities, LORD, who could stand? 4 But there is forgiveness with you, so that you may be revered.	The problem of sin and its resolution
5 I wait for the LORD, my soul waits, and in his word I hope; 6 my soul waits for the LORD more than those who watch for the morning, more than those who watch for the morning.	Repeated pair (2)
7 O Israel, hope in the LORD!	Invocation
For with the LORD there is steadfast love, and with him is great power to redeem. 8 It is he who will redeem Israel from all its iniquities.	The problem of sin and its resolution

Textual points and comparative material from the ancient Near East

Although this Psalm shares some general features with typical laments from the ancient near east (in particular, the sense of sinfulness and inadequacy which only the merciful nature of the deity can overcome), I have not been able to identify any close parallels. The opening plea, 'Out of the depths I cry to you, O LORD', is so deeply embedded in Christian religious thinking that it is hard to recover any sense of its contextual force. The 'depths' referred to are elsewhere always qualified as being 'deep waters' (Psalm 60:2, 14; Isaiah 51:10; Ezekiel 27:34), and thus belong to the familiar language of the cosmic threat posed by the primaeval forces. Only here is the word found as an unqualified substantive, which may be grounds enough to regard it as having a special reference to the sense of sinfulness which is taken up in verse 3.

The question in verse 3, which asks 'who could stand' in God's presence, is similar to those found in the entrance liturgies in Psalms 15 and 24. This may have a bearing on the overall interpretation of the Psalms of Ascents as a sequence associated with a pilgrimage festival. Psalm 24:3 in fact uses the same verb, 'to stand'.

Structure

This is the first of a pair of psalms in which an air of suspense, of expectation, of a certain tension is evident. In the sequence as a whole they represent the build-up to the grand climax in Psalm 132. Perhaps the most obvious technique which drives this atmosphere is heightened repetition, beyond the normal requirements of parallelism. There are three examples in Psalm 130 – in verses 2, 5 and 6 – and their effect is to postpone whatever point the psalmist is addressing. More strikingly, the device is redoubled at its second occurrence – the delay is itself delayed! This produces a strangely tentative overall impact, the elements of which may be summarised as follows (the relevant text can be read on p. 217):

> Invocation – pause – first statement of theme – pause – pause – invocation – second statement of theme

In addition to this dramatic device, we find that the two thematic statements involve an element of chiasmus. In verses 3–4, the first two lines speak of iniquity and the second two of forgiveness. Verses

7b–8 reverse this priority, taking first the motifs of love and redemption, and then ending with a reference to iniquities. This has the effect of leaving the reader in some doubt; for although the sense of the last verse is positive, there is a residue of doubt – an impression which the next Psalm fastens on to when it commences with an almost feverish protestation of innocence.

Psalm 131

	TEXTUAL NOTES

1 O LORD my heart is not lifted up,
    my eyes are not raised too high;
  I do not occupy myself with things
    too great and too marvellous for me.
  But I have calmed and quieted my soul,
	The problem of sin
	and its resolution

2   like a weaned child with its mother;
    my soul is like the weaned child that is with me
    [*or* my soul within me is like a weaned child].
	Repeated pair (3)

3 O Israel, hope in the LORD from this time on and for evermore.	Invocation

Textual points and comparative material from the ancient Near East

There is some uncertainty as to the meaning of verse 2c. The NRSV is perhaps not so good, and I would prefer the alternative given in the footnote: 'my soul within me is like a weaned child'. The only other textual point of any note is that this is one of only three Psalms of Ascents (the others are 122 and 124) to be attributed to David. There does not appear to be anything significant about this.

The metaphor of the weaned child deserves some comment, for it is not as straightforward as a superficial reading might imply. This Psalm is often described as a Psalm of confidence, as though its air were one of calm serenity. However, if the practice of nursing children at the breast into their third year was common in Israel (as 2 Maccabees 7:27 seems to imply[11]) we may wonder whether a newly weaned child might not be fretful and ill at ease, rather than content. In that case, the Psalm would represent a further expression of the tension and suspense recorded in Psalm 130.

INTEGRATED STRUCTURE AND TEXT FOR PSALMS 130–1

1   Invocation   A Out of the depths I cry to you, O LORD

2   Repeated pair 1   B   LORD, hear my voice!
                                Let your ears be attentive
                                     to the voice of my supplications!

3   The problem of sin C If you, O LORD, should mark iniquities,
    and its resolution   LORD, who could stand?
4   But there is forgiveness with you,
                                     so that you may be revered.

5   Repeated pair 2   B I wait for the LORD, my soul waits,
                                 and in his word I hope;
6   my soul waits for the LORD
                                   more than those who watch for the
                                        morning,
                                     more than those who watch for the
                                        morning.

7   Invocation   A O Israel, hope in the LORD!

    The problem of sin C   For with the LORD there is steadfast love,
    and its resolution   and with him is great power to redeem.
8   It is he who will redeem Israel
                                     from all its iniquities.

1   The problem of sin C O LORD my heart is not lifted up,
    and its resolution   my eyes are not raised too high;
                              I do not occupy myself with things
                                     too great and too marvellous for me.
2   But I have calmed and quieted my soul,

    Repeated pair 3   B   like a weaned child with its mother;
                                 my soul is like the weaned child that is
                                   with me.

3   Invocation   A O Israel, hope in the LORD
                              from this time on and for evermore.

Structure

It seems to me appropriate to interpret the structure of Psalm 131 as a direct continuation of 130, and the headings alongside the text of

Psalm 131 are chosen to make this clear. They are, of course, perfectly in keeping with the actual content – the proposal to see a continuity is not imposed from some prior need but drawn from the character of the two Psalms. The perplexing problem which results is to find some reason for their separation (other than the desire to have exactly fifteen Psalms – a fact which appears to be quite secondary, and to have no internal logic). In order to show how they might cohere as a single formal entity providing a tense prelude to 132, I have set out the two Psalms together as an integrated structure.

Psalm 132

Textual points and comparative material from the ancient Near East

The Psalm opens with a reference to David's 'hardships', though it is not clear what is thus intended. It may be that the word anticipates the account in verses 3–5 of his restless search for a suitable place for Yahweh. However, others have seen in this word an indication of a more mythic kind, preferring the translation 'humiliation'. I will return to this point.

There are two very curious phrases in verse three. Where the NRSV reads 'house' and 'bed' the Hebrew has something like 'the tent which is my house' and 'the bed which is my couch'. No really satisfactory explanation has been given for this unique turn of phrase, which is perhaps best taken as one indication (among several) of a certain strangeness characteristic of this Psalm. Another such phrase, often taken to be an indication of antiquity, is the repeated 'Mighty One of Jacob' (verses 2 and 5). Variously described as an ancient divine title or as evidence of the religious traditions of the northern kingdom of Israel, it is nevertheless curious that two of its other three occurrences are to be found in undoubtedly late texts (Isaiah 49:26 and 60:16). The other is Genesis 49:24, in Jacob's deathbed blessing of his sons, and while it occurs as part of the blessing of Joseph, it is by no means clear that either Genesis as a whole or this chapter is pre-exilic.

The place names in verse 6 have also prompted considerable speculation in view of their apparent associations with David (Ruth 4:11; Micah 5:2) and with the traditions about the Ark in Samuel (1 Samuel 6:21–7:2[12]). The parallel references to Ephrathah, like those to 'the Mighty One of Jacob', are ambiguous. While Micah may take us back to pre-exilic Judah, the provenance of Ruth is

PSALM 132

		TEXTUAL NOTES AND STRUCTURE	
1	O LORD, remember in David's favour all the hardships he endured;	For David	A
2	how he swore to the LORD and vowed to the Mighty One of Jacob,	David's oath	B
3	'I will not enter my house or get into my bed,		
4	I will not give sleep to my eyes or slumber to my eyelids,		
5	until I find a place for the LORD, a dwelling place for the Mighty One of Jacob.'		
6	We heard of it in Ephrathah. we found it in the fields of Jaar.	The people's search	C
7	'Let us go to his dwelling-place; let us worship at his footstool.'		
8	Rise up, O LORD, and go to your resting-place, you and the ark of your might.		
9	Let your priests be clothed with righteousness, and let your faithful shout for joy.	Refrain	D
10	For your servant David's sake do not turn away the face of your anointed one.	For David	A1

11	The LORD swore to David a sure oath
	   from which he will not turn back:
	'One of the sons of your body
	   I will set on your throne.
		Yahweh's
		oath
			B1

12	If your sons keep my covenant
	   and my decrees that I shall teach them,
	their sons also, for evermore,
	   shall sit on your throne.'		

13	For the LORD has chosen Zion; he has desired it for his habitation:	Yahweh's search	C1
14	'This is my resting-place for ever; here I will reside, for I have desired it.		
15	I will abundantly bless its provisions; I will satisfy its poor with bread.	Refrain	D1
16	Its priests I will clothe with salvation, and its faithful will shout for joy.		
17	There I will cause a horn to sprout up for David; I have prepared a lamp for my anointed one.	For David	A2
18	His enemies I will clothe with disgrace, but on him, his crown will gleam.'		

far more likely to be the Persian Period or later. In two places (Ruth 1:2 and 1 Samuel 17:12) the adjective 'Ephrathite' is associated with Bethelehem, and these may be relevant to the discussion. However, questions of both relative and absolute dating remain unresolved, so that we cannot draw any useful conclusions from these references about the antiquity or otherwise of Psalm 132. The more general matter of the Ark narratives in Samuel and their significance in Psalm 132 will be discussed in the next chapter.

Regarding possible parallels in the traditions of the ancient Near East, the most interesting (and also the most notorious) is the suggestion that Psalm 132 represents an Israelite ritual similar to that of the quest for Marduk at the Babylonian New Year Festival.[13] The two dramas are not identical, not least because of Israel's mono-theism, but the parallel is none the less intriguing, as Mowinckel points out (1962, I: 176):

> In Babylonia the other gods would go out with the king and the priests, etc., in a cultic procession to search for and deliver the lost, dead, or imprisoned god. In the cultic drama of Israel it is the king, 'David', who with his army marches out to search for the representative symbol of Yahweh, the holy ark;[14] who finds it, and provides a permanent abode for it on Zion.

Frankfort (1948: 320) describes an interesting scene which takes place in the shrine of Marduk prior to the search for the god. The high priest removes the king's insignia and strikes him on the face, after which the king, kneeling, declares his innocence:

> I have not sinned, O Lord of the lands,
> I have not been negligent regarding thy divinity,
> I have not destroyed Babylon.

The high priest then returns the king's insignia and strikes him again.

Johnson (1967: 111ff.) discusses the ritual humiliation of the king as part of a hypothetical enthronement festival of Yahweh in Israel.[15] Without necessarily subscribing to his reconstruction, it is interesting that Psalm 132 begins with a reference to David's hardships, suffering or (possibly) humiliation, and that David then vows to take no rest until he has restored Yahweh to his proper place. If there is any connection between the Babylonian ceremony and the events indicated by Psalm 132, this reading of the opening of the Psalm provides an additional link. However, it must be emphasised that there is considerable uncertainty surrounding both the interpretation of the Babylonian material and the circumstances which might have produced an emulative ceremony in Jerusalem. At any rate, it would presumably have to be a post-exilic relationship, based on the experiences of those who made a new life for themselves in Babylonia.[16]

Structure

Formally, Psalm 132 presents us with something of an embarrassment of riches, at the levels both of individual words and phrases and of overall architecture. Many commentators have remarked upon the detailed parallels between the two halves of the Psalm, though differing somewhat in their view of the precise point at which the division should be made. The difficulty lies in the existence of one threefold pattern (indicated alongside the text by the heading 'For David') which leads to uncertainty as to whether the two stanzas should be defined as verses 1–10 and 11–18 or as verses 1–9 and 10–16, with a coda in verses 17–18. The latter fits better with the positioning of the repeated refrain, but the former provides two stanzas each concluding with the theme of David and God's anointed. I have adopted a middle way which declines a straightforward division into two halves, preferring a broad structure of the form A // B / C / D// A1// B1/ C1/ D1// A2 where two matching stanzas are embraced by the three 'For David' themes. Whichever option is preferred there are several detailed parallels of note. The vow made by David (verses 2–5) is matched by the oath sworn by Yahweh (verses 11–12); the refrain in verse 9 returns (in an expanded form) in verses 15–16; the prayer for the return of the Ark to Jerusalem (verse 8) is matched in verse 14 by Yahweh's positive choice of Zion. The remaining verses of the 'search' sections are less obviously parallel, though certain interesting links can be observed. Verse 6 refers to the place where the Ark was previously located (Ephrathah/Jaar) while verse 13a identifies Yahweh's chosen place, thus contributing to the general movement from an unfulfilled quest in the first part to its realisation in the second. This transformation is seen also in the refrains which constitute a transformation from prayer (verse 9) to affirmation (verses 15–16). Further, verse 7 speaks of the 'dwelling place' of God while verse 13b describes Zion as God's 'habitation'.

The three 'For David' passages illustrate the dynamic of the Psalm, which we have seen in the movement from part one to part two. The first refers only to David, the second to David and the anointed, and the third to both of these and to David's enemies, whose presence affirms the finality of the messianic victory. But the dominant motif of the Psalm is the quest to find a proper place for both Yahweh and the royal dynasty. Only when Yahweh is ensconced in Zion and the messianic dynasty on the throne of Jerusalem can the restless progress of the Psalm find its resolution. Finally, this is a permanent outcome, as the double use of the phrase 'for evermore' reveals. 'Their sons . . . for evermore, shall sit on your throne' (verse 12) and 'This is my resting-place for ever' (verse 14) – both of which remind us of one of the standard formulae of the Psalms of Ascents: 'from this time on and for evermore'. It is significant also that Psalm 133, which forms a coda to the sequence, ends with the phrase 'life for evermore'.

There are several parallel passages elsewhere in the Hebrew Bible which have a bearing on Psalm 132. Numbers 10:35 preserves a kind of battle cry of the Ark which has some relevance to 132:8–17 (*passim*):

> Whenever the ark set out, Moses would say,
>   'Arise, O LORD, let your enemies be scattered,
>   and your foes flee before you.'
> And whenever it came to rest, he would say,
>   'Return, O LORD of the ten thousand thousands of Israel.'

Verses 8–10 are substantially the same as 2 Chronicles 6:41–2, part of the long sequence describing the dedication of the temple in Solomon's reign.[17] Psalm 89, which Johnson discusses in detail (1967: 106–13), has a passage (89:3–4) very reminiscent of Yahweh's oath to David:

> You have said, 'I have made a covenant with my chosen one,
>   I have sworn to my servant David:
> "I will establish your descendants for ever,
>   and build your throne for all generations."'

Lastly we may note that in Proverbs 6:4 there is a saying similar to 132:4; perhaps this was a proverbial usage.

Psalm 133

		TEXTUAL NOTES AND STRUCTURE	
1	How very good and pleasant it is when kindred live together in unity!	The blessing of unity	A

2	It is like the precious oil on the head,
	   running down upon the beard,
	on the beard of Aaron,
	   running down over the collar of his robes.
		First
		comparison
			B

3	It is like the dew of Hermon, which falls on the mountains of Zion.	Second comparison	B1
	For there the LORD ordained his blessing, life for evermore.	The blessing of life	A1
	[Peace be upon Israel. (11QPs^A)]		

Textual points and comparative material from the ancient Near East

There are no textual problems in this short and somewhat odd Psalm. The imagery may strike the modern reader as strange – combining as it does a scene from the ritual anointing of the high priest with a bizarre geographical link (the dew of Hermon, in Syria, could hardly be thought to fall upon Zion, in Jerusalem). We have, of course, seen geographical references employed metaphorically at the beginning of the Psalms of Ascents (Meshech and Kedar in Psalm 120), where their very strangeness was the point of the trope. Hermon may stand for the holy mountain in the north (*Zaphon* – the name also of Baal's sacred mountain in the Ugaritic texts). In Psalm 48:2 Zion is said to be 'in the far north',[18] and Psalm 89:12 speaks of Tabor and Hermon in an enigmatic context[19] which seems to imply a metaphoric use not dissimilar to the present context.

The oil poured over Aaron's head and running down his beard and robe must have been inspired by the ceremonial of the consecration of Aaron and his sons to the priesthood in Exodus 29:1–9, with particular reference to verse 7. I remarked in the previous chapter on the rarity of references to Aaron and to priests in the Psalms. Coming as it does immediately after the celebration of the priests and the messiah/king in 132:16–17, there is surely more to this metaphor than just a pleasing image to conjure harmony.

Dahood (1970) points out a Ugaritic parallel to the conjunction of dew and oil in this Psalm, found in the myth of the palace of Baal,[20] but other biblical metaphorical uses of dew are arguably of greater interest. Thus in Exodus 16:13f. and Numbers 11:9 dew is associated with the phenomenon of manna, while Deuteronomy 32:2 and 33:13 use it to signify God's blessing. There is no other example of the parallel between dew and oil, though Numbers 11:8 does describe the cakes made with manna as having the flavour of 'cakes baked with oil'. Lastly, Psalm 110 (one of the few which speak of the priesthood) has an enigmatic reference to 'the dew of your youth' – though what that signifies is not at all clear. Johnson takes it to be symbolic of the resurrection of the king/messiah at dawn.[21]

Structure

The shape of this Psalm is simple enough: an opening prayer for 'the good life' brackets the piece with the concluding declaration of Yahweh's blessing 'life for evermore'. In between there is a pair of similes, whose context and parallels I have discussed in some detail above. The wording emphasises the downward nature of the blessing. Now that Yahweh is established upon Zion, blessings flow down to all the people from his dwelling.

If the Qumran text is reliable, there is a coda to this Psalm in the form of one of the characteristic phrases, 'Peace be upon Israel'. It must be admitted that the additional phrase does not sit very easily with the structure I have proposed, and I am not sure how to accommodate it. Perhaps it could be seen as introducing an explicit parallel to the term 'kindred' in verse 1. There is a comparable formulation in Psalm 122:8, 'For the sake of my relatives and friends / I will say, "Peace be within you".' 'You' of course refers to Jerusalem, and the Hebrew word translated 'relatives' is the same as that rendered 'kindred' in Psalm 133. This might allow us to interpret the final phrase as part of an extended blessing forming a detailed parallel to the several elements of verse 1.

Psalm 134

	TEXTUAL NOTES AND STRUCTURE	

1 Come, bless the LORD,
   all you servants of the LORD,
   who stand by night in the house of the LORD!
	The pilgrims
	bless Yahweh
		A

2 Lift up your hands to the holy place, and bless the LORD.	Address to the sanctuary	B
3 May the LORD, maker of heaven and earth, bless you from Zion.	Yahweh's closing blessing upon the pilgrims	A1

Comment

There seems little point in going through the motions of the separate headings of our discussion for what is evidently a doxology rounding off the sequence of Psalms of Ascents. There are just two points of some interest in this preliminary commentary: the reference to those 'who stand by night', which might imply an all-night vigil[22] (Psalm 130:6 could be another hint of such a ritual; and see my discussion of Johnson in respect of Psalm 110:3, above); and the action involving lifting up one's hands towards the sacred place, which is apparently an act of homage. The intensity of the poem is revealed by three linguistic features:

1   There are no fewer than six designations of God in its brief compass.
2   The term 'bless' occurs in each verse.
3   A phrase denoting God's dwelling place is found in each verse.

We may perhaps imagine the pilgrims, who first encountered the formula 'maker of heaven and earth' at the outset of the festival sequence in 121:2, now returning to their homes emboldened and encouraged by that final blessing: 'May Yahweh, maker of heaven and earth, / bless you from Zion.'

14

PSALMS 120–34

A contextual overview

In Chapter 13 various features supporting the coherence of the Psalms of Ascents were identified. Among them was a set of words which occurred with unusually high frequency in this collection. I propose now to consider the thematic implications of these terms, in conjunction with a résumé of the main concerns which inform these Psalms, based on the discussion in Chapter 13. I then undertake an interpretation of the whole sequence in the light of this thematic analysis which will give us clues to the kind of hermeneutical framework which may be proposed as we seek an overall view of the nature, function and socio-historical context of the Psalms of Ascents, in accordance with aspect 3 (and to a lesser extent aspect 5) of my general methodology. I will reserve treatment of the main part of aspect 5, and of aspects 6 and 7 for the final chapter.

The significant themes of the Psalms of Ascents

In Table 12.3 the following were picked out as words whose frequency in the Psalms of Ascents implies special significance: *Jacob*, *Israel* and *Jerusalem*; *David*, *anointed* and *throne*; *Zion*, *Aaron*, *priest* and *Ark*; *desire/hope* and *slumber*; *peace* and *blessing*.

Certain themes seem to be already suggested by this list. Thus, *Aaron*, *Ark*, *priest* and *Zion* belong to the realm of the temple cult in Jerusalem, while *anointed*, *David* and *throne* speak of the royal or messianic[1] dimension. *Israel*, *Jerusalem*[2] and *Jacob* point to the third member of the body politic of ancient Judah – the people themselves.

We thus have at the outset an indicative emphasis in the Psalms of Ascents on the 'trinity' of *people*, *priesthood* and *royal dynasty*. The details of *theme 1*, the formal institutions of Judah, including a note of those individuals Psalms in which the themes occur, can be set out thus:[3]

1a the nation and the people (121, 122, 125, 126, 127, 128, 132, 133, 134)

1b the king and the dynasty (122, 127, 132)

1c the priesthood, Zion and the temple (122, 125, 126, 127, 128, 132, 133, 134).

The remaining terms – *desire/hope* and *slumber*; *blessing* and *peace* – will figure in the analysis of other themes drawn from the discussion of individual Psalms in Chapter 13.

A second very important group of motifs from these Psalms comprises *theme 2*, which concerns domestic realm of family and farm. These are very striking, and scarcely paralleled elsewhere in the Psalter. The family scene in 128:3, for example, is matched in only one place, Psalm 144:9, and even there no mention is made of a wife.[4] Three motifs can be identified, concerned with: family structures (wife, children, servants); agricultural and climatic matters; and fruitfulness, both of people and of crops. The details are:

2a the domestic scene – wife, children, servants (121,[5] 122,[6] 123, 128, 131, 133[6])

2b fruitfulness (127, 128, 132)

2c hunting, farming, climate (121, 124, 126, 129, 133).

It is the first of these which is most characteristic of the Psalms of Ascents; the others contribute not to the collection's uniqueness in kind but to the cumulative special character which the constituent Psalms display.

Whether the Psalms of Ascents are pilgrim songs is, as we have already seen, one of the areas of greatest controversy. Despite the uncertainty over this issue, there are themes within these Psalms (not to mention the title itself) which belong to the subject matter of procession on the one hand, and the place to which the pilgrims go on the other. Indeed, it could be said that the drama of finding a proper place for Yahweh is at the heart of the sequence, both in terms of the climax to Psalm 132 but also in terms of an important emphasis on place (or displacement) in several members of the sequence. Part of this process involves hope, expectation, and the suspense of waiting for the right time. Accordingly I have defined three motifs in *theme 3* – the quest for Yahweh:

3a the festival procession (122, 126,[7] 132)

3b the importance of place (120,[8] 122, 125, 132, 134)

3c suspense (130, 131, 132, 134[9]).

This theme of course overlaps with *theme 1*, since the place concerned, the goal of any festival procession, is the sacred place (*hieros topos*) variously known as Zion, Jerusalem and the house of Yahweh. The terms *slumber* and *hope/desire* from my preliminary list of key words are appropriate to theme 3c. The former relates both to Yahweh's constant wakeful vigilance and to David's zeal in the quest for the Ark, and the latter in relation to the hopes of the people and the desire of Yahweh in respect of Zion.

Throughout the Psalms of Ascents there is a recurring motif of conflict, danger, deceit and alienation. It forms the main thrust of Psalms 120, 124 and 129, but is by no means absent from the others. Clearly much of the drama is derived from this sense of danger, rooted (as I have elsewhere suggested) in an inner-Judaean difference of principle rather than the actual threat of external enemies. In part this motif represents an awareness of the culture of honour and shame which has figured largely in recent studies of the Mediterranean world[10] (though it is by no means confined to that geographical region). Putting one's enemies to shame, or being shamed oneself, is an important weapon in the biblical world, as is its converse, the principle of honour (*kabed*). Indeed, the great majority of instances of the concept of shame are to be found in Isaiah, Jeremiah and the Psalms. However, as a caveat, it is remarkable that in the Psalter the two terms 'honour' and 'shame' hardly ever come together as a pair, and the term for 'honour' is not found in the Psalms of Ascents. The best parallel is in Psalm 4:2: 'How long, you people, shall my honour suffer shame'; for the rest, there is one other less explicit parallel in Psalm 97:6–7 where God's glory is to be seen, while worshippers of images are put to shame. I have divided the motifs of *theme 4* – enemies of the faithful – into conflict and danger on the one hand, and deceit and shame on the other.

4a   conflict and danger (120, 124, 125,[11] 127, 129, 132[12])
4b   shame, contempt and deceit (120, 123, 125,[13] 127, 129, 132).

It is in fact the motif of shame and contempt which is striking in the Psalms of Ascents,[14] while the more traditional motif of enemy attack is relatively underplayed. This coheres with the view I have already expressed that we are not dealing here with external enemies but with internal opposition.

The last broad theme which I want to discuss is that which represents responses to the events of the sequence. On the one hand, the gifts of freedom, blessing and prosperity, and protection which come from God and, on the other, those expressions of joy on the part of the people which are presented as their spontaneous response to God's gifts. The motif of protection (terms such as 'keep' and 'watch' are strongly represented in the Psalms of Ascents) is important, and finds an echo where people variously 'watch' or 'observe' (e.g., the Covenant). The last of the key words – *peace* and *blessing* – are taken up at this point. Thus, *theme 5* – God's gifts and the people's responses – can be detailed as:

5a   God's gifts:
- peace, prosperity and blessing (122, 126, 128, 132, 133, 134)
- freedom and salvation (124, 126, 130, 132)
- protection (121, 125, 127)

5b   the people's responses
- expressions of joy (122, 124, 126, 132, 134)
- watching and observing[15] (127, 130, 132).

Certain familiar themes from the Psalter are missing or relatively under-represented in the Psalms of Ascents. There is no instance of any of the terms associated with *holiness*, though these are common in the rest of the Psalter – an omission which is the more surprising given that the 'hill of God' in Psalm 24 (which I have also tentatively linked with an Ark ceremony) is paired with the expression 'his holy place' (verse 3). And although Psalm 132 refers to the faithful along with righteousness and salvation (the refrain, verses 9, 16), this series of expressions, otherwise rather common in the Psalter, is the only instance in the Psalms of Ascents. Together with other absences noted under theme 4, this adds up to a very significant negative feature of the collection: the omission or relative infrequency of the set of terms *righteous/righteousness*, *faithful*, *glory/honour*, *holy/holiness*, *salvation*, *enemy*.

The significant themes: further analysis

Table 14.1 summarises the distribution of the various themes across the whole sequence. Readers may find it helpful to refer to this table in relation to the discussion which follows. But before embarking upon a study of the individual themes it is necessary to comment on certain broad characteristics which pertain to the analysis of the sequence as a whole.

Theme 1 constitutes a synopsis of the primary subject of the psalmist's concern – 'who we are, how we are governed, and what our

Table 14.1 Distribution of the five major themes of Psalms 120–34

	1 Judah's formal institutions			*2 Family and farm*			*3 The quest for Yahweh*			*4 Enemies of the faithful*		*5 Blessings and joy*	
	1a	*1b*	*1c*	*2a*	*2b*	*2c*	*3a*	*3b*	*3c*	*4a*	*4b*	*5a*	*5b*
120							✓			✓	✓		
121	✓			✓		✓				✓		✓	
122	✓	✓	✓	✓			✓	✓				✓	✓
123				✓							✓		
124					✓					✓		✓	✓
125	✓				✓			✓		✓	✓	✓	
126	✓				✓	✓	✓	✓				✓	✓
127	✓	✓	✓	✓	✓					✓	✓	✓	✓
128	✓				✓	✓						✓	
129						✓				✓	✓		
130									✓			✓	✓
131				✓					✓				
132	✓	✓	✓		✓		✓	✓	✓	✓	✓	✓	✓
133	✓		✓	✓		✓						✓	
134	✓				✓			✓	✓			✓	✓

religious institutions consist of' – and in a significant sense it is their security and survival that form the implied intention of the Psalms of Ascents. At the risk of repetition, it is necessary to emphasise the point that this concentration of themes is highly characteristic of *this* collection, and not of the Psalter as a whole, regardless of what one might expect to be the case. *Theme 2*, in contrast, is not a subject of the psalmist's interest, but one of the metaphorical fields which the poet employs in the process of dramatising his/her concerns. The other metaphorical field is *theme 4*, which focuses largely on the threat to a successful outcome of the project. It is not a simple matter of a positive trope contrasted with a negative one since, as we shall see, both are used positively and negatively.

Theme 3, the quest for Yahweh, is the means by which the collection moves from the expression of a desired outcome to the achievement of its resolution. In detail this involves pilgrimage or procession, expectation and tension, and the place at which the drama will be finalised. It could be argued that the last of these belongs to the subject matter of the sequence rather than its process, but at the end of the day it is not Zion or Jerusalem or the temple *simpliciter* which confirm the hopes of the people, but Yahweh on Zion, Jerusalem surrounded by God, and the temple of the LORD. Finally *theme 5* expresses both the blessings flowing from a fully realised political and religious economy based on the idea of Jerusalem as sacred place, and the exuberant pleasure of the people as a whole.

In sum, it is possible to discern a project, a process, two sets of metaphors delineating these, and an outcome, together comprising the framework of a coherent understanding of the Psalms of Ascents as a festival ensuring the success of people, priesthood and dynasty as long as Yahweh remains faithful to Zion. The drama is based in the myth that (each year?[16]) God symbolically withdraws from the temple, thus instituting a quest for the 'lost' deity by king and people. Only when Yahweh returns to Zion can normal business be resumed and the future contemplated with both joy and equanimity. I will now look at each theme in more detail, before returning to the question of a context within which the whole sequence may be set.

Theme 1: the formal institutions of Judah

Three Psalms (122, 127 and 132) present all three aspects of this theme particularly strongly, and it is absent from 120, 123, 124, 129, 130 and 131. The royal motif is not explicit in Psalm 127, but follows rather clearly from the comments in Chapter 13 (p. 211). In some cases one or other of the key expressions is used, but not in such a way as to constitute a thematic emphasis.[17]

Since I have put forward the claim that this first theme is, in effect, the main subject of the Psalms of Ascents, it is perhaps incumbent on me to comment on its absence from six of them. Several observations are in order, not least to recall that since I am treating them as a complete group, the significance of themes must be interpreted within the whole pattern. It is not necessary that everything be represented in every Psalm – I am not making an argument on the basis of the genre coherence of each single composition, rather on the genre of the collection as a whole. Nevertheless, there are useful things to be said. First, there is a more personal tone to the opening sequence of Psalms (120–4), where use of 'I', 'you' and 'we' predominates. This means that for public institutions to be signalled a positive decision is required rather than the use of the natural language of the cult. When we add to this the broadly (though not wholly) negative themes of 120, 123 and 124 it is not surprising that such symbols of confidence as the nation, the king and the LORD are not to the fore.

It is all the more significant, then, that we find in Psalm 122 a resoundingly comprehensive celebration of the full theme; and even more, that in the very personal 121 there is a central passage which uses the effects of climactic parallelism to bring together the individual and the whole people under the aegis of Yahweh (verses 3–5, emphasis added):

> *He* will not let your foot be moved;
>> *he who keeps you* will not slumber.
> *He who keeps Israel*
>> will neither slumber nor sleep.
> *The* LORD *is your keeper.*

Notice the steady progression from the simple unqualified 'he' to the final declaration that it is Yahweh all along who is the protection of Israel.

Psalm 129, though it mentions Israel and Zion, is concerned once again with the dark side of the nation's experience (and returns, interestingly, to the first-person address), and 130–1 focus not on the substantive subject of the sequence, but on the period of waiting and watching which precedes the climax: they form, as it were, a pause in the festival before the drama of the re-enactment of the legend of the Ark described in Psalm 132 – where all three aspects of the theme are finally and resoundingly expressed.

My grouping of these motifs as a single theme suggests the construction of a certain ideology of 'Israel' which is not uncontroversial. The bringing together of an idealised concept of the nation (Israel, Jacob) with a messianic reading of kingship (David as the anointed) has important implications, particularly since the existence of a messianic view of the Davidic 'ideal king' as a topic in the Psalms is not universally acknowledged. When, further, the institution of the priesthood and the emblematic figure of Aaron as High Priest are added to the equation we find ourselves with a heady brew indeed.

The priestly connection derives from the combination of 132:10, 17f. with the graphic depiction of an anointing in Psalm 133, in which Aaron and Zion are combined. This is, as far as I can ascertain, the only place in the Hebrew Scriptures where the anointing of Aaron is linked with Zion. The two names come together in two other places – Psalm 99:2, 6 and Psalm 135:19, 21; but in neither of them does the text make any metaphorical connection. The word for 'priest' is found again in 78:64, 99:6 and 110:4. The first of these has no bearing on our discussion, and the second is a literal statement to the effect that Aaron was a priest. The third is clearly of considerable interest, being the famously obscure reference to Melchizedek within a Psalm which must have strong claims to be messianic[18] and which also uses the form 'Zion'. While it does not lie within my present remit, a much closer examination of this Psalm in the context of the Psalms of Ascents in general and 132–3 in particular might be fruitful.

I have already indicated that the Psalms of Ascents are likely to be from the late post-exilic period and identified compelling grounds for accepting that they were composed as a collection. It follows therefore that the very high incidence of the two royal names, David and Solomon, in these Psalms, together with the prevalence of Zion (a decidedly prophetic, and certainly not historic, term), suggests a thoroughgoing interest in ideal kingship which is (I propose) precisely what the term 'messianism' means prior to the Christian era. This combination of factors – Jewish messianic hopes, high priestly power, and an ideal nation of Israel whose home is Jerusalem – offers a specific and tempting possible historical context, to which I shall return the end of this chapter.

Theme 2: family and farm – domestic metaphors

This is at first sight an odd theme – we are accustomed to think of the Psalms within a grand cultic context, and to see domesticity as rather too commonplace a motif to figure significantly in 'high' liturgy. Be that as it may, it would not be surprising if a predominantly rural and agricultural economy were to express its everyday concerns in its worship.[19] After all, the festivals of which the Bible gives account (Unleavened Bread and Passover; Weeks; and Booths) have at bottom an agricultural origin and *raison d'être*; the historical or cultic meanings are later accretions. And in my own culture, the Celtic tradition of worship has a robust element of the most basic everyday agricultural reality[20] which gives it a force entirely absent from those traditions where the aspiration to liturgical and literary 'excellence' has supplanted the human need to bring the basics to God.

From this perspective, Psalm 122 speaks to us of the village collectively involved in the grand festival visit to Jerusalem, no doubt through its nominated favoured son (or daughter?). Admittedly, this may be a rather romantic view – but it is hard to think of a better reading of verses 6–9. In Psalm 124, on the other hand, the dangers faced by the soul are graphically portrayed in the language of the torrential floods of the wadis in spring – a metaphor given positive form in 126. Equally, the escape from danger uses a rural image: the bird escaping the fowler's trap. Psalms 126, 127 and 128 demonstrate the blessedness of Zion in a series of vignettes from farm, family and farmhouse; then, as if to forestall any premature abandonment of the quest by settling for a lesser form of contentment, Psalm 129 abruptly reminds us of the violence faced by those who struggle to be loyal. The language is that of agricultural practice; it is applied both to the cruelties employed by the wicked, and the punishment wished upon them by the psalmist. Finally, though this is not a major theme in 132, it does appear in several ways: in the finding of the Ark in the 'countryside' around Jaar; in David's depriving himself of bed and sleep; in the reference to 'the fruit of your loins' (verse 11) and in the promise to the poor in verse 15.

If we examine the three motifs individually, a certain structure appears. The motif of family – children, kindred, servants, husbands and wives – turns up in the majority of these Psalms, being absent only from 120, 125, 130 and 134. While it features as a predominantly benign metaphor, there is an ambivalence to its use in 123 (exactly how do the servants regard their superiors?) and in 131 (is a weaned child happy or fretful?). The second motif, fruitfulness, is confined to four of the central members of the collection – 126, 127, 128 and 132 – and is uniformly positive in tone. Finally, the use of metaphors from nature – the climate, agricultural realities, raw forces – reflects the kinds of risk and danger which we still perceive as essential characteristics of 'nature red in tooth and claw'. In 121 and 124 these elements pose a threat to the faithful, and so are negative in tone. In Psalm 126, though there is an ambiguity present (will the waters of the Negeb provide for the harvest, will the tears of those who sow induce the rains they mimic?), the overall tone is positive. Psalm 129 refers to the enemy's barbaric tortures using agricultural implements (a negative note), but then turns the tables by visiting upon them in turn the evils of a failed harvest; presumably a positive effect from the point of view of the psalmist. The final instance, in Psalm 133, is of the dew of Hermon falling on the mountains of Zion. However geographically or climatically unlikely this may seem, it certainly constitutes a positive metaphor. Taking the aggregate of these metaphors gives us a pattern, which I will return to at the end, in which negative (–), ambivalent (0) and positive (+) instances of these metaphors are distributed across the sequence:

121	122	123	124	126	127	128	129	131	132	133
+ –	+	0	–	+ +	+ +	+ +	– +	0	+ +	+

This suggests groups of 'positive' poems (122, 126–8, 132–3) dispersed among those of a negative or ambivalent nature. This schema will be refined when theme 4 is considered.

Theme 3: the quest for Yahweh

Though, as we have seen, the use of the term 'pilgrimage' is questionable in relation to the Psalms of Ascents, I believe that the motif of the quest is unambiguously present. Since there is evidence from other places that pilgrims were conceived of as being on a search for God (compare, for example, Psalms 24:6, 27:7–9 and 77:2; Genesis 25:22; Amos 5:4–6), there is nothing inappropriate about drawing the obvious conclusion from 122 and 132. Psalm 126 is more of a problem, for the reasons set out above; but even so there are plausible grounds on the basis of the general character of the Psalms of Ascents (not to mention the title) for interpreting verse 6 within the framework of some kind of processional. The central point, of course, is that in the Psalms of Ascents the concept of pilgrimage or motion is fundamentally rooted in the idea of finding a safe haven; and, in particular, in finding a proper place for the residence of the Ark as the quintessential representation of Yahweh.

The sub-theme of the importance of place is found in five poems within the sequence. Psalm 120 expresses the negative – dwelling in the wrong place and time – in a most poignant and dramatic fashion. Psalms 122 and 125 affirm the desirability of Jerusalem/Zion as a secure place, expanding in different ways on the theme of stability (built solidly as one; surrounded by mountains) and the place of the people under the shelter of the city. Finally, and as expected, 132 resoundingly brings together these ideas in the motif of the quest for and finding of the place where Yahweh, symbolised by the Ark, may rest. Zion, ruled by the chosen, loyal, messianic dynasty, where the final humiliation of the enemy is confirmed, is revealed as God's chosen seat – thus resolving the dilemma with which Psalm 120 concluded. All that remains is for the company of pilgrims and worshippers to celebrate the sacred place in the closing doxology: Psalm 134.

Theme 4: the enemies of the faithful

Probably no theme is more pervasive in the Psalter than that of complaints against a whole gallimaufry of enemies. Ancient Israelites, it appears, suffered either grievous persecution or extreme paranoia!

The resulting poetry has contributed some of the most melancholy as well as some of the bleakest and most vengeful material in the religious realm. We saw, in our study of Psalm 74, how the writer despairs of the future, surrounded by enemies and abandoned by God. On the other hand, there is the savagery of prayers for vengeance, such as the graphic 'Let them be like the snail that dissolves into slime; like the untimely birth that never sees the sun' of Psalm 58:8, or the horrifying

> O daughter of Babylon, you devastator!
>   Happy shall they be who pay you back
>   what you have done to us!
> Happy shall they be who take your little ones
>   and dash them against the rock!
>   (Psalm 137:8–9)

There are real difficulties with this material. Is it historical, does it represent constant oppression at the hands of Assyrians, Babylonians, Aramaeans, Moabites, Edomites, and so on? If so, can we match these complaints to known historical situations? Many have speculated on these matters, beginning with those who first gave titles and headings to the Psalms and correlated individual compositions with episodes in the life of David. But few in the scholarly world would now wish to press such identifications too far, and we can only hope that 137:8–9 remained an unfulfilled prayer.

We should understand the theme of conflict and of enemies in the Psalms of Ascents as an indication neither of external foes nor of actual physical violence. Psalm 120 is the key, in its very clear use of war as a metaphor for conflicting opinions. This is by no means to minimise the significance of the theme: strongly held views in conflict (whether religious, cultural or political) can lead to the most bitter of consequences, and may well merit the use of tropes based on the language of war. But the important point is that in the Psalms of Ascents it is war as metaphor, as trope, which provides the means to an understanding of what is going on. There is no need to look for international conflict or Judaean wars against her territorial rivals to understand the language of these poems. It is directed against heresies, not armies; the enemy is not some armed foreigner, but your neighbour with whom you cannot exchange the time of day (120:7; 129:8). That still leaves us, of course, unable to identify the 'enemy', for we lack the specific information that would enable us to examine the cause of the dispute (or disputes), the different beliefs which led to such bitterness. We cannot, for example, take the language of Psalm 120 as evidence of a 'hawks versus doves' situation, precisely because the military language is metaphoric. Your enemies are always against peace, even if you are the hawks and they are the doves!

While the themes of conflict and shame represent an inherently negative metaphoric field, there is nevertheless a positive side (just as the seemingly benign domestic metaphors afford examples of negative applications). When your enemies are put to shame, that is a matter of celebration; and conflict is welcome when (as in Psalm 132) it is used by 'the Mighty One of Jacob'. The symbolic presence of the Ark is an important part of this pattern. Traditionally the Ark is linked with battle, with power, and with 'Yahweh Sebaoth' – that is, the LORD of the armies of heaven/Israel.[21]

In the discussion of theme 2 I remarked that its positive and negative aspects were distributed across the sequence of Psalms in a potentially interesting fashion (see the detail note on page 237). We can now add to this pattern the positive and negative applications of theme 4.[22] The first sub-theme (conflict and danger) has a negative aspect in 120, 124, 125 and 129, while in 127 and 132 it is the positive which is accentuated. The second sub-theme (shame, contempt and deceit) is negative in 120, 123, 125 and 127 and positive in 129 and 132. I have combined the results of the analysis of positive, negative and ambivalent uses of metaphor in themes 2 and 4 in Table 14.2. The findings in respect of theme 4 reinforce the pattern suggested above (p. 237), and indicate a trend in the collection as a whole to move through negative expressions to positive, with the final resolution in 132 leading to a wholly positive ending (the feel-good factor?)

There are three 'positive' movements (122, 126–8, 132–4), although the middle one has a negative marking at Psalm 127. This is one of the instances in which theme 4b, though strictly speaking an expression of the enemy's desire to shame the faithful, is present as a denial of the effectiveness of that wish. Each of the three 'negative' sequences is distinctive in character. Psalms 120–1 give expression to

Table 14.2 Positive, negative and ambivalent uses of metaphors (themes 2 and 4)

	120	121	122	123	124	125	126	127	128	129	130	131	132	133	134
2		+	–	+	0	–		+	+	+	+	+	+	–	+	0	+	+	+
4	–	–			–		–		–	–		+	–		–	+		+	+	

240

a deeply felt sense of threat and danger which is not entirely resolved (though the hope of God's vigilance is fully explored in 121). Psalms 123–5 express uncertainty, and (somewhat feverishly) recount the near-escapes which the people have experienced, being rescued just in the nick of time by God. Finally 129–31 stand thematically as the reverse of 123–5. Psalm 131, with its ambiguous use of the domestic metaphor of the weaned child, parallels Psalm 123, where we find servants keeping a watchful eye on their superiors. On the other hand, Psalm 129 returns to the mood of 124–5, with its memories of past injustices and prayer for God's effective intervention. The new element in this group is the note of expectancy which I have already identified as the preparation for the final movement. The result is a chiastic relationship between the two groups, together with a development in the form of the new theme in 130–1.

Theme 5: God's gifts and the people's response

The motif of God's gifts permeates this sequence, missing only from 120, 123, 129 and 131[23] – all placed, for one reason or another, in the negative sections of Table 14.2. The key terms are 'blessing' and 'peace' (*shalom*); 'freedom', 'redemption' and 'salvation'; and 'protection'. The other motif, the people's response, has two distinct aspects: the expression of joy; and participation in the task of watching. I want to stress the first of these now, because the other tends to be the duty of specific 'professionals' (the city guards, or the royal family). The joyful response occurs in 122, 124, 126, 132 and 134 – all but one of which are located in the positive subgroups of Table 14.2. These observations regarding the placement of the motifs of theme 5 (G for gifts, R for response) are included in Table 14.3, which records the results of the assessments of themes 2, 4 and 5.

The 'positive groups' (122, 126–8, 132–4) are strengthened by the addition of theme 5; however, the spill-over into certain other psalms (most particularly 124, where both gifts and response are recorded) requires consideration in relation to the topic of the next section.

Table 14.3 Distribution of the uses of metaphor (themes 2, 4 and 5)

	120	121	122	123	124	125	126	127	128	129	130	131	132	133	134
2		+	–	+	0	–	+	+	+	+	–	+	0	+	+
4	–	–		–	–	–	–		+	–		–	+	+	
5		G	G R		G R	G	G R	G	G		G		G R	G	G R

I would like to make one last comment before taking up the question of an interpretation of the Psalms of Ascents as a complete cycle. It may seem that for God to bless Israel, or to visit peace and prosperity upon Jerusalem, are rather unremarkable things; and so, in a sense, they are. But it is necessary to reiterate the point that they are nevertheless specific to this collection. Maybe such treatment is what, at best, the faithful always hope to receive from Yahweh; here, in Psalms 120–34, they are dealt these gifts in peculiar abundance. It is hardly surprising, then, that certain of these Psalms have a rather special place in the self-awareness of modern Israel. Psalm 122 in particular resonates with that keenly felt desire to establish Jerusalem as the heart, soul and political centre of the Israeli State. This is by no means an unambiguous good: the absence defined by such rhetoric is of course the nature and rights of Arab Jerusalem and the propriety of claiming as the capital of the Jewish State a place which is widely held to have international and inter-religious standing. There are questions here which we will have cause to consider further in the final chapter.

Meaning and function in the Psalms of Ascents

The themes which have been identified and discussed in relation to Psalms 120–34 can be understood as a total framework for their interpretation. To begin with we find a set of topics (theme 1) which constitutes the principal subject of the collection – these are, in effect, what these Psalms are about. Then in theme 3 we discover the process by means of which the subject is realised – pilgrimage to the place of Yahweh in hope and expectation. Two themes encompass the range of metaphors used to enliven and give body to the skeleton of the structure: images drawn from the domestic world and life of the people of Judah, and the dramatic conventions of the perennial conflict between the righteous and the wicked, the faithful and their enemies. Finally the rewards for a successful conclusion to the enterprise envisaged in the Psalms of Ascents are set out in the form of the manifold gifts of God and the mood of enthusiastic celebration which is the people's response.

Since the sequence has a dramatic purpose and builds to a climax, these various themes are distributed through the Psalms in such a way as to lend suspense to the sequence. It is only with Psalm 132 that we reach a lasting resolution, though there are earlier smaller peaks which seem to promise peace, only to be dashed by further set-backs. In part this pattern is revealed by the evidence gathered in

Tables 14.2 and 14.3, and I now endeavour to present the material in a discursive fashion in order to uncover the kind of liturgical programme which *may* have been the function of the Psalms of Ascents.

Table 14.2 gives some schematic grounds for discerning a form of cyclical or undulating pattern in which three thematically positive groups are placed – 122, 126–8 and 132–4. When the instances of theme 5 are added in Table 14.3 a roughly similar pattern remains, though clearly Psalm 124 requires some further consideration. We also observed a chiastic element in the thematic character of the two middle groups, 123–5 and 129–31, which may well support the wave pattern, in which chiasmus is obviously a significant feature. These tentative signs of a discovered structure will be examined now in relation to the thematic content of individual members of the sequence.

Psalm 120 introduces the sequence in the despairing tones of one who sees no hope of escape from despair. There is an appeal to Yahweh, and a hopeless expression of how the psalmist would like to see those who are the source of his or her despair treated. But nowhere in this composition is there the least indication of hope, of any reply by God or lessening of the situation of stress. Were this a piece by itself, it would have to be categorised as a Psalm of despair, the kind of prayer we make when life is grim and the night dark and the dawn endless hours away. Appropriately, then, we begin the 'ascents' from the lowest point, as if in mimesis of the pilgrims gathering at the beginning of their festival at the foot of the hill. The references to night in 121:6 and 134:1, together with the reference to relatives and friends in 122:6, permit the imagined context of folk gathering from their various villages and farmsteads, perhaps at dawn, having travelled by moonlight, or perhaps in the evening ready for a night's preparation before the main events.

With the opening verses of Psalm 121 we encounter both the explicit theme of pilgrimage and the sense of a possible answer to the despair of the previous poem. The upward gaze of the poet elicits the question and answer for which this Psalm is famous. If the question implies the threat posed by the raw forces of nature (forbidding mountains, hot sun and bright full moon), the answer promises help from the very one who made that which threatens danger. Rather than a resolution this constitutes a dramatic movement in which threat and promise, safety and insecurity, go hand in hand. And that 'hand in hand' is surely an appropriate phrase, since part of the Psalm's power lies in the way it hints at the pilgrim–poet as a child seeking (perhaps a little desperately) the constant presence of a parental figure. Thus, though the theme of God's gifts is in place and contributes positively, it is not quite certain. It does not elicit the people's response, because it is a future hope (see verses 7–8) and not, as in the first part of Psalm 126, an assured blessing. The final words of Psalm 121 flow into the opening of 122 (emphasis added):

> The LORD will keep
> *your going out* and your coming in
> for this time on and for evermore.
> I was glad when they said to me,
> '*Let us go* to the house of the LORD.'

Thus as we enter, in literary terms, into the third poem, the pilgrims metaphorically anticipate their entry into Jerusalem, full of antici-pation and charged with the prayers they are to make on behalf of the city and their fellows at home. Psalm 122 is the first of the collection to be devoid of any negative motif, and thus constitutes a sort of climax. But it is important to note that, as a climax, it is none the less tentative in tone. The pilgrims are 'standing within your gates, O Jerusalem'; they have apparently not yet entered the sacred precincts – perhaps they have not even climbed the holy hill yet. They remember (verses 4–5) how the tribes have been accustomed to go up to Jerusalem, and they celebrate its Davidic importance. But their prayers are still (verses 6–9) located in the future ('I will say, "Peace be within you." . . . I will seek your good'). These points raise several possibilities for our imagined reconstruction. Does the 'pilgrimage' take place in stages – a preliminary ascent to the city gates (Psalms 120–2), a second journey to the entrance to the temple (123–8) and a final ceremonial entry into the sacred centre of the city, hinted at by the sequence 129–32?[24] Or, as an alternative, do these early groups represent 'false starts' which serve the dramatic purpose of heightening the actual event when it takes place? The threefold repetition, with only the last being effective, is of course a very common device in both folk-tales and literature, and is well-attested in religious traditions. Consider, for instance, Peter's threefold denial of Jesus, or the three temptations put to Jesus by the devil (Matthew 26:69–75, 4:1–11). In any case, it soon turns out that 122 is not a conclusion or a resolution, but in some ways a calculated disappoint-ment, as the next poem makes very clear.

Psalm 123 begins with a reminiscence of 121, both in the words 'I lift up my eyes' and in the address to God as 'you who are enthroned in the heavens' (see 121:1a, 2b). Further, it displays ambiguity and negativity – for although the similes in verse 2 are often assumed to be positive, in reality they tolerate equally an air of uncertainty, even of threat. This enhances the sense that 123 returns us to the mood of Psalm 121, at least in its first part. As we move on to verses 3 and 4, however, we find ourselves confronting the same sense of despair which infuses 120. The phrases 'we have had more than enough' and 'Our soul has had more than its fill' (verse 3b) reminds us inevitably of that poem's 'too long have I had' (120: 6a).[25] What this amounts to, in short, is a sudden descent in the space of four verses back to the pain of despair with which the sequence began. But it is not quite a matter of 'back to square one', for hopes have been expressed, beliefs in the nature of Yahweh have been affirmed, which enable a new start.

Psalm 124 opens with an expression of thanksgiving by the people for Yahweh's having been on their side in the fight against the enemy – a motif which takes up the despair of 120 and 123 and cancels it by affirming God's presence even in the most desperate of situations. Interestingly, its metaphors represent a liberation in the form of a flight, like a bird's, upwards from the dangerous depths of the waters, thus creating a mimesis of the upward movements implied in 121 and 122. Psalm 124 ends by repeating the formula of 121:2, 'Our help is in the name of the LORD, who made heaven and earth', and this surely suggests an impending return to the more positive note of Psalm 122. We are once again, as it were, on an ascending curve, and this continues through 125 where the celebration of Mount Zion in verses 1–3 is very close to that of 122:3–5.[26] There is a difference, however, in that the presence of evil is felt in a way that is quite absent from the earlier Psalm. Thus, although Psalm 125 is undoubtedly representative of a movement towards a climax, there is further still to go. The prayer for peace, which brought 122 to a conclusion, is now reduced to the formula 'Peace be upon Israel'. In effect it introduces the next climax (Psalms 126–8), and its repetition at the end of 128 creates an *inclusio* which marks off the boundaries of this second group of 'positive' Psalms.

If the first climax, in Psalm 122, celebrated primarily the public institutions of Israel, we find in 126–8 the peak of that celebration of the domestic and the everyday which I identified as one of the characteristic features of the Psalms of Ascents. No doubt, as Table 14.1 makes clear, both domestic and public themes are present in each climax; but the emphasis which I have pointed out is very striking. In addition, the possibility of some allusion to pilgrimage in Psalm 126 makes it a fitting opening to this subgroup, while the suggestion of continuing danger in 127 reminds us once again that the true climax is not yet within reach – not least because of the conditionals in verses 1–2: where Yahweh is not involved, our actions are in vain. The pilgrimage, seen simply as a procession of the faithful, achieves nothing, though it may aspire to great things. This is further reinforced by the persistent note of 'not quite yet' which is sounded by the future tenses and precative moods of 126:4–6, 127:5 and 128:2–5. The concluding 'Peace be upon Israel' is thus still a prayer rather than a firm certainty.

Psalm 129 turns the sequence downwards once more, though just as in 123 the evil of which we read is mitigated by the hope of God's vengeful and redemptive involvement. It belongs, without doubt, to one of the troughs of the drama, but it is now far advanced along the road to fulfilment. The final height is, as it were, within view. It is therefore highly appropriate to find at this point the words of the *De Profundis*: 'Out of the depths I cry to you, O LORD.' This final desolate cry, combining both the consciousness of sin and the fear of the abyss, leads calmly, though not without fretful uncertainty, through the last stages into the great drama of the procession of the Ark. I would regard 129 and 130:1–4 as being uttered, metaphorically, at the foot of the mountain, while 130:5–8 reminds us of the hymn of redemption in 124:6–8. Lastly, in 131 we encounter the same hope, combined with the same ambiguity as that found in 123:1–2. Psalm 131 concludes with a combined formula: 'O Israel, hope in the LORD from this time forward and for evermore.' The first part is repeated from 130:7; the second, significantly, is found in each of the Psalms which directly precedes a climax (121:8, 125:2 and 131:3), as if to give expression to the hope that this time the LORD will finally and fully reveal and make firm all that God promised from time immemorial. It is therefore highly significant that only in Psalm 132 of all the climactic Psalms is a similar phrasing included, applied both to the messianic dynasty and to the settled dwelling place of Yahweh (132:12–14).

Psalm 132 fits so neatly into the hypothesis of a pilgrimage that little needs to be said in support of its plausibility. Its introduction of the active participation of Yahweh, the LORD's definitive choice of Zion, and the inner movement from the first refrain (a prayer for righteousness and an appeal for celebration) to the second (a confident affirmation of salvation and joy[27]), all combine to give this composition an assurance and finality of purpose lacking in 122 and 126–8. It is messianic, at least in the modest pre-Christian sense of the ideal king, and it promises something like the messianic kingdom envisioned by the prophets (abundance, prosperity, joy and secure rule). Lastly, it sees the ultimate disgrace of the enemy, humiliated in the presence of the glorious king (verses 17–18) – compare with this the somewhat troubling passage in Psalm 23:5 ('You prepare a table before me in the presence of my enemies; you anoint my head with oil; my cup overflows'), which is probably best understood as a similar expression of the messianic triumph. The remaining two Psalms bring us, gently, on the plateau of our metaphorical mountain through a celebration of unity, in which the role of the high priest is honoured, to the closing doxology, uttered perhaps at night, at the end the day's pilgrimage, or at dawn, after a final joyful vigil. The possible inclusion at the end of Psalm 133 of the formula 'Peace be upon Israel', indicated by the Qumran materials, would give a further finality, as the prayer which was uttered tentatively in 122, and at the beginning and end of 126–8, is at last confirmed.

Is Psalm 132 the record or liturgy of a real procession?[28] Was something, for example the Ark, actually taken from some hiding place outside the city and borne in triumphant progress to the temple? We will almost certainly never know, though some other Psalms, 24 is an instance, and some parallels in Chronicles, might lend the hypothesis plausibility. One speculation is interesting enough to be put forward. In Chapter 12 I reviewed the evidence both for coherent and unified composition of the Psalms of Ascents and for the period within which such a composition might plausibly have taken place. The best 'fit', I argued, was rather late in the post-exilic period, perhaps within the Maccabean or Hasmonean context. The problem of the seeming antiquity of Psalm 132 is, I would argue, to be resolved by seeing it as a carefully composed piece, quite consciously using existing biblical traditions to forge for the cult of its author's times an apparently hoary festival appropriate to its needs. We do not, for sure, know either who the author was or who commissioned it, but it is not a separate writing brought in to complete the set. Its position as focus and climax, its sharing in the general thematic structure of the collection, and its very obvious messianic, priestly and 'Zionist' interests all confirm that we should with complete propriety allocate it to the same context as the Psalms of Ascents as a whole.

As to what that might be, I will venture (in the interest of providing sport for my fellow academics, if for no better reason) the hypothesis that it was indeed commissioned by some member of that ruling dynasty of Jerusalem which, in Hasmonean[29] times, claimed both the Davidic throne and the Aaronic office of high priest. It could have been Jonathan, or Alexander Jannaeus; it does not matter. All I want to note is that the setting is remarkably good – a dynasty keen to confirm its religious and political credentials, a regime which had shown its 'enemies' the renewed power of 'Israel' in the form of conquests of Galilee and Edom, and a community which was largely centred upon Jerusalem and took the city and its temple to be the focus and affirmation of its identity. Add to this the recent restoration of the temple by Judas Maccabeus after its desecration by the Syrians (which we know gave rise to another festival – that of Hanukkah[30]) and the ground is clear for a temple ceremony such as that suggested by Psalms 120–34. It may have been carried out only once; it may have been held annually while the Hasmoneans ruled; certainly it did not survive the destruction of the temple, and probably did not survive the take-over by the Romans. It would have been too challenging a symbol to Roman rule for that to have been possible.

It is, I think, an attractive story. Let it rest at that, as we move finally to the structural and postmodern interpretation of the Psalms of Ascents.

15

HOME ALONE

Structural and postmodern readings of Psalms 120–34

Structural observations

Towards the end of Chapter 14 various comments were made along the lines of establishing a wave pattern to the Psalms of Ascents. This depended upon similarities of theme running through certain psalms and the existence of peaks and troughs representing both positive and negative thematic elements. In Figure 15.1 this material is assembled in graphic form, revealing a profile which suggests a progression which will be very familiar to anyone who has ever gone hill-walking. The two positive Psalms or groups of Psalms (122, 126–8) represent false summits. They have to be climbed on the way to the top; moreover while climbing them the walker is prevented by perspective from seeing that they are not in fact the true climax. In the interests of verisimilitude I have drawn contours on my profile map which link together those Psalms which share themes or parallel motifs. The result is a 'found' structure which suits the collection with peculiar aptness. What better a metaphor could there be for a sequence of pilgrimage Psalms to the temple on Mount Zion than that of a walk in the hills?

Is this structure 'really there'? Certainly it is in the sense that I have elucidated it from what I trust has been an acceptable literary analysis of these Psalms. Moreover it is highly appropriate to the conclusions drawn from that analysis. But does that render it unacceptably circular? I believe not, and there are two reasons for that claim. First, it was the individual readings of the separate Psalms which built up the graphic profile, so that Figure 15.1 emphatically does not depend upon the conclusions drawn in Chapter 14. And, second, there is no claim of authorial intention being made. The discovery of structure in this way is not bound up

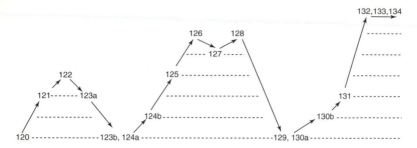

Figure 15.1 The Psalms of 'Ascents': the 'Pilgrimage to Zion'
Note: The 'contours' show where the individual psalms display parallel motifs.

with any suggestion that the author(s) wrote these Psalms with this diagram in mind. It belongs to the category of structuralist analysis where there is recognition of the inherent capacity of language to create, regardless of the writer's desires or knowledge.

The evidence which leads to the diagram in Figure 15.1 is discussed in Chapter 14, but in order to make the pattern clearer I have set it out in tabular form in Table 15.1, which should be considered in conjunction with Table 14.3. The arrangement places together those Psalms, or part-Psalms, which belong to the same contour in the profile. While my discussion of individual psalms above treated them as whole items, following the biblical numbering, in the detail I have already pointed out that many of them consist of two or more parts in terms both of structure and theme. It is important, however, to realise that there is horizontal as well as vertical progression. For example Psalm 131 marks a thematic advance on 121 and 123a, and a similar development can be seen in the sequence in the lowest contour. It may perhaps seem arbitrary to place Psalms 132–4 on a contour higher than Psalms 126–8; the justification rest on the prior argument that the sequence finds its religious and literary climax at this point.

The accounts given of the individual Psalms of Ascents in Chapter Thirteen included a structural diagram for each Psalm which briefly summed up the balance of its mode of composition. I want now to consider these as a whole with a view to analysing their significance for the structuralist reading of the collection. They are listed below on p. 252.

With five exceptions (120, 123, 128, 129 and 132), these structures may be grouped as pairs with similar basic structures. 121–2 have a common A–B–C pattern; 124–5 share A–B–A+B;

Table 15.1 Evidence for a pattern of progression in the Psalms of Ascents

132–4	The climax of the procession, when the Ark enters the temple, and the peak of the Psalms of Ascents, the top-most hill from which the pilgrims may celebrate their God and their good fortune.
126, 128	Poems which celebrate fruitfulness in the context of Zion, framed by the double motifs of 'Peace be upon Israel' (at the end of Psalms 125 and 128) and the fortunes of Zion (126:1 and 128:5).
127	In many ways 127 belongs to the sequence 126–8 in which a generally positive outlook is preserved in the context of domestic motifs. It may be distinguished from them in two ways: its focus on dynastic matters, and its reminders of the risk of fruitless endeavour and enemy attack. It therefore forms a dip in the plateau of this second peak.
122, 125	Celebration of Jerusalem as a symbol of security, unreserved in the case of 122, which forms the first peak, but qualified by the threat of danger from the wicked and the twisted in 125, which is on the way to, but not yet at its intermediate climax.
121, 123:1–2, 131	Anticipation, uncertainty and hope, shot through with the domestic motif of dependence, are the unifying themes here. The overt statement of hope is confined to 131, which links it with 130 in the forward progression of the sequence.
124:6–8; 130:4–8	The shared theme is of redemption or freedom, which in the case of 130 includes the expression of hope, and thus leads into 131.
120, 123:3–4, 124:1–5, 129, 130:1–3	With one exception these all share the motifs in which enemies threaten violence or cause shame. The exception (130:1–3) is a reflection on the psalmist's despair at being in the depths (whether of danger or of sin).

120	A	B	A1						
121	A	B	C						
122	A	B	C						
123	A	B	B1	A1	C	C+	D	D++	
124	A	B	A+B						
125	A	B	A+B						
126	A	B	C	A1	B1	C1			
127	A	B	C	A1	B1	C1			
128	A	B	C	B1	A1	D	E	F	E1	D1
129	A	B	C	D	D1	C1	B1	A1	
130	A	B	C	B	A	C			
131	C	B	A						
132	A	B	C	D					
	A1	B1	C1	D1	A2				
133	A	B	B1	A1					
134	A	B	A1						

126–7 are both of the type A–B–C, A1–B1–C1; 130–1 as a unit displays the permutations A–B–C, B–A–C, C–B–A; and lastly 133–4 are again chiastic.

Of the individual Psalms, two of them are internal pairs: 128 has a double chiasmus, and 132 is made up of two verses (including refrains) with a three-fold *inclusio* (the 'for the sake of David' tropes, marked A). These observations are summarised in Table 15.2.

It will not have escaped the attention of the keen observer that this produces a sequence with three peaks and three troughs at precisely the same places as were found in Table 15.2, where it was themes and motifs which served to identify the underlying framework. Figure 15.2 consists of these new results mapped in the same way as those of 15.1: the results are strikingly similar. The 'negative' Psalms are structurally isolated; otherwise as the sequence progresses we move from simple ABC patterns (121–2), through more elaborate patterns

Table 15.2 Pairings of structures

Mixed					132a,b	
Chiastic			128a,b	130–1		133–4
Enhanced		126–7				
'A, B, C'		124–5				
'A, B, C'	121–2					
Isolates	120	123		129		

252

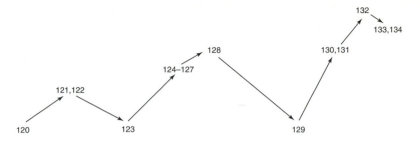

Figure 15.2 The 'Pilgrimage to Zion': pattern of structures displayed by individual psalms in the collection

of this type in 124–7 (ABA+B, ABCABC), to chiasmus and permutation (which employs all the possible chiasmuses of ABC) in 128, 130–1. The final set of Psalms uses both types of pattern in its summing up of the sequence. There is, of course, more than a degree of arbitrariness in this display: placing the three individuals (120, 123 and 129) at the troughs is undoubtedly not a decision independent of their position in Figure 15.1. However, given the coincidence of the same group of three turning up as special cases in both analyses, it is neither absurd nor perverse to align the diagrams in the same way for each set of structures.[1]

Deconstruction of the Psalms of Ascents

It must be admitted at the outset that what follows can be little more than a few tentative moves of a postmodern kind.[2] A thorough treatment would require a book in its own right, though whether such a work would be worth carrying out may be more doubtful. Deconstruction is, after all, a tool like others in the service of hermeneutics; to produce a book entitled (perhaps) *The Psalms of Ascents Deconstructed* would give the impression of a final outcome, rather like those books (and they are plentiful) which include the word 'explained' in their title.[3] Accordingly I will confine myself to the examination of only a few items pertinent to this aspect of my investigation. In particular I want to explore further two of the key themes of the collection: the importance of place and the sense of dependence. The latter is present in 121, 122, 123, 127, 128, 131 and 133, and is characterised by relationships (psalmist–God, parent–child, servant–master/mistress, friends–neighbours) in which some kind of inequality is identifiable. The former is explicit in 120, 122, 125, 132 and 134, so that only 124, 126, 129 and 130 are excluded in this general coverage. The original distribution of the theme of dependence was based on the presence of domestic imagery, which is not a feature of 130; however in a broader sense it does not seem unreasonable to include the opening verses of that Psalm as expressive of a similar kind of dependence as that of 121.

It is interesting to see that the problem of being in the wrong place is very much to the fore, both in Psalm 120 where the poet's alienation is the issue, and in 132, where Yahweh has 'gone missing' and needs to be found so that proper services can continue in the temple. The bringing together of these two elements creates a disjunction, for what is involved is pilgrimage, which is at heart a displacement of people from their homes and their relocation to some religious ideal of home. The sequence ends with the people gathered in the temple praising God ('Come bless the LORD, all you servants of the LORD, who stand by night in the house of the LORD'), but what appears to be a completion is in fact a hiatus – the people have after all to return home, to their kindred, to their domestic lives, to their problems, to live again in Meshech and to dwell in the tents of Kedar. For the problem with pilgrimage is that it represents not a linear progression to a conclusion but either a tantalising glimpse of what can never be, or a reminder of the cycles of life. 'Next year in Jerusalem', that famous rabbinic hope, is also a modern symbol of displacement. Jews of the *galuth* (the diaspora) may see Jerusalem as their true home, but how many having made that journey find it to be a house of strangers – Meshech in Zion, Kedar in the Holy City. Conversely, many who thought of Jerusalem as their own home have either been forced to leave or have found life there so uncomfortable that exile was the only remedy (and both Jews and Arabs have shared these experiences in the twentieth century). If exile is everywhere, we can be nowhere at home – a thought, of course, addressed by Paul in Philippians 3:20 ('our citizenship is in heaven') and by the author of Hebrews, describing in 11:8–10 Abraham's faith in 'the city that has foundations, whose architect and builder is God'.

The problem of placement is not a concern only of the people, for the Psalms of Ascents are equally bound up with the decision about where God should dwell. Yahweh's personal choice of Jerusalem is the thesis and theme of Psalm 132, which is all very well for those who can access the special power of Zion. But there is a supplément, that if Yahweh is in Zion there must be some sense in which Yahweh is not in Hebron, or Galilee, or Babylon, or Rome. It is this theoretical absence of God from the many places where Jews live which sets up a tension akin to that which makes the 'holy land' such a potent symbol and explosive icon (potent because it sustains the myth of a perfect place where a particular people are somehow meant to dwell, explosive because it is shared by more than one people!). Of course we know that in reality God is everywhere if God is anywhere, but the rhetoric of these Psalms (still enormously powerful in modern Judaism) forces us into a kind of 'equal but better' paradox. God is everywhere, but God's presence is in some way richer, fuller, more clearly expressed the closer one comes to Zion. What this entails in turn is a renewed exile of God from everywhere else (perfection cannot be present in part, so the logic of the holy place implies the un-holiness of other places), and an increased empowerment in the religious sphere for those who manage the sacred shrine. In so far as this is a metaphor, it applies equally to any of the vast number of special places, sacred wells, healing pools, saintly grottoes to which the numinous has been confined in all religions. Like the Ark, a symbol of power, all these power systems have the effect (even if they were not intended thus) of disempowering the faithful. The sequel to Psalm 134 ought to be a drama in which the returning pilgrims seize the Ark once more and carry it off into hiding for another year, for only by making exile the shared condition of priest and people alike can the idea of a place for God make sense. God is only to be found when we search, not at the behest of a sacerdotal clique.

This deconstruction of place as a theme in these Psalms is graphically present in the two figures (15.1 and 2) with which I illustrated certain structural features. These figures remind us of one obvious consequence of the metaphor of ascents: that what goes up must come down! The final plateau of 132–4 is all very well, but no one can live forever on the mountain top. There must be a coming down, and it is that rapid descent which has been the metaphor behind my explicit undermining of the apparently satisfactory resolution at which these Psalms arrive. I want, however, to emphasise that deconstruction itself is to be treated with suspicion, and to warn against any comfortable sense that we have now 'come down' to the essence of the matter. Therefore, allow me a further deconstructive remark: there is one important sense in which we *can* remain on the mountain top, and that is by the exercise of the imagination. I have elsewhere reflected on the importance of 'imagined geography' for cultural construction,[4] and the significance of the sense of place as a defining characteristic for individuals and communities is increasingly recognised. Simon Schama's *Landscape and Memory* (1995) explored the same theme on a very broad canvas, and John Kerrigan (1998) has discussed the links between geography as a professional discipline and the literary imagination in a recent review article. The high place at which the Psalms of Ascents arrives may, as Wordsworth argued in *Daffodils*, 'flash upon that inward eye / which is the bliss of solitude', and so enable us, in the context of alienation, to recover the sense of belonging which is the supreme gift of the rightly imagined place.

Dependence, while often construed as one of the many means by which religion exercises control, is also one of the fundamental structures of human society. Neither our physical well-being nor our emotional security is conceivable in terms of isolated individuals. The claim frequently made that it is language which distinguishes humankind from other animals is meaningless without the actuality of interdependence: language is the least solipsistic of phenomena, though we often use it idiosyncratically. The antonym which dependence conjures is, of course, independence – the ironic goal of so many individuals in our intensely interdependent world. It seems that just at the point in human history when the world has become interconnected at every level the myth of freedom (of speech, of action, of thought, of spirit) has taken off as rarely before.

What might such a sequence as the Psalms of Ascents, which 'depends' so strongly on the variety of forms of dependence which humans experience, have to say to this contemporary condition? Perhaps only to mock us with pointed reminders that from childhood (when, weaned or not, we are at the mercy of parental care), through servitude (when politicians, bosses, trend-setters and media moguls order us around) and family life (a relentless network of obligations), to old age (when we in turn find ourselves at the mercy of our children) and death (the end of hypocrisy, the time to stand morally and emotionally naked before God[5]), we are never once truly free, never for a moment independent in anything but the most trivial of senses.

That rather jaundiced interpretation is a modern deconstruction, flowing from modern weariness with duty. Perhaps it is a peculiarly western experience; at any rate we are often told (in somewhat hectoring tones) of the vibrant power of the extended family which still holds sway in non-westernised cultures and which enables its members to mature in the safe arms of a close community. It all sounds rather too good to be true – and there is sufficient evidence of the claustrophobic and sometimes murderous effects of such imposed interdependence to make one wonder whether there is not some special pleading at work. The author(s) of Psalms 120–34 appear to take a wholly positive view of the matter of dependence. At some points (the second part of Psalm 126, for example) we seem almost to be on a Sunday-school outing, 'taking Yahweh for a picnic'.[6]

Traditional interpretations of both 123:2 and 131:2, where I suspect there is at least ambiguity, have been wholly positive, suggesting that English commentators have smoothed over the material in the interests of a rather conventional understanding of dependence. A closer reading of the texts reveals a rather different state of affairs – a sense of tension (interestingly a literal physical consequence when one object hangs from – depends upon – another) which derives from the ancient world's more highly developed knowledge of the risk involved in adherence to God. The root of dependence is the same as that which produces the word 'pendant', and to understand it requires that we have a sense of things left hanging, at risk from either the inattention of the one who holds, or the weakness of the chain which links the two. The myth of the sword of Damocles, hanging by a thread over the king's head, potently expresses what I mean. God (by whatever name) is an uncertain source of comfort, for we never know for sure know what the deity requires, or whether the ties that bind are made of the stuff that suspends bridges or of thread which snaps when it's stretched. Hence the edginess which appears more than once in these Psalms, the feeling that the writer 'doth protest too much' in (for example) Psalms 121 and 131.

When religious people explore the concept of dependence there is often a supposition that it is a one-way process. The psalmists appear to take it for granted that the term is sufficiently defined in terms of our dependence on God and on each other, without realising that there are important ways in which God depends on us. In the ancient world the gods of a city were deemed to have died when the city was destroyed, for when there was no longer anyone to pronounce the god's name or to sing his or her praise, there could be no future for that deity. Psalm 82:6–7 may be making use of that tradition in its warning that the gods will 'die like mortals'. Israel's bold claim that Yahweh of Jerusalem was the god of the whole universe may be regarded as having pre-empted that kind of death of divinity, for now God's existence is to be acknowledged by the whole of humankind.

It would be hard to find any thoughtful approach to religion today which does not in essence accept the universal application of its principles, whether they be theistic or, like many forms of Buddhism, atheistic. Where the appeal is to a single autonomous deity, that being brooks no rivals; indeed, the universal character of such gods renders rivals both impotent and irrelevant.[7] Suppose, however, that humankind were to become extinct. Would 'God' survive? Does God depend for existence upon human belief that there is such a being? Or suppose that the scientific philosophy of Richard Dawkins were to prevail, and a day dawned when no-one any longer gave any credence to the proposition that there is an omnipotent being responsible for and in control of everything. Would God be dead? These limiting situations are not as fanciful or as far-fetched as at first appears, for what they highlight is the extent to which God's character depends upon our depiction of it and our belief in that depiction. Most ethically sensitive Christians no longer believe in a deity who orders the slaughter of whole people – but that was certainly an important characteristic of God in the Hebrew Bible. Most modern western church people no longer believe that God would be pleased by a violent crusade against the Islamic world – so what God was it who was appealed to by a succession of popes, monarchs, preachers and 'soldiers for Christ' from the eleventh to the fourteenth century? Can we be sure that the formulations and characterisations and theological propositions which form our contemporary idea of God will be any more robust?

The Psalms of Ascents present us with a drama of place and of dependence, of alienation and independence, of imagined place and interdependence, in which God and humankind seek together and reach an uneasy compromise. We can return to these poems repeatedly, as the pilgrims perhaps repeatedly returned to the sacred destination. Our journey, like theirs, remains one of hope, of tension, of excitement and of exploration. There are treasures to be found and risks to be faced. I hope than in this brief encounter with the text I have succeeded in suggesting how we each might make our own maps, the better to find our own way into, through and beyond the words which constantly draw us, those fixed marks on the page whose meaning remains forever at the end of journey not yet taken.

NOTES

1 TRANSLATING AND READING

1 It is ironic that the RSV translation itself includes a note to the effect that the first sentence of this quoted passage might also be read as 'Please read therefore with good will and attention, and be indulgent.' We are not told by the RSV translators why they offer an alternative. It may arise from the existence of variant readings; or from an inherent ambiguity in the Greek. The situation thus created is by no means abnormal in the translation of ancient texts.

2 This sentence is so full of indeterminate and ambiguous signifiers as to deserve a chapter in its own right. Few of the readers of this book will be able to decode the Hebrew word: but that is rather the point of the exercise. The notion of a 'standard' edition of the Hebrew text is something of an academic sleight of hand. What we have is an agreed selection from a variety of readings, with a significant proportion of preferred readings given not in the text but in the *apparatus criticus*. And the reference to 'Jewish Bible' is a device to avoid various other well-known problems ('Hebrew Bible' is misleading because part is in Aramaic; 'Old Testament' is a Christian term). But the term Jewish Bible is in its own way biased towards a non-Christian – and, for that matter, non-Muslim – perspective, and I shall revert to the standard form Hebrew Bible after the preliminary discussion in Chapters 1 and 2.

3 It may be of interest to point out that the words *leb* and *lebab*, which refer to the physical organ we know as the heart, in metaphorical situations indicate 'will' or 'mind' and not, as in English, the emotions. Thus to translate *leb* literally as 'heart' (a practice common in many reputable versions) is in effect to misconstrue and to mislead. 'Trust in the LORD with all your heart' (Proverbs 3:5) does not 'mean' in English what its literal equivalent 'means' in Hebrew.

4 Carroll (1981, 1986) discusses this phenomenon as a problematic feature of traditional readings of the Book of Jeremiah, where invention of the character of the prophet is a major industry.

5 It is a remarkable fact that, despite the confidence with which the Psalter is defined as a liturgical collection ('The Hymn Book of the Second Temple' is one such popular description), it is very difficult to identify appropriate liturgical settings in known cultic celebrations in Jerusalem prior to the Rabbinic Period. Many speculative reconstructions have been offered – a covenant renewal festival for one, or a festival of the enthronement of Yahweh. But there is no obvious link with the three great festivals of the Jewish Bible – *Pesach* (Passover), *Shevuot* (Weeks) and *Sukkot* (Booths). Other, more specialist, studies go into these and related questions in more detail – see the bibliography for further reading.

6 'Praise him with trumpet sound; praise him with lute and harp! Praise him with timbrel and dance; praise him with strings and pipe! Praise him with sounding cymbals; praise him with loud clashing cymbals!' Brass, woodwind, strings, percussion and a resident dance troupe suggesting a liveliness and exoticism we do not often associate with worship.

7 Suzanne Haik-Vantoura (1991) and Daniel Meir Weil (1995); see also Gillingham (1994: 45–51).

8 Clearly at least some of these concerns relate to the problem of 'knowing the author and his or her times' to which I have already referred.

9 The best such introduction known to me, and one which has the additional advantage of describing some of the modern literary theories that will concern us, is John Barton's *Reading the Old Testament* (1996).

10 Psalms 1 and 2 'present special problems since *both* are untitled and each possibly functions in an introductory capacity (Psalm 1 to the whole Psalter and Psalm 2 to the first Davidic collection)' Wilson (1985: 173). See also the extended discussion in Sheppard (1980: 136–144).

11 *The Psalms of the Sons of Korah* (1982), *The Prayers of David* (1990), *The Psalms of Asaph* (1996) and *The Psalms of the Return* (1998). These represent a *tour de force* of detailed reconstruction; whether as a project the whole sequence delivers a plausible contextualisation of the Psalms is more doubtful.

12 See, for example, Davies (1992), Garbini (1988), Grabbe (1997), Jamieson-Drake (1991).

13 *Midrash and Lection in Matthew* (1974).

14 In Book I of the Psalter, *Yahweh* occurs 278 times as against fifteen instances of *Elohim*. Similarly, in Books IV and V the proportions are 339:9. However, *Elohim* predominates in Books II and III; in particular Psalm 53 is almost identical to Psalm 14, apart from the substitution of *'elohim* for *Yahweh*.

15 Cf. McCann (1993); Wilson (1985).

16 Thus Psalm 2 is referred to in connection with Jesus's baptism (Matthew 3:17), his transfiguration (Matthew 17:5), and his resurrection (Acts 13:33). Psalm 22 is quoted in connection with his crucifixion

(John 19:24). Psalm 91 figures in the wilderness temptations (Matthew 4:6).

17 The word means literally 'history of salvation' and was coined by members of the Biblical Theology school of thought who regarded the historical materials of the Old Testament as being essentially bound up with the Christian understanding of salvation. Without arguing for the inerrancy of the text, this group affirmed the underlying reliability of the historical narratives; thus, they assumed, though we may not be able to access the actual details of the exodus events, we can be sure that they are essentially correct and serve as a vehicle of God's plan for the human race.

18 The familiar words of 139:7–12 never lose their force, no matter how often they are repeated:

> Whither shall I go from thy Spirit? Or whither shall I flee from
>   thy presence?
> If I ascend to heaven, thou art there! If I make my bed in Sheol,
>   thou art there!
> If I take the wings of the morning and dwell in the uttermost
>   parts of the sea,
> even there thy hand shall lead me, and thy right hand shall hold
>   me.
> If I say, 'Let only darkness cover me, and the light about me be
>   night,'
> even the darkness is not dark to thee, the night is bright as the
>   day; for darkness is as light with thee.

19 This somewhat obscure word which has recently found a place in literary approaches to text (not least through its determined use by my colleague, Robert P. Carroll) – means either 'criminal neglect' or 'undervaluing', though its literary use is more along the lines of a 'deliberate misreading', which could be said to combine aspects of both of the dictionary meanings.

20 The Hebrew text includes a question: 'I lift up my eyes to the hills. From whence does my help come?' which is answered by the affirmation: 'My help comes from the LORD, who made heaven and earth.'

2 WHICH TRANSLATION?

1 Though even this is a matter for debate. As far as we can tell, we do not have anything like a contemporary text for most of the Psalms; though it is possible that some psalms were composed in the third or second centuries BCE, and so are quite close in time to certain of the Qumran texts. But that is only the most obvious problem; for, as is widely known, these texts are without indications of vowels, which makes their interpretation somewhat fraught. This is particularly true

of the characteristically ambiguous language used in poetry. Moreover, there is evidence that both the collection as a whole and individual psalms within it to some extent remained subject to variation until the first century CE. What we generally think of as *the* Hebrew text is a product of scholarly activity between the sixth and the sixteenth century CE – the 'Old' Testament is in certain important respects not really very old!

2 An interesting example of academic assumptions is to be found in the translations given by Mitchell Dahood in his Anchor Bible Commentaries (1965–70), which includes his own versions. Dahood was convinced that the roots of many psalms lay in the language and culture of Canaan, and he found that language and culture clearly expressed in the language scholars know as Ugaritic (which is a Semitic language closely related to Hebrew, used in the city of Ugarit up to its destruction towards the end of the thirteenth century BCE). His translations reflect very strongly this conviction, and those using his versions of the Psalms, whatever merits they may have (and they contain many stimulating and intriguing suggestions) need to be aware of that bias.

3 A particularly furious and ill-tempered public row broke out in the pages the *Times Literary Supplement* when Hans Walter Gabler's Penguin edition was published in 1986, and designated as *Ulysses: The Corrected Text*.

4 A fine Scots word used for interview situations where the original applications have been reduced to those who are serious candidates. In English the standard term is 'shortlist', which is, sadly, much less romantic.

5 The plural is typical, and interesting. None of the versions which have found general acceptance is of single authorship. The only such case of which I am aware is J. B. Phillips' version of the New Testament (1959), which had a considerable vogue in the 1950s and 1960s but which remains an isolated curiosity.

6 An ancient legend has it that the Septuagint, the Greek translation of the Hebrew Bible carried out in Egypt in the Ptolemaic Period, was produced by seventy-two elders of Israel working independently for seventy-two days to produce (miraculously) virtually identical translations.

7 Thus, 'The Revised Standard Version Bible is an authorized revision of the American Standard Version of 1901, which was a variant of the English Revised Version of 1881–5 and a revision of the King James Version of 1611' (pp. iii–iv); and 'In 1937 the revision was authorized by vote of the [International Council of Religious Education], which directed that the resulting version should "embody the best results of modern scholarship as to the meaning of Scripture, and express this meaning in English diction which is designed for use in public and private worship and preserves those qualities which have given to the King James Version a supreme place in English literature"' (pp. iv–v). A similar statement may be found in the preface to the NRSV.

8 'And what marvel? the original thereof being from heaven, not from earth; the author being God, not man; the inditer, the Holy Spirit, not the wit of the Apostles or Prophets; the penmen, such as were sanctified from the womb, and endued with a principal portion of God's Spirit . . .'(p. 2b).

9 The NIV adopts a very curious translation: 'God presides in the great assembly; he gives judgement among the "gods".' This preserves the KJV understanding of *el* as metaphorical, and introduces a deeply anachronistic device in the form of 'scare' or 'ironic' quotes in its translation of *'elohim*.

10 Both the KJV and the NRSV have the reading 'breasts' in Proverbs 5:19, while RSV translates 'affection'. However, both the JB and NJB use the literal word 'breast' in Proverbs 5:19. In 1 Kings 21:21, however, only the KJV is strong enough to report the literal meaning of the Hebrew: 'him that pisseth against the wall'. The others all use a euphemism, such as 'male'. Clearly we are not yet ready for the roughness of the Hebrew original!

11 RSV: 'Sometimes it is evident that the text has suffered in transmission, but none of the versions provides a satisfactory restoration' (p. vi); NEB: 'In spite of [the] wealth of ancient versions, and even when the earliest known form of the text has been established, many obscurities still remain in the Hebrew Scriptures' (p. xvii); NIV: 'As in other ancient documents, the precise meaning of the biblical texts is sometimes uncertain. This is more often the case with the Hebrew and Aramaic texts than with the Greek text' (p. xii); etc.

12 Sometimes, for what seemed sufficient reasons, the order of the verses has been changed, as will be seen from the verse-numbering. Occasionally passages have been brought together if a common refrain or other evidence shows that they have been wrongly separated; such changes are recorded in the notes (see pp. xvii–xviii).

13 The New Jerusalem Bible, General Editor's Foreword: 'The biblical text of the first edition was occasionally criticised for following the French translation more closely than the originals. In this edition the translation has been made directly from the Hebrew, Greek or Aramaic. . . . [A]ccuracy of translation has been a prime consideration. Paraphrase has been avoided more rigorously than in the first edition' (p. v).

14 I do not discount the recent World's Classics' edition of the KJV edited by Robert Carroll and Stephen Prickett (1997). The former, responsible for the editing of the OT, would certainly not claim any divine inspiration for the Bible – but the translation is (of course) not his. Occasional editions of the Psalms appear (for example Levi (1976), Frost (1977), Slavitt (1996), Davie (1996) and Jackson (1997)), some of which emphasise their poetic nature; but these editions do not meet the requirement for a readily available and widely used version of the whole Bible.

15 Thus the NIV:

Like all translations of the Bible, made as they are by imperfect man, this one undoubtedly falls short of its goals. Yet we
are grateful to God for the extent to which he has enabled us
to realise these goals and for the strength he has given us and
our colleagues to complete our task. We offer this version
of the Bible to him in whose name and for whose glory it
has been made. We pray that it will lead many into a better
understanding of the Holy Scriptures and a fuller knowledge
of Jesus Christ the incarnate Word, of whom the Scriptures
so faithfully testify.

(p. xiii)

Notice how the strongest claims concerning divine activity in the
work of translation (a characteristic of the fundamentalist tradition) are
combined with an exclusively Christological view of the purpose of
scripture as a whole.

16 As does the final statement: 'It is the hope and prayer of the translators
that this version of the Bible may continue to hold a large place in
congregational life and to speak to all readers, young and old alike,
helping them to understand and believe and respond to its message.'
The emotive and quite pious shape of this expression of the translators'
motivation should alert the reader to the fact, already evident from
what we have examined so far, that there is a very significant baggage
in attendance on any biblical version.

17 The Editor's Foreword to the JB is quite blunt:

The form and nature of this edition of the Holy Bible
have been determined by two of the principal dangers facing
the Christian religion today. The first is the reduction
of Christianity to the status of a relic. . . . The second is its
rejection as a mythology. . . . What threatens the mother
threatens her two children even more seriously: I mean
Christianity's adopted child, which is the Old Testament,
and her natural child, which is the New.

(p. v)

The General Editor's Foreword to the NJB is less blunt, but still firmly
within the tradition of the Bible as a Christian resource: 'The character
of the *Jerusalem Bible* as primarily a study Bible has been kept
constantly in mind. . . . At the same time the widespread liturgical use
of this version has been taken into account' (p. v).

18 A striking example may be found in Proverbs 6:22. The Hebrew text
unambiguously indicates the third-person singular feminine 'she, her',
presumably a reference to Wisdom (a feminine figure). Yet almost all
the other versions avoid this translation. The KJV has 'it'; the NIV, the
RSV and NRSV, the JB and NJB all have 'they' (with occasional footnote

references to the alternative 'it'). The NEB and REB are the notable exceptions. The former transposes the verse to 5:19, and makes it refer to a wife's care; the REB makes explicit the reference to Wisdom, and uses 'she'.

19 The NRSV Preface states:

> During the almost half a century since the publication of the RSV, many in the churches have become sensitive to the danger of linguistic sexism arising from the inherent bias of the English language toward the masculine gender, a bias that in the case of the Bible has often restricted or obscured the meaning of the original text. The mandates from the Division specified that, in references to men and women, masculine-orientated language should be eliminated as far as this can be done without altering passages that reflect the historical situation of ancient patriarchal culture. As can be appreciated, more than once the Committee found that the several mandates stood in tension and even in conflict.
>
> (pp. xiii–xiv)

Compare also the NJB: 'Considerable efforts have also been made, though not at all costs, to soften or avoid the in-built preference of the English language, a preference now found so offensive by some people, for the masculine; the word of the LORD concerns women and men equally.'

20 The NEB declares

> Finally, the translators have endeavoured to avoid anach-ronisms and expressions reminiscent of foreign idioms. They have tried to keep their language as close to current usage as possible, while avoiding words and phrases likely soon to become obsolete. They have made every effort not only to make sense but also to offer renderings that will meet the needs of readers with no special knowledge of the background of the Old Testament.
>
> (p. xviii)

21 The Hebrew of Isaiah 7:14 speaks not of a virgin who will become pregnant, but of a young (married) woman who is pregnant. It is a sign for Isaiah's own time, and only through special pleading can it be read as a mystical sign of the nature of Jesus's birth. It certainly does not *prove* the Matthaean story of the virgin birth.

22 'Sometimes, for what seemed sufficient reasons, the order of the verses has been changed, as will be seen from the verse-numbering. Occasion-ally passages have been brought together if a common refrain or other evidence shows that they have been wrongly separated' (pp. xviif.).

23 Significantly, the Preface to the REB is at pains to counsel caution in the use of cognate languages to elucidate obscurities in the Hebrew. Thus: 'It is a method which has led to valuable results, but its application demands both skill and particular caution; the revisers have been aware of the dangers of an over-zealous use of it'! (p. xvi). This is very close to being a rebuke to the excesses of the NEB.

24 I am aware that Jewish versions have not been considered. The Jewish Publication Society's *Tanakh: The Holy Scriptures* has many virtues (not least being the complete absence of Christian bias!). It does make disconcertingly frequent use of the rubric 'Hebrew uncertain'; but the principal reason not to employ it as the main text is (as also for the REB) that its use is considerably less widespread than that of the NRSV.

25 Carola Kloos (1986: 16–23) provides a detailed and convincing account of the phrase *bny 'lym*, in the course of which she argues that the form *'lym* is a later misunderstanding of the Ugaritic *il* with enclitic —*m*, and so should be read as the proper name El, not as a plural form "gods"'.

26 There is a Hebrew word – *mal'ak* – whose root meaning (like that of 'angel') is 'messenger'. It is not used in this Psalm; and even where it is used in the Old Testament, it rarely has that later theological implication.

3 READERS AND READING

1 See below, Chapter 6, pp. 78f.

2 See, for example Boone (1989), and Barr (1981, 1983, 1984).

3 The furore raised by the so-called 'revisionist school' of historical writings on ancient Israel testifies to the sensitivity of this point. Lemche (1988), Davies (1992), Thompson (1992), Whitelam (1996), Grabbe (1997) and others are labelled 'deconstructionists'. In particular Whitelam (1996) led to the (wholly unjustified) charge of anti-Semitism being brought against him.

4 The king is described as a shepherd in 2 Samuel 5:2, 7:7; Jeremiah 3:15, 10:21, 22:22; Ezekiel 34:23; Isaiah 44:28; Micah 5:4. The great Hammurabi, ruler of Babylon ca.1700 BCE, is described as 'the shepherd' (ANET 164b) or 'the shepherd of the people' (ANET 165b; cf. 177b).

5 In this context it is interesting to note how Mays (1994) argues for 'Yahweh reigns' as the central controlling metaphor for the whole Psalter, and goes on to make the case for this being a relevant *modus interpretandi* for modern readers. I am not persuaded by this latter point; but he may be right in recognising a prevalence of royal imagery wider than we are accustomed to allow.

6 Incidentally, a clear ritual of kingship – compare Psalm 2:2. Note also the reference in verse 4 to 'your rod and your staff' which are descriptive of God's sceptre of office as king. The first of these terms is

found in Psalm 2:9 and the second occurs in the same parallel in Numbers 21:18, and as a sign of office in Judges 8:4, 2 Kings 4:29,31, 2 Kings 18:21 (= Isaiah 36:6) and Ezekiel 29:6. The last three symbolise the *broken* power of The Pharaoh.

7 Literally, 'crossed', indicating that the order in the second line is at least partly inverted.

8 'Some statistician has computed that in this Elohistic Psalter (Psalms 42–83) the divine name Elohim appears 200 times and Yahweh only 43, whereas in the rest of the Psalter, Yahweh appears 642 times and Elohim only 29' Anderson (1983: 27). Since Psalm 14, which uses Yahweh, is repeated as Psalm 53, where Elohim is used, it seems probable that a specific editorial policy substituting the one for the other was at work in this group of Psalms.

9 The Hebrew word is *yadid*; compare 2 Samuel 12:24–5: 'Then David consoled his wife Bathsheba, and went to her, and lay with her; and she bore a son, and he named him Solomon. The LORD loved him, and sent a message by the prophet Nathan; so he named him Jedidiah, because of the LORD.' *Jedidiah* means, literally, 'beloved of Yahweh'.

10 See the critique by Childs (1970) and Smart (1970).

11 Despite conservative rhetoric, the evidence upon which the Documentary Hypothesis was founded is still as compelling; the difference now is that the proposal to explain that evidence in terms of a series of documents reworked by editors is not generally held to be satisfactory. Some of the alternatives are much more radical – for example Davies (1992: 94–113) posits a school of professional writers in post-exilic Jerusalem composing (partly out of their imaginations) a set of 'historical' texts for the use of the recently established cult of the returnees.

12 For example, Barr (1983: 130–71) is critical of Brevard Childs' 'canonical criticism' on these grounds.

13 This is not an idle example. Many of the most enthusiastic practitioners of deconstruction are to be found among the rabbinic ranks, not least because traditional rabbinic modes of exegesis have always been 'playful' (in the most honourable sense) with the text. Yet a formal belief in the Mosaic origins of Torah remains common in traditional Jewish circles.

14 Prothero (1913: 261).

15 Psalm 48:1–3 speaks eloquently of God's mountain (as does Isaiah 2:2–4). Psalm 68:15–16 portrays the mountain of Bashan looking with envy upon God's mountain. Negative connotations of both Israelite and foreign worship on high places are found (for example) in Deuteronomy 12:1; 1 Kings 11:7; 2 Kings 15:4, 18:22 and 2 Chronicles 34:3ff. Gunkel (1926: 540) understands *harim* (the hills) in verse 1 in a negative cultic sense as referring to mountain sanctuaries dedicated to different gods, in contrast with the true God of verse 2.

16 A palinstrophe is a composition in which verses or sections form an overall pattern of one of the types A B C B A or A B C C B A.

17 Out of interest I append here a brief word-pattern analysis of Psalm 121 which could be the basis of further interpretation:

- The word 'help', occurring twice, has a *mediating* function.
- Words relating to Yahweh ('LORD' is found five times) are characterised by *inertia*: keep, etc. (6x); slumber (2x); sleep; shade.
- Terms relating to humankind indicate *energy and activity*: eyes; right hand; life; day; night; this time; evermore; lift up; come, etc. (3x); move; go.
- Finally, a set of terms indicating *that which requires mediation*: hills; heaven; earth; sun; moon.

4 THE LANGUAGE OF POETRY

1 My source for this story is a lecture given at the University of Glasgow by Dr Sandra Kemp in the late 1980s.

2 It is assumed throughout that our concern is with readers of poetry. A related but distinct set of problems surrounds the issue of oral reception of written material. In oral-reception situations the response of the hearer is to a considerable degree controlled by the speaker; whether the material is heard as poetry or prose will therefore depend on the speaker's interpretation of the material, not to mention the his or her communication skills!

3 This insight is essentially that of Roman Jakobson. I discuss aspects of his theory of language and poetry later in this chapter.

4 Dorothy Wordsworth (1978: 193). I have deliberately chosen this unusual source for the poem since it is set there alongside the prose account.

5 Jakobson (1987: 124) has an interesting comment to make on this point: 'Where the poetic function dominates over the strictly cognitive function [i.e. where the language is perceived to be poetry rather than prose], the latter is more or less dimmed, or as Sir Philip Sidney declared in his *Defence of Poesie*, "Now for the Poet he nothing affirmeth, and therefore never lieth." Consequently, in Bentham's succinct formulation, "the Fictions of the poet are pure of insincerity."'

6 The translation adopted follows fairly closely the NRSV, with certain modifications (indicated by the use of italic type and specified in notes 8–10).

7 The order of lines 1 and 3 follows that of the Hebrew text; and I have used past tenses reflecting more accurately (in my view) the mode of the Hebrew verbs. 'Yahweh' is used for the traditional 'LORD'.

8 The active forms are truer to the Hebrew.

9 As with lines 1 and 2, the English past tense is better here.

10 The Hebrew is somewhat cryptic here. My proposal is designed to highlight the drama implied by the poem of a verbal conflict between rival opinions.

11 Petersen and Richards (1992: 37–47) provide a useful discussion of metre and rhythm in Hebrew, and reach the conclusion that while rhythm certainly exists, as it does in all poetry, metre in any strict or regular sense is unknown.

12 Accounts of these, should the reader be interested, will be found in most of the general introductions to the Psalms listed in the bibliography.

13 The term *induced similarity* refers to the fact that metaphor often works not by using an already existing likeness but by creating a new 'likeness' which reveals something not previously thought of in connection with the object of the metaphor.

14 Jakobson (1987: 83) identifies only the first four. Hopkins suggests that the semantic level results from the formal levels. It seems useful to identify the semantic level separately, partly because it is in many respects the easiest to recognise, and partly because it may occur in the absence (in a particular instance) of any of the other four.

15 This issue is discussed in Saussure (1916: 147–9). Those familiar with Hebrew will know very well that what seems to constitute a single 'word' in that language often requires several 'words' in English.

5 A FRAMEWORK FOR READING I

1 See Adam (1995), Collins (1987), Culley (1967), Detweiler (1982), Ingraffia (1995), Johnson (1979), Polzin (1977).

2 Aramaic, as the language of the Assyrian, Babylonian and Persian Empires, became the *lingua franca* of Canaan some time in the sixth century BCE. It is assumed that Hebrew was Israel's everyday tongue to that point, and that it continued as a sacred language long afterwards.

3 The consonants of the Hebrew Leviathan are *lwytn*; those of the Canaanite equivalent are *lwtn*: they are, in effect, dialect variants of each other.

4 For example Proverbs 6:16–19, 30:15–31, Amos 1:3, etc.

5 Compare Gibson (1977: 68):

[Y]ou smote Leviathan the slippery serpent
and made an end of the wriggling serpent,
the tyrant with seven heads.

And

Did I not destroy Yam the darling of El
did I not make an end of Nahar the great god?
was not the dragon [*tanin*] *captured and vanquished?*
I did destroy the wriggling serpent,
the tyrant with seven heads.

(ibid.: 50)

(The word *Nahar* means 'river' in Hebrew, and Yam means 'sea'; the passage is thus an account of victory over watery enemies – a typical motif of Canaanite mythology.)

6 See, for example, Cross (1950) and Gaster (1946).

7 Structural*ism*, as a specific modern literary theoretical approach, has in some of its forms developed very specific formulaic techniques of analysis. I refer to these in discussion of aspect 6, but do not develop them as hermeneutical approaches.

8 The Hebrew word *shalom* expresses a much more comprehensive idea of well-being, success, prosperity and calm than its usual English equivalent 'peace'. A good example of this is the parallel in Psalm 122:6–7 (emphasis added):

> Pray for the *peace* of Jerusalem:
>   'May they *prosper* who love you.
> *Peace* be within your walls,
>   and *security* within your towers.'

9 Kloos (1986: 59f.) suggests a reference to the slaying by Baal of a mythological monster, 'Fire', which might be indicated in 'The Palace of Baal' 3D 38–46 (see Gibson 1977: 50). This would make it possible to take the verb in its natural sense, to cut or to kill, and could be further supported by the fact that the same Ugaritic passage, just before the reference to 'Fire', names 'the calf of El' as another monster. 'Calf' is, of course, referred to in the preceding verse of our passage. Finally, Kloos also notes that in Baal and Mot 5 i 1–5 (see Gibson 1977: 68) Baal acts as a dragon-slayer.

10 I cannot resist one more Hebrew reference. The word for the 'oaks' in verse 9 is similar in Hebrew to the name El – the action of verse 9, therefore, hints at the final destruction of any residual credibility the old gods may have had. They are not even fit to worship Yahweh – a conclusion not unlike that of Psalm 82, which is discussed in Chapter 11.

6 A FRAMEWORK FOR READING II

1 In this chapter a number of texts will be referred to frequently. For convenience, the following abbreviations will be used: LENT = Lentricchia and McLaughlin (eds) (1995); SS = Harland (1987).

2 'Structuralism in this view is neither a theory nor a methodology. Rather, an analysis is "structural" to the extent that an analyst consciously constructs a model of which he has subsidiary awareness of its relationship to the very set of procedural tools he used to construct it in the first place' Polzin (1977: 34).

3 I have made use of the arguments set out in Chapter 6 of Harland (1987) in this passage.

4 Harland (SS: 77) writes:

> Before Saussure, language was traditionally viewed in terms
> of a physical sound on the one hand, and a mental idea on
> the other: the former existing in the world of objective
> things, and the latter inside individual subjective minds. But
> Saussure's signifier, in so far as it is taken up into 'langue', is
> not a thing but . . . a category of sound, a conceptualized
> 'sound–image'. And Saussure's signified, in so far as it is
> taken up into 'langue', is not an event inside individual
> subjective minds but . . . an ever-present, pre-existing social
> reality. In the realm of 'langue', the traditional dualism
> between objective things and subjective ideas simply falls
> away.

5 Quotations of Husserl which follow are from this edition.
6 In my own attempts to introduce students to Derridean hermeneutics,
this is the most common sticking point. The fervour with which
the notion of the priority of thought is clung to partakes of religious
enthusiasm rather than rational appraisal.
7 The grandiose terms in which this is put belong to Derrida, not to this
author!
8 In this context the alternative readings which suggest premature birth
(or even abortion) as one of the effects of Yahweh's anger in Psalm 29
are worthy of note.

7 PSALM 2

1 Throughout this section, I will use the form 'verse X' when referring
to a verse within the Psalm under discussion. All other references,
including those to other Psalms, will be given in full.
2 De Vaux (1961: 100–14) provides a detailed summary of the biblical
evidence on the king in general, and on the coronation rituals in
particular (pp. 102–10).
3 RSV text. It is curious that the NRSV reads at this point 'I will be a
father to him, and he shall be a son to me', a rendering which is rather
indirect, and seems to owe something to theological caution on the part
of the translators.
4 Bar Kochba, acknowledged as messiah by Rabbi Akiva, led the Jewish
revolt against the Romans which established a short-lived independent
Jewish State from 132–135 CE. Zvi was proclaimed as messiah in 1665,
won a considerable following among Dutch Jews, but eventually
apostasised under Turkish authority in 1666. His movement continued, however, followers regarding his apostasy as a fulfilment of the
'suffering servant' prophecies in Isaiah.
5 Who, between 168 and 165 BCE succeeded in overcoming the far

superior forces of the Syrian Seleucid empire, ultimately establishing an independent (if short-lived) kingdom.

6 See Acts 5:36f.; Josephus, *Antiquities*, xvii.x. 4,6,7; *Wars of the Jews*, vi. verse 3.

7 Matthew 26:52.

8 Matthew 3:17.

9 We may observe here another twist to the tale, with the claim in about 1992 by some members of the Lubavitcher Hasidic movement that their Rebbe Menachem Schneersohn was the messiah. Schneerson died in 1994. See Coughlin (1997: 160); his book is an excellent commentary on many aspects of modern Jerusalem.

10 The former is the muse of sacred lyrics, the latter of music and lyric poetry.

8 PSALM 8

1 Though Briggs and Briggs (1906–7) think that the relationship is evident. They argue that the description of God's use of his fingers in creation owes more to Genesis 2:7 and 19, and so the Psalm is indebted to the final form of Genesis 1–2. This seems to me to be a considerably bold claim on the evidence presented.

2 1 Samuel 15:3 and 22:19; Jeremiah 44:7; Joel 2:16; Lamentations 2:11 and 4:4.

3 For the metaphor of grass, see Psalms 90:3–6 and 103:13–16; Isaiah 40:6–7, and Job 7:7 and Isaiah 2:22 for the metaphor of breath.

4 See my discussion of this in Bigger (1989: 110–16).

5 Thus Davidson (1998: 37).

6 There might be an echo of the horrors of the flood in the cosmic language of Psalm 18, where terrible dangers are faced by God's anointed, whose righteousness is the source of his salvation. Moreover, the selection of Noah, who 'was a righteous man, blameless in his generation; Noah walked with God' (Genesis 6:9), has a striking resemblance to the description in Psalm 15:1–2 of the person who is fit to dwell on God's holy hill: 'Those who walk blamelessly, and do what is right, and speak the truth from their heart.' If Psalm 18 is to be associated with the flood, Psalm 19 (whose words form the basis of Haydn's great celebration in *The Creation*) takes up the metaphoric language of the sign of the covenant in Genesis 9:1–17, particularly in verses 4b–6. Although the Psalm does not speak directly of the covenant, in verses 7–10 the language is full of covenant words (law, decrees, precepts, commandment, ordinances), as though the writer had consulted a thesaurus from the Book of Deuteronomy!

7 See, for example, Brueggemann (1982: 1–39, *passim*).

9 PSALM 24

1 There are, of course, exceptions. Certain types of verb (usually described as *stative*) have meanings in their 'complete' forms which are necessarily continuing in effect. Thus 'he was old' may legitimately be rendered 'he is old', and 'it became' as 'it is'. The opposite situation is much less sustainable – that a form which 'naturally' means 'is . . . ' or 'continues to . . . ' or 'will . . . ' could be translated with an English past tense. It is the latter (mis-)translation to which I take exception in verse 2.

2 See the discussion in Chapter 1, Note 3.

3 Gillingham (1994: 250) provides a useful summary of proposals as to the meaning. We might also add Goulder's (1982: 102–6) typically interesting but eccentric suggestion that the word marks a place where the performance of the Psalm would be interrupted by some appropriate lection.

4 See the Akkadian creation Epic (*ANET*: 67b–8a, 501b–2a).

5 The implication is that by the time the Psalm is written the city and temple are long-established. It is not clear, however, whether this suggests a post-exilic composition looking back to the past, or a writer during the monarchy gazing at structures which date back to Jebusite times. The vagueness of such proposals is evident.

6 'Hosts' renders a Hebrew word which means, literally, 'armies'. Used as an epithet of Yahweh it may refer to the armies of Israel, the heavenly bodies, or the cosmogonic forces at the disposal of the deity.

7 I have given a very literal version of the last phrase, 'his holy place', to unpack the actual structure of the Hebrew, in which 'holy' could be read as a substantive.

8 Gendered pronouns are deliberate in what follows.

10 PSALM 74

1 Studies carried out by Goulder (1982) and Nasuti (1988) are of some relevance, while McCann (1993: 95–100) provides a brief but explicit defence of the thesis.

2 For example, verses 4–7, compare 79:1; verse 19b, cf. 79:2; verses 18 and 22, cf. 79:4; verse 1 'the sheep of your pasture', cf. 79:13a.

3 The only other instances of this formulation are to be found in Psalm 100:3 and Ezekiel 34:31, and there is a similar form in Psalm 95:7. Thus all the occurrences are in Books III and IV of the Psalter and in Jeremiah and Ezekiel – together forming a rather tightly defined time-scale in the late sixth/early fifth centuries BCE.

4 I would not rule out the possibility of some psalms dating from the second century as the discussion of the Psalms of Ascents in Part III of this book will make clear.

5 A similar explanation helps us to understand what is happening in Deuteronomy 5:2–3, where the making of the covenant is dramatically

re-presented by 'Moses' (the fictional persona of the author of the book), who revealingly begins as follows:

> The LORD our God made a covenant with us at Horeb. Not with our ancestors did the LORD make this covenant, but with us, who are all of us here alive today.

We are not to understand this as a historical recital, but rather as a contemporary address in which each new generation, as it were, stands where the ancestors stood, and hears again how 'Moses' brings to them the covenant.

6 Note that three of them belong to more than one of these structural sets. Thus in the phrase 'your covenant' in verse 20 the word 'covenant' is also part of the fourth set; and in the phrases 'your foes' and 'your adversaries', in verse 23, both nouns belong also to the sixth set. I have not included the expression 'Yours is the day, yours also the night' in verse 16, since this really belongs to the lyric poetry of the section rather than to the complaints in the rest of the Psalm.

7 The NRSV has nine; I have slightly modified the NRSV text (on p. 145) to reveal the Hebrew, which uses the pronoun only once each in verses 13 and 14, not twice as in the NRSV.

11 PSALM 82

1 It is my view that Genesis 1–11 is the latest part of Genesis, and that the book as a whole is a supplement (or 'prequel') to the older Exodus–Kings complex, which probably came into being in the sixth or fifth centuries BCE.

2 In the discussion which follows I read the text as amended in verses 1 and 6, but do not assume the amendment suggested for verse 8.

3 See the NRSV footnote to Ezekiel 28:3.

4 The reading 'gods' was originally based on the Septuagint. However, with the discovery of the same reading in the Dead Sea Scrolls, it has been generally agreed (with the exception of the NIV) that the MT reading 'sons of Israel' was a theological euphemism, and that the best text is that which has 'gods'.

5 The existence of 'evil' of course is an unnecessary hypothesis in an atheist view of the world – but in that case, of course, theodicy is also a meaningless problem.

12 THE PSALMS OF ASCENTS AS A UNIT

1 In Geza Vermes's translation (1997: 306).

2 The quotation marks are used to make the point that the adjective *Davidic* can be used of the idealised messianic monarchy as well as the historic dynasty of early Israel.

3 The dedication of the temple, described in 2 Chronicles 5–7, takes place in the seventh month, at the time of the festival of Sukkot, and involves the ceremonial placement of the Ark in the temple. The direct quotation of Psalm 132:8–10 in 2 Chronicles 6:41f. and other clear echoes and references suggest strongly that the Chronicler's account of this ceremony is influenced, in a manner not true of that of Kings, by the Psalms of Ascents. I return to this point later.

4 See, for example, Davies (1992: 94–154).

5 I can find only one other study of the subject – Freedman (1977), and that does not refer to Culley. Strange that such a widespread assumption should be so little studied!

6 The common use of the term 'Second Temple Period' for the time beginning with the 'return' from exile and running through to that of Herod is questionable not least because it is increasingly unclear that there was in Jerusalem, at any time before the late sixth century, a temple properly dedicated to the religion associated with Yahweh.

7 See, for example, Childs' explanation (1979: 513–17) of the placing of Psalms 1 and 2 *before* the first Davidic collection, and Westermann's proposal (1989: 292–6) that Psalms 1 and 119 may have formed, at one time, the boundaries of just such a book of meditations.

8 Is this also true of the appearance of verbal or thematic elements which appear to be late? It is now notorious that nineteenth-century commentators routinely reported Wisdom material as late because it had to depend on Greek philosophical thinking – a conclusion thoroughly discredited by the subsequent discovery of very early examplars of the genre from Egypt and Mesopotamia. Perhaps linguistic features are more reliable, but the debate between dialect difference and chronological difference is unresolved.

9 The *Letter of Aristeas* is a good non-biblical example. In the Bible Genesis 14 may be the most striking, but both Jonah and Ruth probably also reflect later attempts to give an ancient patina to post-exilic stories.

10 He offers nine words or phrases characteristic of the Korah Psalms (1982: 3f.); in *The Prayers of David* (1990: 20–4) a general case is made for shared features, with the promise that more will be dealt with in the detailed exegesis; in the case of the Asaph Psalms he reviews the work of Delitzsch and Nasuti, and offers a range of connecting features (1996: 17–36). In none of these, in my view, is the evidence (suggestive though it undoubtedly is) anywhere near as strong as that for the Psalms of Ascents.

11 There is a very good account of Gunkel's ideas in Hayes (1976: 123–30, 139–43), where the key role of the cult as the fundamental *Sitz-im-Leben* for the Psalms is spelled out.

12 In McCann (1993: 78).

13 See, for example, the readiness with which Delitzsch (1887: 14–17) allows the possibility of Maccabean psalms, and compare with this the

implications of the work of Gunkel and Mowinckel, which seems to demand a pre-exilic cultic context for the bulk of the material. Thus Mowinckel (1962, II:154f.):

> At one time scholars used to refer a great many psalms to the Maccabean age. There is no need to do this with any single psalm. From the point of view of the history of the canon such a reference is most unlikely; for the Maccabean age the Psalter was a 'canonical' book; already at that time a comparatively finished collection.

Briggs and Briggs (1906–7: xcii), with the legendary precision of the ICC, attribute exactly eight psalms or part-psalms to the Maccabean period, one of them (129) being from the Psalms of Ascents.

14 It is hard to resist one remark, however. It is well known that in later Hebrew the form *she-* replaces the older *'asher* as the relative conjunction. It is found ten times in the Psalms of Ascents, a further eleven times in Psalms 135–46, but nowhere else in the Psalter – surely strong circumstantial evidence of characteristic language of a late period.

15 The instances in Psalms 113 and 115 are within the sequence of Hallel psalms whose general tone is of praise to the eternal and sustaining God of Israel.

16 As a matter of interest, five of the other seven references to David are in just two Psalms – 78 and 89 – each of which is described as a *maskil*. Without wishing to make too much of this, it is more than a little odd to discover just how few of the Psalms (only seven out of 150) refer to David! Psalm 89 is a rather interesting case, since it shares with the Psalms of Ascents a similar concentration of references to David, the anointed and the throne (respectively in verses 3, 20, 35, 49; 20, 51; 4, 14, 29, 36, 44). As the likely climax to a different collection – the Psalms of Korah – its similarity to Psalm 132 may not be accidental.

17 The last part of the Hebrew form *yerushalaim* is similar to *shalom*.

18 See, for example, Allen (1983: 219), Anderson (1972: 847), Davidson (1998: 405), Dahood (1970: 194), Keet (1969: 7). The phenomenon is, of course, not unique to the Psalms of Ascents, and both Kraus (1988: 23) and Briggs and Briggs (1906–7: lxxix, cf. xxxvii), while recognising it as a phenomenon of these Psalms, give examples of others where step-parallelism occurs (93, 96, 103, 118 – Kraus; and 3.1–2, 12.3–4, 24.7–10, 25.1–7 – Briggs and Briggs).

13 PSALMS 120–34: PRELIMINARY EXEGESIS

1 I have had occasion to make connections with 1 Kings 18 and 19 more than once – with reference to Psalm 29, for example, and the broom bush in Psalm 120. Given that this episode is also a clear sparring-partner for the text of Jonah, we may wonder whether it has a rather

particular place in the religious literature of the post-exilic period. Could it be that its particular theme (how should the old gods be opposed – through violence or through reason?) was peculiarly relevant to the more cosmopolitan world in which the Jews of the late sixth century onwards found themselves? It is certainly a feature of other Scripture of the period (Deutero-Isaiah, for example).

2 The translation depends also upon attaching the first word of verse 2 ('Jerusalem') to the end of verse 1.

3 It may not be an accident that just as the Psalm as a whole is resolved by the use of one of the stock formulae of the Psalms of Ascents, so is the first section (see also 121:8 and 131:4).

4 A technical observation may be appropriate here: the words for 'tears' (verse 5), for 'weeping' (verse 6), for 'laughter' (verse 2) and for 'rejoicing' (verse 3) in Psalm 126 are cognate with those found in the Ugaritic texts quoted – a close verbal similarity which seems suggestive.

5 Although this comment may more properly belong to a later stage of the interpretation, I cannot forbear from mentioning at this point the well-known spiritual 'Bringing in the Sheaves', which uses the language of these verses as a metaphor for the entry of the faithful into paradise.

6 Dahood (1970) goes further, proposing the reading 'like the sands of the waters' in place of 'like those who dream', on the basis of a different interpretation of the Hebrew consonants. While this has not found scholarly support, it certainly reinforces the bond between the two parts, by making water a shared motif.

7 We might speculate that the mysterious final line of the second stanza contains an innuendo: it is better to stay in bed and procreate than to work furiously to no point, for only by parenting children can the dynasty be assured!

8 It is noteworthy that Psalm 129:3 employs a rare word for 'furrow', elsewhere found only in 1 Samuel 14:14, a cognate of which is used in this passage.

9 The scene in Psalm 2:3 where the rebellious rulers want to break Yahweh's cords may be another example of this metaphor, as also is the positive use of the image in Hosea 11:4.

10 I will reserve the symbolic structural description for the combined illustration (p. 220) in which both of Psalms 130 and 131 are set out together.

11 A mother seeks to persuade the last of her seven sons to accept death at the hands of Antiochus rather than abandon his religion: 'My son, have pity on me. I carried you for nine months in my womb, and nursed you for three years . . . '. The story of Hannah and Samuel (1 Samuel 1:21–2:11) seems also to imply a child of a few years' age rather than a baby.

12 It is assumed that 'Jaar' in Psalm 132 and 'Kiriath Jearim' are the same place – the term *Kiriath* simply means 'town'.

13 Mowinckel (1962, I: 174–7). He bases his case on the material evaluated by Frankfort (1948: 318ff.).

14 The putative source for this story, the material in 1 Samuel 4–6, describes the captivity of the Ark in Philistine territory – perhaps a suitable analogy to the imprisonment of Marduk in the Babylonian rite.

15 Having discussed in detail Psalm 89:38–51, Johnson concludes (1967: 113):

> Thus we see that at this autumnal festival the Davidic king, for all that he is the specially chosen Servant of the omnipotent, heavenly King, is a suffering Servant. He is the Messiah of Yahweh; but on this occasion, at least, he is a humble Messiah. What we see, however, is a ritual humiliation which in principle is not unlike that suffered by the Babylonian king in the analogous New Year Festival.

16 However, see Van der Toorn (1989), who does make the connection but regards it as having pre-exilic provenance.

17 Since the parallel account in 1 Kings 8 does not incorporate this text, we may wonder if this is to be explained by a late provenance for Psalm 132 – it was (we may guess) available to the Chronicler, but not to the Deuteronomists.

18 There is one other passage which might imply the north as Yahweh's dwelling, but it is in Isaiah 14:13, part of a notoriously obscure text.

19 'You created the north and the south; / Tabor and Hermon sing for joy at your name.' From a Galilean perspective, Hermon would be in the north and Tabor in the south (though both are northern from the standpoint of Jerusalem).

20 See Gibson (1977: 48): 'She scooped up water and washed [herself], / dew of heaven [and] oil of earth.' Unfortunately the context has no bearing on Psalm 133.

21 Johnson writes:

> The fact is that it deals in a perfectly straightforward way with the rebirth of the Messiah, which . . . takes place on this eventful day with his deliverance from the Underworld, apparently at the spring Gihon, at dawn or 'as the morning appeareth'; and this carries with it the implication that the Messiah, in all the fresh vigour of his new-won life (which is here symbolized by the morning dew), has been elevated for all time not only to the throne of David but also to the traditional priesthood of Melchizedek.
>
> (1967: 131)

Johnson refers in a note to Psalm 133:3 as a clarificatory example.

22 Compare Isaiah 30:29: 'You shall have a song as in the night when a holy festival is kept; and gladness of heart, as when one sets out to the sound of the flute to go to the mountain of the LORD, to the Rock of Israel.'

14 PSALMS 120–34: A CONTEXTUAL OVERVIEW

1 The English word 'anointed' is of course a translation of the Hebrew which produces the term *messiah*. The theme of anointing has pertinence also to the cultic dimension, since the high priest was also anointed. This is the ceremony to which Psalm 133:2 refers.

2 Although Jerusalem may be thought to be in some sense a synonym of Zion, I regard it as symbolising the political identity of the people, whereas Zion specifically denotes a religious emphasis.

3 In most cases I leave it to the individual reader to check the specific verses in each Psalm which belong to a given theme. Occasionally, if the evidence is unclear, I give further detail.

4 Many readers may be surprised to discover that the word for 'woman' occurs three times only in the entire Psalter!

5 This reference is not obvious. It derives from the belief that behind Psalm 121 lies essentially a child–parent form of dependence, almost as though a worried child seeks reassurance that 'the parent' will always be there to provide protection, and will never fall asleep at the wrong moment.

6 In both 122:8 and 133:1 I treat the references to family, friends and kindred as being appropriate to this motif.

7 I include 126 with considerable hesitation. The only overt indication of a processional element is in verse 6: 'Those who go out weeping . . . shall come home with shouts of joy . . . '. While, as I argued in Chapter 13, this might relate to a cultic fertility drama, it is doubtful that the verbs of motion here are to be interpreted as a pilgrim procession. The classic argument that verse 1 refers to the return from captivity was also assessed (negatively) in Chapter 13. In any case, even if the old interpretation were to stand, it refers not to a festival setting for the Psalms as we now read them but to a one-off return of exiles – a quite different matter.

8 The motif is manifested in this Psalm in a negative form, as the poet bewails his/her fate as an alien in Meshech and Kedar, living among those who reject peace (verses 5–6).

9 While the significance of waiting and hoping is evident in 130–2, as the sequence approaches its climax, I include 134 with some hesitation. It seems to me that the picture of worshippers 'who stand by night in the house of the LORD' could be understood as a vigil – though not now one which is mounted suspensefully pending an outcome of the drama, but rather a contemplative response to what has taken place – which will reach its final expression in the doxology of verse 3. Readers

may find all this far too fanciful, a response with which I have every sympathy.

10 This is a subject too remote from my present concerns to merit further discussion. However, as a sample bibliography might I mention the following: D. A. DeSilva (1995) *Despising Shame: Honor Discourse and Community Maintenance in the Epistle to the Hebrews*, Atlanta, GA: Scholars Press; V. H. Matthews and D. C. Benjamin (eds) (1995) *Honor and Shame in the World of the Bible* (Semeia 68), Atlanta, GA: Scholars Press; J. G. Peristiany (1966) *Honour and Shame: the Values of Mediterranean Society*, London: Weidenfeld & Nicolson. In addition to these, a quick trawl of one of the standard databases (Religion Index) produced a dozen or so articles on this subject published in the last eight years.

11 The phrase 'the sceptre of wickedness' refers metonymically to the power and authority of the wicked.

12 Several themes and sub-themes occur in both positive and negative forms. In the case of the motif of conflict and danger, it is important to recognise that God's power is negative or dangerous from the point of view of Israel's enemies. Hence the sequence of terms referring to God's power or might in Psalm 132 indicates the presence of this sub-theme here.

13 I take the description 'those who turn aside to their own crooked ways' to be an indication of the deceitfulness of the wicked.

14 Words like 'shame', 'scorn' and 'contempt', and their associated verbal forms, occur up to ten times more often in the sequence 120–34 than would be expected.

15 These are not strictly *responses* in that where the terms for 'watching', 'keeping' and so on are used of the people it is either of their mounting guard (127, 130) or keeping the law (132) – and all of these are more properly conditional than responsive. Only if God is watching will the city's guard be effective; only if David's sons watch out for the terms of the Covenant will their throne be secure. However, this does answer to the important theme of God's protection, and this seems to be the best place to locate the motif.

16 There is no indication of any kind that this festival (if my speculation is plausible) was held only once, at the coronation of a monarch, or on a regular basis.

17 124 and 129–31 fall into this category. This observation does not reduce the significance of the frequency of certain key terms – their use even where the theme with which they are associated is not developed is a sign of the general context of composition.

18 See Chapter 13, note 21.

19 Other examples from the Psalter may be found in 22:9 and 23; 32:9; 35:13–14; 37:25–6; 58:6–9; 144:12–15 and the Psalm of creation, 104. The theme is not so unusual; once again, it is the density of its use which impresses us in the Psalms of Ascents.

20 See, for example, Alexander Carmichael (1928–71) *Carmina Gadelica*, Edinburgh: Oliver & Boyd, 6 vols; reprinted as a single volume in 1992.

21 A particular Hebrew term for power (*'oz/'ezuz*) is associated with the Ark (thus for example Psalms 24:8 and 68:29, 34ff.). It occurs often as a designation of God's might. See also the sinister play on the name Uzzah, who comes to a sticky end for tampering with the Ark in 2 Samuel 6:6–11.

22 This is difficult. I have taken an instance to be negative if it describes what the enemy has done or wished to do, even if thwarted. Hence 'thanks be to God that they did not . . . ' is taken as a negative instance. Positive examples are those where God, or the psalmist, initiates action against the enemy.

23 The expressions 'peace' or 'blessing' are in fact present in 120 and 129, albeit as gifts *not* available.

24 I am anticipating somewhat the analysis still to come; but since there are three places where pilgrimage seems to be indicated (121–2, 126 and 132), the threefold construction I am proposing matches that pattern. These also occur where the positive themes are most pronounced.

25 It is significant that the underlying Hebrew also uses the same unusual form in both places.

26 One detail of the Hebrew is worth highlighting: it is well known that one of the common words for 'tribe' is the same as that for 'sceptre'. Hence the 'tribes of the LORD' in 122:4 are echoed negatively in the 'sceptre of wickedness' in 125:3.

27 I am aware that I have noted future tenses in the earlier 'positive' Psalms as one sign of lack of resolution. The difference in 132 is that the future tenses in verses 15–16 and 17–18 are, first, emphatic and, second, in the context of (at last!) God's definitive action (verses 13–14, 17b).

28 That is certainly the view expressed in Van der Toorn (1989: 339–43), where the Akiti Festival of Marduk and Nabu at the Babylonian New Year is closely linked with the Israelite Autumnal Festival.

29 Around 140–65 BCE.

30 The post-exilic period saw the introduction also of Purim, based on the story of Esther, itself a late composition. It was a powerfully formative period for Jewish religion.

15 HOME ALONE: STRUCTURAL AND POSTMODERN READINGS OF PSALMS 120–34

1 To the cynical reader who will no doubt by now have asked her/himself whether these structures would have sprung to mind if the word 'ascents' were not already in the frame, I can only answer: 'Who knows and does it matter?'

2 Readers might at this point also revisit the more detailed deconstruction of Psalm 121 which was carried out in Chapter 3 (pp. 41–5).

3 A trawl of the Glasgow University Library database using the keyword 'explained' produced 562 items covering four centuries of publication and an equally wide range of subjects. I note four of them here (in chronological order): *The Acts of the Apostles Explained* (1857); *The Apocalypse Explained for Readers of Today* (1936); *Archaeology Explained* (1988); and *Explaining Auschwitz and Hiroshima* (1993). We seem to have an insatiable appetite for explaining even the inexplicable!

4 'Defining culture: a challenge for pluralism', to be published in the proceedings of the conference *Studies on Cultural Meaning* at Chantilly and Cergy–Pontoise, November 1997.

5 Consult, respectively, Psalms 131, 123, 122, 127:3–5, 130.

6 To borrow an idea from Black (1981) '"Taking Bel by the hand" and a cultic picnic'.

7 There are still those who regard the god of rival religions as either demonic or idolatrous. But this is a different matter: Christians who denounce 'Allah', for instance, do not reject the idea that God has universal power, what they reject is any suggestion that that universal deity might equally be called 'Allah' or 'God'. It is further ironic that in certain languages the distinction cannot be made. Indonesian Christians use the word 'Allah' as the normal word for the being English refers to as 'God'; after all, Allah derives from the same root as El, the Hebrew word usually translated 'God'.

BIBLIOGRAPHY

The titles are arranged the titles in three sections for ease of use. Sections 1 and 3 are self-explanatory; section 2 consists of all the other titles referred to in the book.

1 Standard commentaries and introductions

Briggs and Briggs (1906–7) and Delitszch (1887) are classic commentaries from the period when the practice of biblical criticism was at its height, and they are still useful for their detailed attention to linguistic matters. Their successors in the modern period are Dahood's Anchor Bible Commentaries (1965, 1968, 1970) and Allen (1983), Craigie (1983) and Tate (1990), all Word Commentaries. While Dahood is idiosyncratic in his extensive use of Ugaritic parallels, Davidson (1998), Kraus (1988) and Weiser (1962) focus more on theological issues, and Anderson (1972) represents the critical approach, but at a level more accessible for the general reader. The remaining titles in section 1 are general introductions to the Psalter. Gillingham (1994) is probably the most comprehensive.

Allen, L. C. (1983) *Psalms 101–150*, Waco, TX: Word Books.
Anderson, A. A. (1972) *The Book of Psalms*, London: Marshall, Morgan & Scott.
Barth, C. F. (1966) *Introduction to the Psalms*, Oxford: Blackwell.
Briggs, C. A. and Briggs E. G. (1906–7) *A Critical and Exegetical Commentary on the Book of Psalms*, Edinburgh: T. & T. Clark.
Craigie, P. C. (1983) *Psalms 1–50*, Waco, TX: Word Books.
Dahood, M. (1965) *Psalms I: 1–50*, Garden City, New York: Doubleday.
—— (1968) *Psalms II: 51–100*, Garden City, New York: Doubleday.
—— (1970) *Psalms III: 101–150*, Garden City, New York: Doubleday.
Davidson, R. (1998) *The Vitality of Worship: A Commentary on the Book of*

Psalms, Grand Rapids, MI, and Edinburgh: Eerdmans and the Handsel Press.

Day, J. (1990) *Psalms*, Sheffield: Sheffield Academic Press.

Delitzsch, F. (1887) *Biblical Commentary on the Psalms* (3 vols), London: Hodder & Stoughton.

Gillingham, S. E. (1994) *The Poems and Psalms of the Hebrew Bible*, Oxford: Oxford University Press.

Hayes, J. H. (1976) *Understanding the Psalms*, Valley Forge, PA: Judson Press.

Kraus, H.-J. (1988) *Psalms 1–59*, Minneapolis, MN: Augsburg.

—— (1989) *Psalms 60–150*, Minneapolis, MN: Augsburg.

Seybold, K. (1990) *Introducing the Psalms*, Edinburgh: T. & T. Clark.

Tate, M. E. (1990) *Psalms 51–100*, Waco, TX: Word Books.

Weiser, A. (1962) *The Psalms*, London: SCM Press.

Westermann, C. (1980) *The Psalms: Structure, Content and Method*, London: SCM.

—— (1989) *The Living Psalms*, Edinburgh: T. & T. Clark.

2 General bibliography

Anderson, B. (1991) *Imagined Communities: Reflections on the Origins and Spread of Nationalism*, rev. edn, London: Verso.

Anderson, B. W. (1983) *Out of the Depths: The Psalms Speak for Us Today*, Philadelphia, PA: Westminster Press.

Auffret, P. (1982) *La Sagesse a bâti sa maison: Etudes de structures littéraires dans l'Ancient Testament et spécialement dans les Psaumes*, Göttingen: Vandenhoek & Ruprecht.

Barr, J. (1981) *Fundamentalism*, 2nd edn, London: SCM Press.

—— (1983) *Holy Scripture: Canon, Authority, Criticism*, London: SCM Press.

—— (1984) *Escaping from Fundamentalism*, London: SCM Press.

Barton, J. (1996) *Reading the Old Testament*, 2nd edn, London: Darton, Longman & Todd.

Beaucamp, E. (1979) 'L'unité du recueil des montées: Psaumes 120–134', *Studium Biblicum Franciscanum, Liber annus* 29: 73–90.

Berlin, A. (1985) *The Dynamics of Biblical Parallelism*, Bloomington: Indiana University Press.

Beyerlin, W. (ed.) (1978) *Near Eastern Religious Texts Relating to the Old Testament* (NERTOT), London: SCM Press.

Bigger, S. (ed.) (1989) *Creating the Old Testament*, Oxford: Blackwell.

Black, J. A. (1981) 'The New Year Ceremonies in ancient Babylon: "Taking Bel by the Hand" and a cultic picnic', *Religion* 11: 39–59.

Boecker, H. J. (1980) *Law and the Administration of Justice in the Old Testament and Ancient East*, London: SPCK.

Boone, K. (1989) *The Bible Tells Them So*, New York: SUNY Press.

Brueggemann, W. (1982) *Genesis*, Atlanta GA: John Knox Press.

Carmichael, A. (1992) *Carmina Gadelica*, Edinburgh: Floris Books.

Carroll, R. P. (1981) *From Chaos to Covenant*, London: SCM Press.

—— (1986) *Jeremiah: A Commentary*, London: SCM Press.

Carroll, R. P. and Prickett, S. (eds) (1997) *The Bible: Authorized King James Version*, Oxford University Press.

Childs, B. S. (1970) *Biblical Theology in Crisis*, Philadelphia: Westminster Press.

—— (1979) *An Introduction to the Old Testament as Scripture*, London: SCM Press.

Collingwood, R. G. ([1946] 1993) *The Idea of History*, ed. Jan van der Dussen, Oxford: Clarendon Press.

Coughlin, C. (1997) *A Golden Basin Full of Scorpions. The Quest for Modern Jerusalem*, London: Little, Brown & Company.

Cross, F. M. (1950) 'Notes on a Canaanite psalm in the Old Testament', *Bulletin of the American Schools of Oriental Research* 117: 19–21.

Crow, L. D. (1996) *The Songs of Ascents (Psalms 120–134): Their Place in Israelite History and Religion*, Atlanta, GA: Scholars Press.

Culley, R. C. (1967) *Oral Formulaic Language in the Biblical Psalms*, Toronto: University of Toronto Press.

Davie, D. (ed.) (1996) *The Psalms in English*, Harmondsworth: Penguin Books.

Davies, P. R. (1992) *In Search of 'Ancient Israel'*, Sheffield: Sheffield Academic Press.

De Vaux, R. (1961) *Ancient Israel. Its Life and Institutions*, London: Darton, Longman & Todd.

Frankfort, H (1948) *Kingship and the Gods*, Chicago, IL, and London: University of Chicago Press.

Freedman, D. N. (1977) 'Pottery, poetry and prophecy: an essay on biblical poetry', *Journal of Biblical Literature* 96: 5–26.

Frost, D. L. (1977) *The Psalms: A New Translation for Worship*, London: Collins Liturgical.

Garbini, G. (1988) *History and Ideology in Ancient Israel*, London: SCM Press.

Gaster, T. H. (1946) 'Psalm 29' in *Jewish Quarterly Review* 37: 55–65.

Gelineau, J. (1965) *The Psalms: A New Translation. Translated from the Hebrew and Arranged for Singing to the Psalmody of Joseph Gelineau*, London: Collins.

Gibson, J. C. L. (1977) *Canaanite Myths and Legends*, Edinburgh: T. & T. Clark.

Goulder, M. D. (1974) *Midrash and Lection in Matthew*, London: SPCK.

—— (1982) *The Psalms of the Sons of Korah*, Sheffield: JSOT Press.

—— (1990) *The Prayers of David*, Sheffield: JSOT Press.

—— (1996) *The Psalms of Asaph*, Sheffield: Sheffield Academic Press.

—— (1998) *The Psalms of the Return*, Sheffield: Sheffield Academic Press.

Grabbe, L. L. (ed.) (1997) *Can a 'History of Israel' Be Written*, Sheffield: Sheffield Academic Press.

Gunkel, H. (1926) *Die Psalmen*, Göttingen: Vandenhoek & Ruprecht.

—— ([1930], 1967) *The Psalms: A Form-Critical Introduction*, Philadelphia, PA: Fortress Press; trans of vol. I of the 2nd edn of *Die Religion in Geschichte und Gegenwart* (1930).

Haik-Vantoura, S. (1991) *The Music of the Bible Revealed: The Deciphering of a Millenary Notation*, Berkeley, CA: BIBAL Press.

Hopkins, G. M. (1959) *The Journal and Papers of Gerard Manley Hopkins, edited by Humphrey House, completed by Graham Storey*, London: Oxford University Press.

Jackson, G. (1997) *The Lincoln Psalter: Versions of the Psalms*, Manchester: Carcanet.

Jamieson-Drake, D. W. (1991) *Scribes and Schools in Monarchic Judah: A Socio-Archaeological Approach*, Sheffield: JSOT Press.

Johnson, A. R. (1967) *Sacral Kingship in Ancient Israel*, 2nd edn, Cardiff: University of Wales Press.

Keet, C. C. (1969) *A Study of the Psalms of Ascent*, London: Mitre Press.

Kerrigan, J. (1998) 'The country of the mind' (review article), *TLS*, September 11 1998: 3–4.

Kloos, C. (1986) *Yhwh's Combat with the Sea*, Leiden: Brill.

Kuntz, J. K. (1994) 'Engaging the Psalms: gains and trends in recent research', *Currents in Research: Biblical Studies* 2: 77–106.

Lemche, N. P. (1988) *Ancient Israel. A New History of Israelite Society*, Sheffield: JSOT Press.

Levi, P. (1976) *The Psalms*, Harmondsworth: Penguin Books.

Liebreich, L. J. (1955) 'The Songs of Ascent and the priestly blessing', *Journal of Biblical Literature* 74: 33–6.

Lord, A. B. (1960) *The Singer of Tales*, Cambridge, MA.: Harvard University Press.

Lowth, R. (1839) *Lectures on the Sacred Poetry of the Hebrews*, 4th edn, London: Tegg; originally published at Oxford (1753) under the title *De sacra poesi Hebraeorum. Praelectiones academicae*.

McCann, J. C., Jr (ed.) (1993) *The Shape and Shaping of the Psalter*, Sheffield: JSOT Press.

Mark, J. (1987) *Zeno Was Here*, London: Jonathan Cape.

Mays, J. L. (1994) *The Lord Reigns*, Louisville, KY: Westminster John Knox Press.

Mowinckel, S. (1962) *The Psalms in Israel's Worship* (2 vols), Oxford: Blackwell.

Nasuti, H. P. (1988) *Tradition History and the Psalms of Asaph*, Atlanta, GA: Scholars Press.

Petersen, D. L. and Richards, K. H. (1992) *Interpreting Hebrew Poetry*, Minneapolis, MN: Fortress Press.

Phillips, J. B. (1959) *The New Testament in Modern English* (Schools Edition), London: Geoffrey Bles.

Pritchard, J. B. (1969) *Ancient Near Eastern Texts Relating to the Old Testament* (3rd edn with Supplement), Princeton, NJ: Princeton University Press.

Prothero, R. E. (1913) *The Psalms in Human Life*, London: John Murray.

Reed, H. (1991) *Collected Poems*, Oxford: Oxford University Press.

Saggs, H. W. F. (1984) *The Might that Was Assyria*, London: Sidgwick & Jackson.

Schama, S. (1995) *Landscape and Memory*, London: HarperCollins.

Sheppard, G. T. (1980) *Wisdom as a Hermeneutical Construct: A Study of the Sapientalizing of the Old Testament*, Berlin: Walter de Gruyter.

Slavitt, D. R. (1996) *Sixty-One Psalms of David*, New York: Oxford University Press.

Smart, J. D. (1970) *The Strange Silence of the Bible in the Church*, London: SCM Press.

Thomas, D. W. (ed.) (1958) *Documents from Old Testament Times*, Edinburgh and London: Thomas Nelson & Sons.

Thompson, T. L. (1992) *The Early History of the Israelite People: From the Written and Archaeological Sources*, Leiden: Brill.

Van der Toorn, K. (1989) 'The Babylonian New Year Festival: new insights from the cuneiform texts and their bearing on Old Testament study', in J. Emerton (ed.) *Congress Volume: Leuven 1989*, Leiden: Brill.

Vermes, G. (1997) *The Complete Dead Sea Scrolls in English*, Harmondsworth: Allen Lane at the Penguin Press.

Weil, D. M. (1995) *The Masoretic Chant of the Bible*, Jerusalem: Rubin Mass, Ltd.

Whitelam, K. W. (1996) *The Invention of Ancient Israel: The Silencing of Palestinian History*, London: Routledge.

Wilson, G. H. (1985) *The Editing of the Hebrew Psalter*, Chico, CA: Scholars Press.

Wilson, G. H. (1986) 'The use of royal psalms at the "seams" of the Hebrew Psalter', *Journal for the Study of the Old Testament* 35: 85–94.

Wordsworth, D. (1978) Home at Grasmere, Harmondsworth: Penguin English Library.

3 Postmodern and structuralist

Adam, A. K. M. (1995) *What is Postmodern Biblical Criticism?*, Minneapolis MN: Fortress Press.

Aichele, G. (*et al.*) (1995) *The Postmodern Bible: The Bible and Culture Collective*, New Haven, CT and London: Yale University Press.

Childers, J. and Hentzi, G. (eds) (1995) *The Columbia Dictionary of Modern Literary and Cultural Criticism*, New York: Columbia University Press.

Collins, T (1987) 'Decoding the Psalms: a structural approach to the Psalms', *Journal for the Study of the Old Testament* 37: 41–60.

Derrida, J. ([1967] 1973) *Speech and Phenomena*, Evanston, IL: Northwestern University Press; trans. D. B. Allison from *La Voix et le phènomène: Introduction au problème du signe dans la phénoménologie de Husserl*, Paris: Presses Universitaires de France (1967).

Detweiler, R. (editor) (1982) *Derrida and Biblical Studies*, Chico, CA: Scholars Press.

Grossberg, D. (1989) *Centripetal and Centrifugal Structures in Biblical Poetry*, Atlanta, GA: Scholars Press.

Harland, R. (1987) *Superstructuralism*, London and New York: Methuen.

Hauge, M. R. (1995) *Between Sheol and Temple: Motif Structure and Function in the I-Psalms*, Sheffield: Sheffield Academic Press.

Husserl, E. (1900) *Logische Untersuchungen*, Halle: M. Niemeyer; rev. edn 1913; *Logical Investigations*, trans. J. N. Findlay, London: Routledge & Kegan Paul (1970).

Ingraffia, B. D. (1995) *Postmodern Theory and Biblical Theology Vanquishing God's Shadow*, Cambridge and New York: Cambridge University Press.

Jakobson, R. (1987) *Language in Literature*, ed. K. Pomorska and S. Rudy, Cambridge, MA: the Belknap Press of Harvard University Press.

Johnson, A. M., Jr, (ed.) (1979) *Structuralism and Biblical Hermeneutics: A Collection of Essays*, Pittsburgh, PA: Pickwick Press.

Kamuf, P. (ed.) (1991) *A Derrida Reader: Between the Blinds*, Hemel Hempstead: Harvester Wheatsheaf.

Krasovec, J. (1984) *Antithetic Structure in Biblical Hebrew Poetry*, Leiden: Brill.

Lentricchia, F. and McLaughlin, T. (eds) (1995) *Critical Terms for Literary Study*, (2nd edn), Chicago: University of Chicago Press.

Norris, C. (1987) *Derrida*, London: Fontana Press.

Polzin, R. (1977) *Biblical Structuralism: Method and Subjectivity in the Study of Ancient Texts*, Philadelphia: Fortress Press.

Raabe, P. (1990) *Psalm Structures: A Study of Psalms with Refrains*, Sheffield: JSOT Press.

Robey, D. (1973) (ed.) *Structuralism – An Introduction*, Oxford: Clarendon Press.

Saussure, F. de (1916) *Cours de linguistique générale*, Paris: Payot; *Course in General Linguistics*, trans. R. Harris, London: Duckworth (1983). (This edition helpfully indicates the pagination of the French. In the text I have used the date 1919 and the original pagination.)

GENERAL INDEX

Aaron 160, 176, 186, 226, 229, 235–6, 248
Abram (Abraham) 125, 184, 254
Akkadian *see* Assyria
Allen, L.C. 210, 214
anadiplosis see step–parallelism
anointing 10, 36f, 103, 106, 108–10, 167, 185, 190, 195, 224–6, 229, 235, 247; *see also* Messiah
Anderson, A. A. 42, 136
aporia 93, 95, 113f, 126, 139f, 169
Aramaic (Aramaeans) 18, 20, 25–7, 46, 50f, 64, 105, 109, 239
Ark 7, 72, 76, 132–3, 136–8, 140f, 175, 177, 179, 186, 190, 193, 221, 223–5, 229, 231–2, 235, 237–8, 240, 246–7, 251, 255
aspects *see* reading
Assyria (Akkadian) 26, 105–6, 112–13, 131f, 143, 197 208, 239
Auffret, P. 176

Baal (Hadad) 27, 43, 66–8, 70, 73, 75–6, 96–7, 121, 132, 143, 195, 199, 207f, 215–16, 226f
Babylon: myths and beliefs 9, 65, 125, 143, 146, 153, 166, 195, 201, 223–4; people and place 8, 26, 74, 106, 112–13, 147, 197, 207, 211, 223–4, 239, 254
Barthes, R. 79–81
Beaucamp, E. 176, 179
Berlin, A. 60–1
Beyerlin, W. 68,143
Bible, versions: JB 17, 19, 22, 25, 27–32, 72; KJV 7, 17–19, 21–5, 27–32, 38, 42, 105, 119, 131,

177, 216; NEB 17, 19, 21, 23, 25–32, 119; NIV 17, 19–21, 23–5, 27–9, 31–2, 119; NJB 17, 19, 22, 25, 27–32; NRSV[1] 17, 19, 21, 23–9, 31–2; REB 17, 23, 25, 27–9, 31–2, 119; RSV 17, 21, 23–9, 31–2, 119
Bible: authority 35; Christian 22; cross-references 25; free translations 17; inspiration 19; Jewish 3, 6, 8, 10f, 23; prefaces 17–26
blessing 32, 72, 76, 108, 111, 122, 176, 183, 186, 196, 198f, 202, 212, 214, 216f, 221, 227–32, 234, 237, 241f, 244, 254
Boecker, H.J. 211

Canaan: myths and beliefs 19, 28, 39, 67–70, 75, 96, 143, 153, 160, 164–6, 201, 207, 215; people and place 22, 27–8, 43, 76, 97, 107, 162, 170, 178, 197
chiasmus 39, 109, 123, 200, 205, 209f, 218, 241, 243, 252f
Christianity: christology 11, 40, 61, 81, 114f, 127, 168; and Psalms 11f, 23, 37, 48, 111, 114–16, 141, 168, 178, 218, 246, 258
closure 57, 62, 126, 135, 182, 200f
Collingwood, R. G. 35
Collins, T. 77
combination *see* parallelism

1 Since the NRSV is used as the standard text for this book, references to it after Chapter 2 are not indexed.

224, 227, 235, 244f; *see also* step-parallelism

peace (*shalom*) 56, 58, 72–4, 95–7, 99, 106, 138f, 152, 156, 183, 186, 193f, 198, 206, 214, 227, 229–30, 232, 240–2, 244–7

philosophy: Cartesian 83–4; empiricism 83, 87; Hegel 83, 92; metaphysical 83f, 88; Plato 83, 88, 168; Spinoza 83

pilgrimage 42–4, 132–9, 177, 188, 196–9, 218, 228, 230, 233, 236, 238, 242–9, 254f, 258

poetry (*see also* Psalms: poetry) 46–61, 116; and prose 47–53; and reference 47f, 52f; semantic features 54, 59–61; structure 50f, 54f, 58–61

Polzin, R. 80–2

postmodernism 6, 41, 74, 77–99

post-structuralism *see* deconstruction

priest(hood) 107, 126, 132f, 136, 146, 148, 155, 176, 186, 190, 198, 223, 226f, 229–30, 234–6, 247f, 255

Propp, V. 77

Prothero, R.E. 41

Psalms of Ascents *see* Psalms 120–134

Psalms: comparative material 67–9, 105f, 119–21, 131f, 142f, 146, 161f, 194f, 207f, 215f, 227 (*see also* Assyria, Babylon, Canaan, Egypt, Mesopotamia, Ugarit); critical approach (source, form, redaction) 8, 11, 64f, 181f; 190f, 211, 218, 261 n.1; groups 10, 175–91, 229–58; Hebrew text 15, 103, 105, 119, 129, 131, 142, 160f, 182, 188, 193, 196, 199–201, 203f, 206f, 211, 219, 221; history 7f; 10, 36f, 65, 75f, 146–8, 177–82, 222f, 239, 247f; lections 11; liturgy 7, 9, 13, 116, 122, 132f, 148–50, 162, 169, 177f, 236, 260 n.5; music 7; orality 163, 177f, 268 n.2; personal use 12, 98f, 116f, 128, 141, 157f, 170f; poetry 13f, 30, 53–61, 71–4; social context 65,

70f, 200, 211–14, 216, 219, 228, 230, 236f, 242–5; structure 42, 71–4, 107–10, 123, 133f, 150–2, 163, 182–5, 193f, 196, 198f, 200f, 202f 205f, 209f, 212, 214, 217, 218f, 221f, 224f, 227, 237, 240f, 243, 249–52; theology 11f, 40, 98, 122–5, 128, 183

Qumran *see* Dead Sea Scrolls

reading: aspects, seven 62–5, 67, 72, 75–7, 82, 95, 110, 176, 191, 229; authorial intention 5f, 74; contextual 35–7; critical 37–40; dialogical 33, 40; reader's agenda 6, 80–2; textuality 34; traditional approach 62–76

Reed, Henry 47

repetition *see* parallelism

rhetoric 63f, 70–2, 79, 93, 96, 111, 113, 115, 122, 138, 161, 165f, 242, 255

Saggs, H.W.F. 208

Saussure, F. 77–9, 82, 90, 92

Schama, S. 255

Scotland 7, 12, 41f, 44f, 116, 158

selah 11, 131, 139f

selection *see* parallelism

Septuagint *see* Greek

seven, significance 66, 68f, 72f, 142f, 150f, 154, 156f

sign, the 78, 84–99, 93

Sitz-im-Leben see form-criticism

Solomon 40, 107, 178, 211, 225, 236

speech 78f, 85, 87–92, 94

step-parallelism 176, 184, 188–90, 198

structuralism 41, 77–82, 94, 176; applied to Bible 80–2; heuristic approach 79f, 270 n.2

suffering 111, 155, 162, 165

superstructuralism 82–4

supplément 91, 93f, 97, 114, 254

Tanin 69, 143

temple 7f, 29, 36f, 40, 46, 54, 70–2,

INDEX OF BIBLICAL CITATIONS

21:13–17 193
24:21–2 167
27:1 154
40:10–26 165
42:11 193
44:9–20 76
44:13–20 166
45:20 165
49:2 57
49:26 185, 221
51:10 218
55:10–13 209
59:21 184
60:7 193
60:16 185, 221

Jeremiah
2:21 213
8:13 213
9:8 57, 194
10:16 147
10:25 147
23:1 147
49:2a 193

Lamentations
1:10 147
2:3 147
2:7 147
2:9 147

Ezekiel
17:1–10 213
27:34 218
28:1–10 164
28:2 162
28:14 167
38:2 193

Hosea
10:1 213
11:1, 8–9 153
14:4–7 213

Amos
5:4–6 238

Micah
4:7 184
5:2 221

Habakkuk
1:5–11 112

Sirach
Prologue 3

1 Maccabees
1 148
4:38 147
4:46 147
7:16f 147
9:27 147
14:41 147

2 Maccabees
1:8 148
7:27 219
8:33 148

Matthew
1:23 25
4:1–11 244
26:69–75 244

Luke
1:31 25
2:41–4 197
2:41–51 133
10:29–37 43

Romans
16:20 25

Galatians
4:4 25

Hebrews
2:14 25

1 John
3:8 25

Revelation
12:9 25
12:17 25
20:2 25